AN AMERICAN
IN THE MAKING

The Life Story of an Immigrant

by

M . E . R A V A G E

with a new Preface by
LOUISE RAVAGE TRESFORT

Dover Publications, Inc.
New York

Published in Canada by General Publishing Company, Ltd., 30 Lesmill Road, Don Mills, Toronto, Ontario.
Published in the United Kingdom by Constable and Company, Ltd., 10 Orange Street, London WC 2.

This Dover edition, first published in 1971, is an unabridged and unaltered republication of the work originally published by Harper and Brothers, Publishers, in 1917. To this have been added two chapters (Chapters XXII and XXIII) first published in the Harper Modern Classics edition of 1936. A new Preface has been written by Louise Ravage Tresfort especially for the Dover edition.

International Standard Book Number: 0-486-22013-3
Library of Congress Catalog Card Number: 73-125869

Manufactured in the United States of America
Dover Publications, Inc.
180 Varick Street
New York, N. Y. 10014

PREFACE

TO THE DOVER EDITION

An American in the Making, my father's first book, was an instantaneous success when it was published in America, his adopted home, in 1917. Apparently his account of how one young man from Vaslui, Rumania, became an American found a ready response both among those Americans attempting to understand their immigrant neighbors and among those former Europeans who had taken the route themselves. America was then crowded with people who had just arrived—"Americans by grace of an act of Congress," my father called all our family; and his book, written when he was in his thirties, chronicles all the agony and occasional hilarity of what it is like to be born in one world and grown to manhood there, only to have to adapt to a totally different one.

My father, born Marcus Eli Ravage (in Rumania it was Revici), the son of Judah Loeb and Bella Rosenthal Revici, came to America in 1900 at the age of sixteen. He thus followed the lead of the relative he calls Couza, who had returned briefly to Vaslui from America wearing such rich clothes everyone thought he was a millionaire. The truth about the new world proved to be more grim than my father imagined. He found here a world

v

of pushcarts, nightmarish, littered slum streets, sweat-shops, crowded window-sills that looked directly onto the beams of an elevated trestle. He describes his spiritual journey in the pages of this book: how, having thrown off his mother's apron strings, he set out to conquer America; how, "finding his tongue, shedding his steerage trappings, wrenching himself loose from the foreign colony altogether," he "dived down into the seething rapids of American life and came up again—as a student at a Middle Western college"—to become "an American, not to be distinguished from his fellows, kneaded out of East European dough."

The Middle Western college was the University of Missouri, from which he was graduated in 1909. In 1910 he received a Master of Arts degree from the University of Illinois, and studied at Columbia University inter-mittently from 1910 to 1913. Meanwhile he was doing settlement work in New York, in an attempt to relieve the same conditions of ignorance and isolation among immigrants that he had found after his own arrival. It was at the end of this period, and partly as a result of it, that he wrote *An American in the Making*, a book that has always seemed to me very much alive and that has been hailed by many as an American classic.

Its best pages, I feel, are those that capture the actual feel of the Lower East Side of New York in 1900: the crowded, steamy Rumanian restaurants near Tomp-kins Square; the overflowing apartment on Rivington Street (the "street with a pretty name") which turned

vi

PREFACE TO THE DOVER EDITION

into a dormitory at night housing an indeterminate number of relatives. One does not soon forget my father's harrowing description of the squalor that lay between Couza's apartment on Attorney Street and the Rivington Street building.

If these newcomers had much to learn from Americans, they had much to teach Americans as well, and it was always very important to my father that the richness on both sides of this cultural interchange be recognized. "The alien only begins to feel at home," he wrote, "when he has succeeded in blending his own culture and ideas and mode of life with those of the people who were here before him." The old culture was to be blended, not overcome.

In 1936 my father revised the book, adding the last two chapters included in this edition. Here he tells of giving into the temptation (unlike my French mother, Jeanne, who refused to do so) of revisiting one's birthplace. He returned to Vaslui, Rumania, optimistically, expecting to find it as appealing as he remembered it. The inevitable disappointment was not just a product of growing up; it was also that he had seen a better life in America. My father never lost his admiration for America as a country where men were not shunned because of accidental differences of externals.

My father continued to write to the end of his life. In 1919 he wrote a narrative of the treatment of Jews in Eastern Europe, as well as *Democratic Americanization: A Criticism and a Policy*. In 1923 he wrote *The*

LOUISE RAVAGE TRESFORT

Malady of Europe, which dealt with World War I, and in 1924 *The Story of the Teapot Dome*, an account of the scandal that rocked the Harding Administration. *Five Men of Frankfort*, the story of the Rothschilds, followed in 1929. He also wrote articles for the *New Republic* and the London *Nation and Atheneum*, and *Le Petit Parisien* of Paris. As he grew older he became more and more interested in nineteenth-century European history and wrote a biography of Marie-Louise, Napoleon's second wife, which was widely translated in Europe.

In growing up, I knew my father always as an established writer, and I have often wished I could have known him during the tumultuous period described in the pages of this book. We heard of those days often enough, usually to the accompaniment of much laughter, particularly when my father would run into any of his friends from that period. I remember summer trips we would make on the Hudson River Line—my mother, my father, brother, sister, and I, the middle one—to Loon Lake in the Adirondacks to join Harvey, the roommate from the University of Missouri who had shown my father the essence of his adopted country. Harvey and he had worked out their relationship during that grim college year, and there was no doubt that now they thoroughly delighted in each other's company. I can still see them: my father arriving in some exotic outfit and soon borrowing a more suitable but outsized one from his host, and Harvey, a jolly giant I remember mostly for his laugh.

PREFACE TO THE DOVER EDITION

It was Harvey who introduced us to the least American breakfast, froglegs, and the most unusual way of obtaining them—with a shotgun—but at an hour that saw my father still in bed. He loved to sleep late when he got the chance, and no frog was going to get him out of bed at so hideous an hour in the morning. We would have let him sleep late anyway, for we loved spoiling him lavishly; he was that kind of father.

This book is only the first chapter in a long life that spanned nearly eighty years, but it recalls my father as I remember him—the buoyant, surging nature, on the move, seeking new goals. As a child I was conscious that he was always looking for the highest and noblest among those who surrounded him. To the end of his life he never stopped learning.

It was this characteristic which carried him through the initial turmoil and disappointment to the final triumph in this story of the central moment of his life: that hour in 1900 when, lured by stories about the wealth to be had in America, he cast himself free from Vaslui, Rumania, to find, in his own words, "things Vaslui never dreamed could be found."

LOUISE RAVAGE TRESFORT

Brookline, Massachusetts, 1970

INTRODUCTION

WHEN I hear all around me the foolish prattle about the new immigration—"the scum of Europe," as it is called—that is invading and making itself master of this country, I cannot help saying to myself that Americans have forgotten America. The native, I must conclude, has, by long familiarity with the rich blessings of his own land, grown forgetful of his high privileges and ceased to grasp the lofty message which America wafts across the seas to all the oppressed of mankind. What, I wonder, do they know of America, who know only America?

The more I think upon the subject the more I become persuaded that the relation of the teacher and the taught as between those who were born and those who came here must be reversed. It is the free American who needs to be instructed by the benighted races in the uplifting word that America speaks to all the world. Only from the humble immigrant, it appears to me, can he learn just what America stands for in the family of nations. The alien must know this, for he alone seems ready to pay the heavy price for his share of America. He, unlike the older inhabitant, does not come into its

inheritance by the accident of birth. Before he can become an American he must first be an immigrant. More than that, back of immigration lies emigration. And to him alone is it given to know the bitter sacrifice and the deep upheaval of the soul that are implied in those two words.

The average American, when he thinks of immigrants at all, thinks, I am afraid, of something rather comical. He thinks of bundles—funny, picturesque bundles of every shape and size and color. The alien himself, in his incredible garb, as he walks off the gang-plank, appears like some sort of an odd, moving bundle. And always he carries more bundles. Later on, in his peculiar, transplanted life, he sells nondescript merchandise in fantastic vehicles, does violence to the American's language, and sits down on the curb to eat fragrant cheese and unimaginable sausages. He is, for certain, a character fit for a farce.

So, I think, you see him, you fortunate ones who have never had to come to America. I am afraid that the pathos and the romance of the story are quite lost on you. Yet both are there as surely as the comedy. No doubt, when you go slumming, you reflect sympathetically on the drudgery and the misery of the immigrant's life. But poverty and hard toil are not tragic things. They indeed are part of the comedy. Tragedy lies seldom on the surface. If you would get a glimpse of the pathos and the romance of readjustment you must try to put yourself in the alien's place. And that

INTRODUCTION

you may find hard to do. Well, try to think of leave-taking—of farewells to home and kindred, in all likelihood never to be seen again; of last looks lingering affectionately on things and places; of ties broken and grown stronger in the breaking. Try to think of the deep upheaval of the human soul, pulled up by the roots from its ancient, precious soil, cast abroad among you here, withering for a space, then slowly finding nourishment in the new soil, and once more thriving—not, indeed, as before—a novel, composite growth. If you can see this you may form some idea of the sadness and the glory of his adventure.

Oh, if I could show you America as we of the oppressed peoples see it! If I could bring home to you even the smallest fraction of this sacrifice and this upheaval, the dreaming and the strife, the agony and the heartache, the endless disappointments, the yearning and the despair—all of which must be ours before we can make a home for our battered spirits in this land of yours. Perhaps, if we be young, we dream of riches and adventure, and if we be grown men we may merely seek a haven for our outraged human souls and a safe retreat for our hungry wives and children. Yet, however aggrieved we may feel toward our native home, we cannot but regard our leaving it as a violent severing of the ties of our life, and look beyond toward our new home as a sort of glorified exile. So, whether we be young or old, something of ourselves we always leave behind in our hapless, cherished birthplaces. And

the heaviest share of our burden inevitably falls on the loved ones that remain when we are gone. We make no illusions for ourselves. Though we may expect wealth, we have no thought of returning. It is farewell forever. We are not setting out on a trip; we are emigrating. Yes, we are emigrating, and there is our experience, our ordeal, in a nutshell. It is the one-way passport for us every time. For we have glimpsed a vision of America, and we start out resolved that, whatever the cost, we shall make her our own. In our heavy-laden hearts we are already Americans. In our own dumb way we have grasped her message to us.

Yes, we immigrants have a real claim on America. Every one of us who did not grow faint-hearted at the start of the battle and has stuck it out has earned a share in America by the ancient right of conquest. We have had to subdue this new home of ours to make it habitable, and in conquering it we have conquered ourselves. We are not what we were when you saw us landing from the Ellis Island ferry. Our own kinsfolk do not know us when they come over. We sometimes hardly know ourselves.

Affectionately dedicated to

JEANNE AND SUZANNE

and to

LOUISE AND JOHN

who had not arrived in time for

the original edition

CONTENTS

PART I

THE ALIEN AT HOME

PART II

THE ALIEN ABROAD

PART III

THE EDUCATION OF AN AMERICAN

xvii

CONTENTS

PART I

THE ALIEN AT HOME

I

THE PROPHET FROM AMERICA

EVEN an imaginative American, I suppose, must find it very hard to form anything like a just idea of the tremendous adventure involved in the act of immigration. The alien in our midst is too elusive an object for satisfactory study. He changes too rapidly. But yesterday he was a solid citizen in his particular village of Sicily or Rumania, of a piece with his ancestral background, surrounded by friends and kindred, apparently rooted in his native soil. To-day he is adrift in a foreign world, mute and helpless and tragically ridiculous—a soul in purgatory, a human creature cut from its moorings, the most pitiable sight to be met on this earth. To-morrow? Who knows? To-morrow very probably you will find him a prosperous citizen again, very earnestly devoting himself to some strange—until recently undreamed-of—business, giving

orders or taking them, even now perhaps a bit discordant against his new setting, and, except for one or two well-hidden scars, none the worse apparently for his translation. Who shall find the patience to follow him in his tortuous career?

What is surely most amazing is that he should have started out at all. Considering the pangs of separation and the risks that warn and threaten him and beset his path, why, you might ask, should he want to emigrate? Is it the dream of avarice? Yes, in part. And the hope of freedom? Without a doubt. But these are general motives and remote. The far-flung clarion call of American liberty and her promise of equal opportunity are the powerful lodestones that draw all immigrants alike. There are more particular motives than these to spur him on. Even freedom and economic independence have a varying meaning to individual aliens. Station in life, and nationality, and age, all play their part in composing his mental picture of America. And, as in war, so also in emigration, there are always immediate causes as well as remote and general ones.

I have myself been asked hundreds of times why I have come to America, and I trust that there was no malice in the question. As a rule, I have pointed to the usual reasons. I explained that at home in Vaslui, and in Rumania generally, there was very little opportunity for a young man to make anything of himself. My parents had ambitions for me which their clinging,

hopeless poverty made impossible of attainment. And I was only a child of sixteen, and I longed for the great world with its rich prizes and its still richer adventures. My soul was thrilled with the dream of conquest and the pious hope of delivering my family from want and oppression. But while all this is true, it was not the whole truth. In fact, I quite omitted from my account the most vital, because it was the most direct, cause of my migration.

The remainder of the truth is that in the year of my departure from Vaslui America had become, as it were, the fashionable place to go to. Hitherto it had been but a name, and by no means a revered name. But suddenly America had flashed upon our consciousness and fanned our dormant souls to flames of consuming ambition. All my relatives and all our neighbors—in fact, everybody who was anybody—had either gone or was going to New York. I call it New York, but you as Americans ought to be informed that the correct spelling is Nev-York, as every refined person in Vaslui knows.

I did not, then, as you see, come alone, to America. I came with the rest of the population of Vaslui. And Vaslui was merely a sort of scouting-party, to be followed directly by the main army. It has probably been forgotten in this country, if indeed it was generally noted at the time, that about the year 1900 there was what, to my eyes, appeared to be a national migration from Rumania to New York, a migration which seemed

literally to include well-nigh the whole Rumanian race.

What had so suddenly raised the prestige of New York among the Vasluianders and the Moldavian traveling public generally, I am in an excellent position to relate, for it so happened that the principal agent in this grand scheme of advertising among us the attractions of New York was a not distant relative of my own. I am well aware that such services as his ought not to go unrewarded, and I know that already your curiosity about his identity is getting the better of you, but until a committee of representative New-Yorkers assures me of its appreciation of mine and my countrymen's patronage, I feel in honor bound to respect my kinsman's modesty and to guard his secret. Meantime you shall know him by the name of Couza. Couza is a royal Rumanian cognomen, and my relative, whether by divine gift or forethought, had an unmistakable royal air, at least while he was in Vaslui.

Couza, then, put in an appearance in our town during the winter of 1899, after an absence in America of some fourteen years. For months before, if you had put your ear to the ground, you might have heard the distant rumble of his approach, and Vaslui held not only its ear to the ground, but its breath. It seemed to us that our life had been hitherto dull and common, but that at last it was to be tipped with glory and romance. Couza's brother Jacob became overnight the first citizen of the town, and this reflected glory was

6

shared by all our family. Those daily letters that
Jacob received were inquired after by the whole community. They became, in the truest sense, Vaslui's
first newspaper, for they contained the only intelligence
we cared to hear about. Now he was embarking at
Nev-York, and now he had landed at Havre. A long
succession of bulletins reported him at the various
capitals and great cities of Europe. He was coming,
coming, coming. The air was growing too thick for
respiration. On the street, in the market, at the
synagogue, we kept asking one another the one question, "When will *he* arrive?"

At last the long-awaited telegram flashed over us,
and I shall never forget my terrible disappointment on
learning its message. For weeks I had been training
in the boys' chorus which was to welcome the guest on
his arrival. And now, at the last moment, he had cold-
bloodedly decided to come in on the midnight train.
The choral reception had, therefore, to be abandoned.
Vaslui must content itself with a mere representative
committee of citizens and restrain its pent-up enthusiasm as best it might till the morrow. I have a very
vivid recollection of that night of Couza's arrival, for,
although I was deprived of a direct share in the reception, I had a partial reward for my disappointment in
the reflected splendor that fell upon me through my
father. He, being one of the guest's family, was
chosen a member of the welcoming committee; and
toward two o'clock in the morning he burst into the

house trailing clouds of glory from his rare experience. We had been tossing about for several intolerable hours, wondering whether he ever would get back. No sooner did we hear his key in the door than we leaped up in our beds and greeted him with a chorus of inquiry that nearly frightened him.

"Is he here?" we yelled all together.

"Is he? Well, I should rather say so!" father cried, breathlessly, and still in the dark.

Then followed things amazing. For hours that seemed like brief moments we sat agape, listening to a detailed account of the arrival and a somewhat bewildering word-picture of the personage himself.

"You should see the old boy," my parent began. "It seems only like yesterday when I used to see him in these very streets, a slouchy, unprepossessing youngster, with his toes out at his gaping boot-tips, carrying heavy cans of milk around for his mother. Remember, mamma, he used to bring us our liter every morning before we got our own cow? And do you remember how your brother Samuel never tired of telling us what a dunce the urchin was at school? Ah, this Nev-York must be a wonderful place. Why, I did not know him at all when he stepped off the car, not until Jacob rushed up to him and was followed by the whole cheering lot of us. At first I thought he was a *rov* [rabbi]; he is so large, and stout, and dignified. He wore a long, black frock-coat and a high hat—just the kind that Reb Sander wears on Saturdays at the

services. But when I got up nearer to him, I noticed
that he was clean-shaven. Would you believe it? He
did not even have a mustache. I never saw so many
trunks and bags in all my life as they unloaded for him.
And jewelry! He had diamonds in his cravat and
brilliants on his fingers, and a magnificent gold chain
from which hung a great locket stuck full of more
diamonds. He is a millionaire, if ever there was one in
America."

This was very exciting and altogether astonishing in
many ways. It suddenly revealed America to us in a
new light; for you must not suppose that we were so
ignorant as never to have heard of the place at all.
The name Nev-York was, indeed, rather new, and we
admired father a good deal for throwing it so glibly into
his account. But then you could not expect us to
know the whole map of America in detail. Of America, however, we had heard considerable on several
occasions. Whenever a Vasluiander went into bankruptcy, and whenever a soldier wearied of the discipline
and deserted, it was bruited abroad that he had "run
away to America." There was a female beggar in the
town whom mother always singled out for special
kindnesses. I used to wonder about her, until one day
I learned that she had once been the well-to-do mistress
of a home of her own, but that her husband had tired
of her and escaped to America. I had thus come to
think of the place as a city of refuge, an exile which men
fled to only in preference to going to prison.

I had heard of people going to Vienna and Germany and Paris, and even to England for business or pleasure, but no one, to my knowledge, had ever gone to America of his own free will. And of those who went, considering the circumstances of their departure, none ever returned to tell us what it was like, any more than if they had gone to the other world. In fact, a person gone to America was exactly like a person dead. That was why, on those rare occasions when a family followed its breadwinner to that distant land, the whole community turned out, and marched in slow time to the station, and wept loudly and copiously, and remembered the unfortunates in its prayer on the next Saturday.

I said that no one had ever returned from America. But there was one exception; and I mention it here because the individual was destined to become the villain in the piece which I am here transcribing. It was commonly gossiped in Vaslui that Itza Baer, who was hand-in-glove with officialdom, and whom every one feared and flattered as a notorious informer, had years before returned from America, where he must have had a stormy and ignominious career, because whenever anybody ventured to ask him about it, he would merely say that he preferred to serve his term than to live a dog's life in exile, and forthwith change the subject.

This Itza Baer was at first decidedly friendly to the news of Couza's coming. When the time arrived he even went so far as to consent to serve on the committee,

and at the station he was, according to father's report, one of the first to greet the arrival. Father went into circumstantial detail in his account of this historic greeting. He said that the rest of the committee drew back a step and stood around in solemn awe while the two Americans exchanged compliments in English. But the odd thing was that Itza Baer ever after had an ironical smile about his lips and an impish twinkle in his eye when referring to that English conversation. He was never seen speaking to Couza again, except at the temple on the Saturday following the event, and then it was neither in English nor in friendship. A mysterious coldness seemed to have developed between the two men almost from the start; and when Vaslui fell down on its knees and worshiped Couza as the great man he was, Itza Baer's jealousy—for jealousy was all it could be—turned into whispered threats at first, and finally into open hostility.

On the morrow after the arrival I saw *him.* I saw him on the first of those impressive progresses which were to become a regular, but not a common, sight in the daily life of our town for the next fortnight. He was riding slowly in a droshka, smiling happily, and bowing unpretentiously to the populace. The streets were lined with craning, round-eyed, tiptoeing Vasluianders, open-mouthed peasants, and gay-attired holiday visitors from neighboring towns who, having heard of the glory that had come to Vaslui, had driven in in their ox-carts and dog-carts to partake of it. I have sometimes seen

the king ride in state through these same streets, and have heard the throng shouting, "*Trâiascâ Regele!*" But this occasion was not boisterous, but dignified and solemn. Vaslui seemed too full for idle noisemaking. It seemed to feel that while the king was no doubt a fine fellow and all that, he had not come all the way from Nev-York, he had not brought with him any dozen trunks, he did not speak English, and wear diamonds, and dress in a different frock-coat every day. Quite the contrary: the king had on the same uniform every time he came to Vaslui. He was, after all, a sort of exaggerated army officer with an unnecessary amount of gold lace and other trappings about his person. He, like all military folk, might care for show and shouts. But an American millionaire was not a clown or a bear to be clapped at.

Why, he was the most modest and the simplest of men. Any other man of his great wealth would have put on airs and gone to the Hotel Regal, the exclusive stopping-place in Vaslui for all mere aristocrats. Instead, he went to his brother's home and unassumingly shared the humble quarters of his family. That appeared to be his way. Whatever was good for one man was good enough for every man. He never spoke of his wealth; indeed, he looked embarrassed and uncomfortable whenever the subject was alluded to. He positively disliked to talk about himself in any fashion.

He let his actions speak for him and all that he represented, and from his actions Vaslui was forced to

THE PROPHET FROM AMERICA

draw the right conclusion. The sheer extravagance of that trunkful of presents he had brought from America for the immediate members of his family spoke volumes for his generosity and the abundance of his means. There was the neat little razor in the leather case for his brother Jacob which a child could use without cutting himself and which was reputed to cost no less than ten francs. Then came the wonderful penholder for his sister-in-law, which, as Couza explained at some length, dispensed with ink-wells and drew its life-fluid from some mysterious source. The children, too, were by no means forgotten. There were railways that were wound up like clocks and ran around in their tracks like real trains, and dancing negroes, and squawking dolls, and jews'-harps, and scores of other delights for the palate as well as the fancy. And then the climax was capped when Couza himself drew forth out of that trunk of wonders the final package and proceeded to unwrap therefrom endless reams of tissue-paper, and just as his spectators were about to succumb to the torments of breathless curiosity, held it up and presented it to his old mother—a musical box to the value of twenty-five francs.

Moreover, no one but a millionaire could have behaved as he behaved in the synagogue on the memorable Saturday following his arrival. It was the usual custom for a distinguished guest to be honored with a reading of the Law, and it was expected from him, in turn, to make a suitable offering in return for the

honor. But when the official reader paused for the donor to fill in the blank, Couza calmly and very distinctly said, "One hundred and twenty-five francs," and looked modestly about at the astounded faces of the congregation. That donation simply transcended our imagination. The high-water mark until that day and for years past had been recorded by Eliezer Kaufman, the wealthy merchant, now dead, who had once in an extravagant moment subscribed five francs; and the old men in Vaslui still talked of it in awed tones. A hundred and twenty-five francs! Why, even when crops were bumpers a grain-merchant could garner no more than that in a month. The sum would bring a team of oxen, pay two years' rent for a house in town, or very nearly buy a modest dwelling in the country.

From that day on Vaslui became a changed town. Hitherto we had been content to gaze in abstracted admiration at the splendid phenomenon and the dim, romantic land that lay behind him. But now the shimmering apparition had become a solid reality. We had seen with our own eyes, and had heard with our own ears, the concrete thing that it meant to be an American millionaire, and Vaslui suddenly felt a vast ambition stirring in its galloping heart. Gone was the languor, the easy-going indifference, the resignation, the despair that once dwelt in the lines of our faces. We became a bustling, seething, hopeful community. A star had risen in heaven to lead us out of the wilderness.

II

THE very next day my father took me by the hand and marched me straight up to Great Headquarters. He had done some deep thinking all night and had apparently worked up an exceedingly clever scheme. At least I supposed it was clever until we reached our destination. I had been given only the broadest outline of it, but I gathered from that that it was essentially a plan to induce Couza to take me to America with him when he returned, details to be worked out later. When, however, we got within a block of Cousin Jacob's store my heart sank and father turned very pale. Here was a line of similarly clever fathers with equally shamefaced sons and daughters, extending from Jacob's store in the front, all the way around the little circular park which was in the center of the shopping district; and another shorter column in the rear, starting from the back door and ending a block away at the gate of the court-house. The total effect was of two opposing armies struggling for the capture of Jacob's store and the great prize within. And every father and son there claimed relationship with Couza, and was ready, I suppose, to

15

back it up with documentary evidence and a flourishing family tree. I had never realized that all of Vaslui belonged to my family.

It was just at this time that the notorious Itza Baer entered upon the scene in real earnest. To the shame of Vaslui be it confessed that he had succeeded in gathering about him a very considerable following, and, strangely enough, among men who had hitherto been held in high esteem for their integrity and shrewdness. It is at such stirring times as these that men go astray. When one or two of those whom Couza had felt obliged to discourage in their emigration plans chanced to speak of their disappointment, Itza Baer suggested that they might offer to share their first million with Couza in return for the passage across. He and his followers organized themselves into an anti-Couza committee, which made ridiculous claims of seeking to save Vaslui, and in the end they very nearly succeeded in ruining the hope of the town.

From the day of the great incident at the synagogue rumors of an infinite variety had gained currency regarding certain phases in Couza's career in America. No one was able to trace them to their source, but they kept issuing with ever-increasing frequency and with the emphasis of unquestionable truth. We tried to discuss them with Couza himself, but he could not be induced either to confirm or to deny them. He would simply smile confusedly, and declare that everything was possible in New York. But at the end of that

week a report of the most stupendous sort reached our ears. It was to the effect that our guest was not merely a millionaire, but that he held a very high government position in America, something resembling a prefect or a minister. This time we besieged him and insisted on knowing the truth. For this news was no matter of mere personal glory for an individual. It revealed one side of that wonderful America that we had not thought of before. One could get rich, once in a while, even in Rumania. But that our humble, downtrodden people could not only vote, but be voted for and hold office in New York, was a revelation of the most startling and inspiriting kind.

This time, I say, we would not be put off with modest blushes. Couza, of course, tried to hedge about by admitting that people of our kind might become members of the Government, that religion in America was a private matter unconnected with politics, and that he had himself heard of an American President by the name of Abraham (he could not remember his other name). But while all this was gratifying to a degree, Vaslui demanded to know the whole truth. Was it true that he himself was the prefect of Nev-York? If it was, then nothing else mattered, because everything was as clear as day. Finally the conference ended in a compromise. Of the prefecture of New York he could by no means be persuaded to speak, but after long and cruel drilling and cross-examining he did confess that his visit to Vaslui was only a side-trip incidental to his

commissions in Paris as a special representative of the American Government to the World's Exposition and the Procès Dreyfus.

After that confession Couza's modesty dropped from him like a mask. Once his mouth had been forced open, he found great difficulty in closing it again until we knew as much about New York as he did, which is to say everything. He seemed eager now to make us realize how dull and circumscribed and enslaving was our existence in Rumania, and then point in contrast to the freedom and the wealth and the beauty of that City of God which was New York. There were many ways of getting rich in America, he told us. People got paid, it seemed, even for voting. A mere slip of a girl could earn fifty francs a week at making blouses. Girls, indeed, were not a burden there as they were in Vaslui. In America the richest young ladies earned their own living, fed and clothed themselves, and saved up the necessary dowry to get a husband with. In fact, girls were altogether an enviable asset to their parents. A man who had a half-dozen grown daughters, or even a skilful wife, could be independent and free for the rest of his natural life.

One of the trunks that Couza had brought with him, we were to learn, was filled with American newspapers, and with their help he preached to us the gospel of New York. Seated on the divan in that vast room at the rear of his brother Jacob's store which constituted the family's apartment, he would spread before him

one of those extensive sheets and delight his open-mouthed callers with a message from the great world he had come from. I do not know what other people got out of those readings, but I myself was terribly excited by them, so that for months afterward I dreamed of nothing but ingenious murders and daring robberies committed in broad daylight by clean-shaven desperadoes in frock-coats and silk hats. I conceived of New York as a brave, adventurous sort of place where life was a perilous business, but romantic for that very reason.

Those American newspapers puzzled us considerably. We had expected that they would naturally be in English, but we discovered with surprise that for the most part they were printed in our own familiar Yiddish, although it was a Yiddish somewhat corrupted, like Couza's own speech, with a curious admixture of strange barbarisms. Couza laid great emphasis, as was most natural, on the unlimited opportunities for earning money in New York, and to that end he invited our attention to the pages upon pages of frantic appeals from America for every variety of help. It was vastly encouraging to hear him read those appeals and to know how badly we were wanted in America. But we were a little obtuse at times. We could not understand, for instance, why any one should want a dozen girls to keep on working at blouses day after day without end. What did a body want with so many waists, we asked our interpreter. But we got little satisfaction in

this regard. He seemed to delight in filling his mouth with those strange long words that somehow got into every sentence and spoiled its meaning for us. And he showed, I thought, decided resentment at being interrupted with a request to explain. When his own brother Jacob asked to be told what was meant by a stenographer, Couza contented himself with pointing the moral as to the brutalizing effect of living in such a place as Vaslui, where grown men did not know the things that every child in New York knew. That was perhaps a bit hard on my poor cousin, but even he could not help agreeing with Couza and hoping all the more deeply, in consequence, that his children at least might some day get out into the civilized world.

If any proof were needed of Couza's high character and noble interests, and if anything could effectively give the lie to the unwarranted, ill-tempered slurs of Itza Baer and his anti-Couza party, we got it in Couza's constant references to education. He pointed with profound scorn to the inferiority of the Rumanian schools, and denounced our Government bitterly for forcing us to pay an annual tuition rate of thirty francs for each pupil in the elementary schools. In New York, it appeared, education was to be got altogether without cost, by Jew and Gentile alike, by day or by night. The Government of America not only did not exact charges for instruction; it compelled parents to send their children to school, and it begged grown-ups to come and be educated when their day's work was

over. Couza cited instances of young men of his acquaintance who had become doctors and lawyers, and of young women who had become teachers by studying at night and earning their living in the daytime. He had himself obtained his remarkable education in that way.

After these sessions my father would come away flushed with enthusiasm and repeat, excitedly, "America is good, America is good!" He had long been cherishing the hope of making a doctor of me, but he had not even succeeded in getting me into the public school. Every fall he would take me around from No. 1 to No. 2, and always he would get the same answer: "No room." I knew of hundreds of other cases like my own. There was nothing for us to do but to go to the little private institutes and pay heavily for the scanty instruction we got. When we reached the high-school stage matters got even worse. Vaslui did have a gymnasium, but a poor fellow had not a chance in the world of getting in. The tuition was high, the school was overcrowded, and it was necessary to have a certificate of graduation from a public school to be admitted. The nearest university was at Bucharest, and it would take a small fortune to go there and a very large one to make ends meet during the seven or eight years of instruction, supposing that one succeeded in getting in. Father had almost given up the idea in despair when America appeared in the nick of time to save the situation.

Unhappily, these glorious chats about America were to be cut short with tragic swiftness. Some of our townsfolk were too insistent about their own selfish interests, and kept pestering him with their requests to be taken to America. One night, I recall, the widow Shaindel came with her eight children, and coaxed and begged and cried. She promised that she would slave for him, and clean his shoes, and scrub his mansion, and care for his horses, and weed his gardens, if only he would save her from the poverty and the tax-gatherer by taking her and her children away to Nev-York. When poor Couza could no longer endure the painful scene, he ended it by the sacrifice of his own dignity. "My dear woman," he said, "do you take me for a millionaire?" Then he grew very confused and grunted something in his deep, bass voice. But I admired him for the splendid way in which he said it. It gave me a last glimpse of the fine modesty of the old Couza of the pre-donation period. Yet it was very clear that scenes of that sort were cruelly wearing to his sympathetic spirit, and that he was getting restless to leave.

At the end of Couza's second week Itza Baer became shamelessly hostile. He declared that he could no longer stand by in silence while "this braggart" was bringing misery and discontent upon poor people just to feed his own vanity. And he let it be known that he intended to denounce Couza as an old fugitive from the recruiting officer. When Couza heard of this he declared, with a smile, that he would like to see any

little Rumanian king lay hands on an American citizen. To which Itza Baer retorted that he was ready to bet his beard and earlocks that the pretended American citizen did not even have his first papers. No one took him up on that because of the obvious technical points involved. But the next morning Vaslui awoke to learn with bitter disappointment that a telegram from Paris had recalled the special representative to his duties. He had left in such haste, the official statement added, that he had not even taken his trunks. The glory of our city was gone forever, for, although the hope was held out to us that he would return for another short stay and for his costly baggage as soon as Captain Dreyfus had had his trial, we never saw him again. He did not even come to get his niece whom he had promised to take with him to America, but contented himself with meeting her on the Hungarian border. The evident dislike he had taken to Vaslui hurt us sorely and puzzled us not a little, although we might have understood that a man of his caliber could not long put up with the annoyances he had been subjected to. Nothing but fear of the law prevented my infuriated fellow-townsmen from wreaking terrible vengeance on the unspeakable Itza Baer, who had the cheek to go around boasting that we owed him a debt of gratitude for having saved us from a dangerous impostor.

But if Itza Baer or any one else had imagined that Couza's mission would end with his departure, he was

to learn differently. Indeed, it was only then that our great guest's preaching and example began to have their real effect. Now that he was gone, Vaslui could stand off and see the vision that had passed over it in true perspective. It became quite clear to us that, for one thing, Couza had done something with his fourteen years in America, something very enviable and magnificent. We realized, of course, that he was a fine and clever fellow, and that not every one could aspire to his attainments; but, we argued, if a man of genius could in so short a time become a millionaire *and* an ambassador, then an average chap ought at least to have no difficulty in becoming, say, a police commissioner, and in keeping his cellar perpetually well stocked with red wine.

This much had, at any rate, become certain. There was a country somewhere beyond seas where a man was a man in spite of his religion and his origin. If Couza's career and transformation proved anything, they proved that in America a human being was given a chance to live his life without interference, to become rich and influential if he could, and to develop whatever talents were in him to the best advantage. Even if the informer were right, and Couza were a sham, America surely was no sham, and the message that Couza had conveyed to us was honest. Anyhow, no one from Rumania could go to America and do the things that Couza had done in Vaslui. No, it did no good for Itza Baer and his mournful followers to go around

howling that Couza was an impostor, that New York was not at all what he had cracked it up to be, and that we would find life so hard and so sordid there that we would walk back. We let them talk, and proceeded in feverish haste to put our enthusiasm into acts.

Now I must confess that I have a very grave doubt as to whether it had been a part of Couza's original plan to effect anything like an exodus from his native land to that of his adoption. Those who censure and traduce him have said so; but then so have they said a lot of other slanderous, contradictory things about him. Perhaps I am wrong; but really I do question it. Surely it was not his fault that my fellow-townsmen were so literal and so simple. Let us remember that he was cautious to the point of taciturnity about his own achievements and accomplishments, particularly when he perceived the drift of the impression he was making. A less noble character than he could not have resisted the temptation of bragging about his own wealth and influence as he resisted it.

And let us further remember that it was no voluntary misrepresentation on his part when in a moment of metaphorical excitement he let it be known that he was an envoy of the American Government in Paris; that the statement was forced upon him by my fellow-townsmen; and that in the deepest spiritual sense it was not a misrepresentation at all. The truth is that he was but a member of the great American democracy on a lark. When I got to New York the next year I

found him inhabiting the fraction of a flat on Attorney Street, the remainder of which constituted a thriving dressmaking establishment. Mrs. Couza was making the dresses, and paying the rent, and otherwise attending to the material side of life, while Couza himself was keeping more or less busy as a foreman in a bed-spring factory, and saving enough from his earnings to get another frock-coat very soon.

In a merely literal sense, therefore, it may be said that he had, after all, not been an envoy. But he had been something nobler than that; he had caught a glorious vision of America where any man *might* be a millionaire, an ambassador, or a President—what did it amount to that he, as a matter of crude fact, was not?—and he had traveled all the way to Vaslui to share his vision with us.

III

THE EXODUS

WITHIN three months after Couza's departure the America-fever had spread to the confines of the kingdom. The contagion arose simultaneously in Vaslui and Berlad, and stalked with the pace of lightning, northward through Jassy to far Dorohoi on the Russian frontier, south and westward through the Danube cities of Galatz, Braila and Turnu-Severin to the very doors of the royal palace in Bucharest, until scarcely a hamlet was left untouched by its ravages. During the early spring Vaslui had the appearance of a town struck by war or revolution. By the merciful justice of Providence it befell that the rich and the grasping were among the earliest victims. Forest-owners and land magnates got rid of their holdings, students abandoned their books, reputable merchants took the habit of bankruptcy and made off with their creditors' funds to the nearest foreign port. Houses were sold at such sacrifice that the value of real estate dropped to one-fourth its customary level, and a time soon arrived when no one could be induced to buy a home or a farm at any price. Household furniture was consumed as fire-

wood; personal property, including kitchen utensils,
cradles, prayer-books, and even clothing, were given
away in such quantities that shops and manufactories
had to close their doors. Trade was completely at a
standstill. The streets witnessed a continual procession
of trays and carts bulging with comically shaped bales
of feather-bedding, because rumor had it that the commodity was unobtainable in America. The railway
station had never been so crowded before. There were
cheerful farewells, and those who stayed behind cried
to those who departed, "I'll see you in Nev-York
soon." And what took place in Vaslui was only typical
of what had come to be the state of affairs everywhere
in Rumania.

I am certain that in any other country such a general
exodus, bringing the serious consequences in its wake
that this did, would have been stopped by the police.
Was not the thing assuming the character of a national
disaster? But the Government of Rumania was far
from any thought of interference. It stood by idly
while the caravans kept moving on, apparently only too
happy to be rid of an element of its population for which
it had always entertained a quite frank antipathy. In
fact, it did the reverse of stopping it. Ordinarily the
getting of a passport had been a matter of endless
trouble and very considerable expense. But in this
Messianic year 1900 the bars were unaccountably let
down, and every person not of military age who made
application for a passport was cheerfully sped on his

way by the officials and granted the document with the minimum of cost and almost no trouble at all.

As the movement advanced from one astonishing stage to another our information about America kept growing vaster and vaster, until the few seeds of knowledge that Couza had scattered among us seemed like a primer beside an encyclopædia. This remarkable country, so newly discovered for us, was infinitely more wonderful than it had appeared from first reports, and infinitely more puzzling. To be sure, Couza had made some passing allusion to a President, but it had never dawned on us at the time that this official was the ruler of the land. Surely no government had ever been known to dispense with the guidance of hereditary kings. Countries, no matter whether they did call themselves republics, were, after all, not charity societies to be managed by mere presidents. No wonder it was said that the Government of America was powerless to prevent troublesome persons from carping and poking fun at it, that newspapers had free rein to plot its overthrow, and that the ruler's position was so insecure that he never knew just when his enemies might supplant him. The geography of the place was even more surprising, since by all accounts New York stood exactly beneath Vaslui, "on the under side of the earth," and that would seem to mean that the inhabitants walked head downward like flies on the ceiling. It was regrettable that we had learned this only after Couza had gone, or we might have asked him

to explain how it was managed. We might also have been told in an authoritative way whether it was true that in New York the railways ran over the roofs of houses, that the dwellings were so large that one of them was sufficient to house an entire town in Rumania, that all the food was sold in sealed metal packages, that the water came up into people's homes without having to be carried, and that no one, not even a shoemaker, went to the temple on Saturdays without wearing a stovepipe hat.

By the end of April the greater part of the town's men of means and distinction had rolled away in carriage and railway car and steamboat, and the great problem of emigration gradually loomed up in all its enormity. How were the rank and file of the community—the small grain-merchants, the poor shop-keepers, the hundred varieties of go-between, all of whom lived on the peasant and depended on the brief harvest season for their whole year's income—how were they to make their way to New York? The most conservative estimate showed that two hundred francs would barely pay the passage of a single person; and families in Vaslui were of the traditional, respectable type, consisting usually of father and mother and an average of five descendants, not to mention such odd members, commonly appended to all households, as grandfathers, invalid aunts, orphaned second cousins, and the like. To fit out and transport such a party in its entirety would require a fortune as incalculable as

everything else connected with America was. Now, who among this great middle class was in a position, at the tapering end of the year, to produce anything like such a fortune all at once? Supposing even that one was content to let a mere representative of the tribe go forth to blaze the trail, and that the remaining ones could summon up the patience to wait until he had wrung enough out of New York's fabulous millions to send for them, where was *his* equipment to come from? Now that the moneyed class had gone, it was not even possible to sell or pawn the family heirlooms. The rare few who still had a bit of ready cash clung to it with a tenacity amazing even for Vaslui. So my native town, harassed and floundering, scratched its head and pondered its tremendous problem until it solved it—or I should say, until it would have solved it if relatives in America had been what they ought to be.

Who the clear-headed realist that hit upon so simple a way out of our difficulties was I cannot now recall, if indeed I ever knew. I rather incline to the theory that there was no such person—that, like all beneficial discoveries bringing relief to suffering mankind, the solution was arrived at by all of us at the same time, distilled, as it were, out of the charged air. At any rate, and however that may be, it seemed as if all at once every one in Vaslui suddenly remembered the obvious fact that Couza was not the only one of our fellow-countrymen to have gone to America. Why, there was hardly a family in town that had not a kins-

man of one degree or another in that land of millionaires. It did not matter now what the disgraceful circumstance had been that had driven him there, and it was altogether beside the point that he had hitherto been an outcast from our respectable hearts and our respectable world. Our views had broadened; we had come to regard America in a more charitable light, of late. Thank Heaven for providing us with a refuge in our extremity! And so there followed an eager searching of our memories for exact names and more or less definite addresses, and an immediate despatching of lengthy, affectionate communications to beloved uncles and very dear cousins and most precious nephews, with introductory "why haven't we been honored with news of your valued health all these years" and salutatory "times are hard here; won't you send us a ticket and a few dollars for our Yankel or Moishe, who is now a fine big boy, and you ought to see him." Unhappily, the endeared ones who were addressed somewhere in America had either migrated somewhere else, or were dead or had become hardened by excessive wealth; for very few answers came back and those few of the most discouraging sort. Times were equally hard in America, they invariably said, the country had just been at war, work was scarce, and they would therefore advise us to remain where life was simpler, easier, and freer. No doubt, they expected us to believe all this. But we quite readily perceived their motive—they feared our competition; America was so good that they wanted

her all to themselves. Ah, well, we had Couza's word and example for the truth about New York. Nothing that these selfish ingrates, whom prosperity had rendered unsympathetic to their own kin, might tell us could move us from our resolve. And then just as everything began to look once more as black as possible and the great problem bade fair to remain as unsolved as ever, help appeared from the least expected quarter. The youth—the fantastic, impractical youth—seeing the muddle their elders were in, took matters into their own hands, and one fine morning Rumania awoke to hear the startling news that the Walking Movement had begun.

IV

IT must have been along toward the middle of May that the intelligence reached Vaslui of the strange new turn that the emigration craze had taken; and while I am about it I shall let no amount of civic pride prevent me from recording that it was out of the neighboring and rival town of Berlad that salvation came. It was to the effect that a band of young men had formed themselves into an organization for the purpose of walking to America. I remember how incredulous we were when we first heard of it. In the first place, we had learned entirely too much about America during and since Couza's visit to swallow any such absurd notion as that it could be reached by walking. And besides that, the report was brought to us by a woman whom Vaslui credited with neither too much truthfulness nor complete sanity. The person was a neighbor of ours, whose husband had served a term at the prison of Dobrovetz, justly or unjustly, for arson, and she had built up a trade in convict's work in beads and leather. She used to travel about to all the fairs, and often returned with a great assortment of wild tales. We

34

little dreamed that before many weeks we were to have a To-America-on-Foot Society in our own town.

Yet that is precisely what happened. We had hardly had time to make up our minds as to whether there could be anything in the strange story from Berlad, when a number of the boys in our own set held a meeting and announced that they had formed a walking group right in Vaslui. I do not wish to be immodest, but historical truth demands I should confess that I had the glory of being present at that meeting and becoming one of the charter members of the organization. We assembled, about twenty-five of us in all, in Monish Bachman's grain-shed just outside the town gate. The place was well chosen, for that shed had already become sacred in our hearts by many tender associations. It had been the scene of a long series of theatrical performances in which the present organizers had been both actors and audience. And although we were now practical men and quite done with childish things, our instincts must have guided us in selecting this sentimental spot for our adult activities. We ranged in age from fifteen to eighteen, with the exception of young Frankel, the druggist's son, who, having spent a year at the university of Bucharest, was looked up to as a man of the world, and was, therefore, asked to give us the benefit of his parliamentary training.

The meeting was a thunderous one. As in all parliaments, the body, which had gathered as a very harmonious one, soon split up into a number of factions.

There was the extreme left, which advocated secret procedure and the exclusion of parents from our councils. They were in favor of immediate action, a nocturnal departure with French leave, and not a word to our families until we had reached New York, when a telegram would suffice to inform them of what had happened. That plan had in its favor the element of romance. But it was forthwith howled down by the extreme right, the reactionaries, who laughed at the whole scheme and declared that if we could not travel like gentlemen we might as well abandon the idea of America entirely. Finally the moderates won out. Led by the chairman himself, they argued that it would be wiser to take the townspeople into our secret, and gain the benefit of their advice and support.

Before adjourning, we took up, at Frankel's suggestion, the matter of permanent organization. We elected a president and invested him with tyrannical powers over our bodies and souls. He was to preside at the meetings while we remained in Vaslui, and to act as the captain of the band on the march. He could dismiss a member from the group for a capital offense, or punish him with reduced rations and solitary marching forty meters behind the column for minor misdemeanors. A number of us objected to making the captain into a king, pointing out the patent fact that he was called a president, and crying vehemently that this granting of wholesale privileges to a president was totally out of harmony with the spirit of the great

country to which we were going. Next we turned to the choosing of a treasurer, and experienced tremendous difficulties in deciding what one of us could most safely be intrusted with our prospective common funds. Then the temporary chairman suggested that we ought to have a secretary, "just for the dignity of the organization," even though we may find no duties for him. Last of all, I was myself picked for the post of commissary-general, with powers to purchase supplies and apportion the rations—always, of course, under orders from the president and captain.

But, alas! the irony of fate and the cruelty of parents! No sooner had we each retired to our own homes, and no sooner did we break the news to our several fathers, than we found good reason to repent of our failure to adopt the program of the leftists. The ingrate Monish Bachman, unmindful of the glory that had fallen upon his grain-shed, promptly deposed the powerful tyrant, who was his own son Yankel. Neither he nor my parent would hear of the "absurd" idea. Monish, having once been wealthy, and being still very proud and something of a power in the community, could see no reason why his son should undergo the hardship and the indignity of having to tramp to America. "If Yankel must go away," he declared, with a flourish, "I am not yet so poor but that I could afford to have him travel as befits my position." But Yankel need not leave home at all, he insisted. The youngster was very useful to him in his business. In vain did the boy

object that he cared nothing about dignity and position, that he thought the railway and steamboat were tiresome, uninteresting, grandfatherly modes of travel, unworthy of a boy. Monish had put his foot down.

With me things went quite as badly, if not worse. My father was a cleverer man than Yankel's, and therefore he had no difficulty in trumping up a whole chain of causes why he could not let me go. Number one: had I forgotten that no more than a week before, while I was bathing the horse down at the swimming-hole, I had very narrowly escaped drowning, and a whipping afterward into the bargain? With that exhibition of my incapacity still fresh in his memory, how could I expect him to trust me to take care of myself on such a journey and in a distant country? Number two: I was the youngest in the family, and probably for that reason mother's favorite child— he was not talking about himself now. Paul was in the army at Hushi, and Harry was in business at Constantza. Was I cruel enough to go away and leave mother to die of longing? Number three: The crops last fall had failed; times were woefully hard; there was not money enough in the house to fit me out for any kind of a journey, however inexpensive.

All this array of logic I might have met, but before long father's arguments were reinforced by mother's pleadings. Had I forgotten Annie, my only sister, who had died but three years before, a flower struck down in the midst of spring? How could I think of abandoning

father and mother in their sorrow and quit the precious soil where Annie lay buried? Against the logic of bereavement, I saw, I had no hope of prevailing. Even though my reason did not yield, my heart did, and the session ended in tears.

In the mean time Vaslui generally showed a very different disposition toward the new emigration. In spite of its deposed president and commissary-general, the group had managed to grow both in numbers and in public approval. It had been joined by several older men, so that the roster contained, by now, some forty-odd names. The organization held daily meetings—no longer in the grain-shed, but in one of the town halls—the preparations for the journey were being rushed and enthusiasm ran very high, not only among the members themselves, but especially in the community. If the earlier emigration had aroused interest, this new and strange development had in it the picturesqueness andthe heroic pathos which could not but appeal to the imagination and touch the heart. The majority of those who composed the reorganized group were preparing to walk to America out of real necessity, not for adventure. Vaslui gave them the homage and the sympathy that a nation gives its army marching off to war.

The most striking evidence of the community's interest in the movement appeared right at the start. Before matters had proceeded very far a few prominent citizens of the town undertook to guide the destinies of

the group in a more systematic fashion. They per-
petuated the old committee which had been chosen to
welcome the man Couza, whose missionary zeal had
started the whole migration. The purposes of this
higher organization were at first purely decorative. It
made arrangements to give the group a suitable send-
off on its departure, with flags and speeches and the
like; and it instituted preparations for the welcoming
of such groups from other towns as might happen to
pass through Vaslui on their way to New York. But
once the committee had been formed it found a multi-
tude of unforeseen avenues for its activity. It was
discovered, in the first place, that such funds as had
been gathered from the contributions of the members
themselves were absurdly inadequate to the needs of
the journey. Furthermore, it was out of the question
for the boys to camp out or stop at hotels in the towns
where the night might overtake them. The most
serious problem of all arose over the question of how the
young people were to be cared for in the foreign countries through which they must journey.

Thus there came into being a whole succession of
institutions which the original organizers of the walking
movement had not even dreamed of. The home committee of Vaslui was soon duplicated in every town
where groups were forming, and before long these
separate bodies became merged into a really formidable
national committee, with branches in every corner of
Rumania and activities that covered every possible

need of the emigrants. And then the process of organization was carried to the last climactic step when the newly born national committee entered into correspondence and ultimately became affiliated with the great charitable alliances of Vienna, Berlin, Paris, and London. So that the marching group which had started out as an almost grotesque, childish fancy of merely local scope, had in a short time evolved into a world movement, with agencies in the principal capitals of Europe and even in New York itself.

By far the most noteworthy by-product of this amazing movement was the advent of the newspaper. Hitherto Vaslui had been content to get its news second-hand. Journalism was a thing unknown, not only in Vaslui, but in all the other cities of Rumania except Bucharest. There may have been newspapers in Jassy, but I never heard of them. Even the Bucharest dailies were taken only by the coffee-houses of Vaslui, where they hung on racks clamped into their holders, and were glanced at sporadically by the merchants who congregated there. But all this was now changed. In the last month or two Vaslui and Rumania generally had passed through a cycle of changes the like of which had taken, elsewhere, centuries to effect. The mere thought of New York had somehow in a moment of time raised us to the level of Western civilization.

I have often heard it said since, in school and college, that the genuine art and literature of a people are the direct result of its history and invariably reflect the

popular soul. If this be true, I have myself been present at the birth of a little movement which may—who can tell?—prove a real contribution to the development of a genuine national art. For these daily and weekly papers that arose so suddenly among us were no mere purveyors of the world's daily scandal. They were essentially of the stuff of which literature is made, although I dare say they never found their way into books or libraries. They were filled with poems and passionate eloquence, words of cheer and hope, eulogies of the land of our aspirations, which for some reason or other was continually referred to as Jerusalem, encouragement to those who were left behind, and praise to the Almighty for delivering his people from the bondage of the modern Egypt (Rumania). Nearly all the contents were the work of the members of the groups themselves. And for the first time in their lives our humble, simple people had found an interest in journalistic endeavor. They eagerly devoured every issue from the first word to the last.

The ancient arts of music and oratory likewise came in for their share. We had never dreamed of the profusion of talent that lay fallow in our own midst. Moritz Cahana, the owner of the Hotel Regal, acquired a reputation overnight for impassioned public utterance which reached far out of Vaslui and extended even beyond the frontiers of Rumania. All the meetings of the group consisted in large part of songs, with Hebrew, Yiddish, and Rumanian words, whose airs were adapta-

tions of ancient melodies—tender lullabies, melancholy yearnings for Zion, and solemn chants of the synagogue. Some had been borrowed from the *doinas* of the shepherd, and others had filtered in, after many vicissitudes, from the *cafés chantants* of Vienna. The martial airs were quite recognizable plagiarisms from the military composers. But all of the compositions had been blazoned with the heroic spirit of the young men who sang them and the fervid enthusiasm of the times.

In this immense burst of literary and artistic fire the practical side of the undertaking was, I am afraid, somewhat neglected. I attended the majority of the meetings, but I cannot recall ever having seen a map at any of them. In fact, I am pretty certain that not even the captain of the expedition had the faintest glimmer of a notion about routes. It was the broad, magnificent idea of the thing that occupied all minds. No one seemed to be in the least interested in mere details. As far as I can now determine, there was not a member in the whole group who could tell just which way he was headed, except that the initial stop was to be Berlad—some forty miles away—and the ultimate destination, New York. It was never made clear in the speeches or the newspapers how the Atlantic was to be inveigled into suffering the foot-voyagers to bridge its chasm. Only once had there been an allusion in biblical phrase to the cleaving of the sea and the rising of its waters like a wall, but as that came out in a poem it was not remarked.

AN AMERICAN IN THE MAKING

It was early in May that this first group, having completed its preparations, set out on its strange adventure. The day was a clear and balmy one. The marchers assembled at the gate of the little circular park in the center of the town, and from the earliest hour of the morning vast throngs of people came out to greet them. Promptly at ten o'clock the bugle sounded and the procession began. It was headed by Moritz Cahana, the orator of the occasion, and some other members of the committee in a droshka. Then followed the group in double file, clad in brown khaki, military leggings, and broad-brimmed canvas hats, each with an army knapsack on his back and a water-bottle slung jauntily over his shoulder. Last in order came well-nigh all that remained of the community of Vaslui. We marched and sang through the main thoroughfare, and then we swung off to a by-road that led to the southern gate of the town. There we halted, and Moritz Cahana made a speech that caused the whole throng to cheer and brought a lump into my throat and the tears into my eyes. Finally came the long last farewells, with tears and sobs from other people besides myself. The bugle sounded again, the captain gave the command, and the column was off on its way.

I have sometimes debated with myself whether it was really the enthusiasm for America and the vague yet marvelous things she meant to me, or whether it could have been that fascinating uniform of my fortunate boy friends and the romantic glories that I saw lying so

near before them that made my heart ache when I heard that bugle sound and beheld those feet lifted for the march. Whichever it was, the sight of that column on its way, the eloquent words of the speaker, and the dreary walk back home have remained among the saddest experiences of my boyhood.

V

I HAD given my word that I would not again ask to go with that group, and I had kept it, in spite of the fact that Monish Bachman had withdrawn his objections and allowed my friend Yankel to go. But when, several days later, the papers began to publish exciting accounts of the progress of the group I quite frankly began to be sorry for having been so good. It made me desperate to think that here I was condemned to inactivity, my hopes and my ambitions turning sour within me, while the boys who had been my friends and companions were plucking rich adventure, seeing the world, and daily drawing nearer to that magic city of promise, New York. They had, according to a letter to me from Yankel, reached Berlad; the whole town had turned out to welcome them, had fought for the privilege of entertaining them at their homes, and had banqueted them for three days as if they had been princes. From Berlad they had gone on to Tecuci, where their reception had been even more lavish than in Berlad. Can you wonder, after this glowing report, that I was getting restless and repenting of my good behavior?

Therefore, when, toward the middle of June, the second Vaslui group was organized, I returned to my attack on father. I threatened to run away and join the group at the next town. I reminded my parent of his ambitions for me, and asked him, after all the rebuffs his efforts had met, whether he could still hope to make anything of me in Vaslui. Just what did he expect to turn me into? I painted a gloomy picture of our life in Rumania—the poverty, the absence of every variety of opportunity, the discriminations of the Government against us. Whichever way one turned there were prohibitions and repressions. Supposing I wanted to study law, then "aliens" were not eligible to the bar. The ministry? Rumania forbade the establishment of rabbinical seminaries. Well, I could go in for medicine, if only the Government allowed him to earn the means of seeing me through. But justice had taken precious care that he should not. When he had engaged in storekeeping in the country and had, by hard toil, succeeded in making a comfortable living, a new law had legislated him and all his kind back into the towns. Later on, when he had entered the family occupation of candle-manufacturing, an import tax on the raw materials and a heavy export tax on the finished product suddenly rendered the trade unprofitable. Wine and tobacco still brought tolerable incomes, but he was no more permitted to deal in these articles than I was to study and practise the profession of the law. He was thus doomed to stay forever in the petty business of

grain brokerage, which, being the only occupation open to thousands of others, was in a state of such cutthroat competition that even the most competent were hardly able to support their families by it, let alone send their sons to the universities.

Yes, it was about time that he should look the stern facts in the face and abandon his lifelong dream of a learned career for his youngest and most studious son. Why, as a matter of fact he *had* abandoned it. Hadn't I left school more than a year before and gone into trade? Well, what had I accomplished? I had tried grain for six months and had made a total profit of eighteen francs for the entire period—just about enough to pay for my salt and water. I had been willing to compromise with our family traditions by condescending to buy eggs and poultry from the peasants for export, but he had objected to that and had reminded me that I was not brother Paul, that it was enough to have one boy in a decent family fall below the level of his peers, and that he would rather have me idle the rest of my life than see me hobnob with market-women and butchers' journeymen. Even mother's self-humiliation with her well-to-do brother Pincus, of Berlad, had availed her nothing. I was by no means certain that I would have greatly relished sweeping his dry-goods store and cleaning lamps and running errands for all his clerks by way of a stepping-stone toward some day becoming one of his clerks myself; but thanks to my newly acquired aunt Rebecca, I had been spared the

pains and the shame of it, for she had threatened Uncle Pincus to run away back to her parents and never come back if he started in by filling the place with his own relatives.

My argument gathered momentum as it swept on. Knowing my audience as I did, I turned next with merciless emphasis to another subject. There was the dreadful horror of the recruiting officer constantly lurking in our path like a serpent, ready to spring on a young man just when he had reached the stage where he could be useful to himself and of help to his family. My brother Paul was a case in point. He had struggled for years—ever since he had been twelve—to learn a trade; had served a three-year apprenticeship for his mere bed and board; had then toiled like a slave first for fifty, then for a hundred francs a year. And when at last he had become master of his calling and was about to become independent, along came the scarlet monster and packed him off to its musty barracks, to be fed on black bread and cabbage, to learn senseless tricks with his feet and a gun, to spend days and whole weeks in prison cells, as if he were a criminal, to be slapped in the face like a bad boy, and to live in constant terror of war and the manœuver for the rest of his life. "If this is the sort of future you want for me," I concluded, dramatically, "you are right in trying to keep me here."

It was cruel, this relentless logic of facts. Mother began to weep quietly, and father bit his lip and turned

to look out of the window. But with the single-eyed selfishness of youth I looked only to the advancement of my own cause. I perceived that my speech had had its effect. So I followed up the argument with a brilliant sketch of the great things that were awaiting me in New York. Had they forgotten the wonderful man from New York who had recently visited us? Had they forgotten his jewels, his clothes, his trunks, his fine, impressive appearance, his cultured manners, his official position? That was what America was making out of *her* men. For our visitor, by his own confession, was not the only one who had been so marvelously transformed in that great country. Everybody who went there became a millionaire overnight, and a doctor or a teacher into the bargain. There, in America, was my future as well as theirs. For it would take me only a few weeks to make enough money to send for the whole family.

So at last I conquered. But my victory turned out to be only a partial one. In fact, by the time it was finally won the best part of the glory had been extracted from it. Although father and mother were both completely won over, the chief difficulty still remained to be overcome. When father had previously told me that there was not money enough in the house to fit me out for the journey he had touched on a real obstacle, as I now learned. The costume alone would cost about fifteen francs, the passport about ten more, and I must have a few francs in cash. I suggested selling the cow,

and father consented. But by the time that could
be accomplished the second group had left Vaslui, and
me at home, a thoroughly broken and disappointed
boy.

Meantime mother set about with a heavy heart to
prepare for the great day which I looked forward to so
impatiently and which she so horribly dreaded. For
the next four weeks she knitted socks, and made me
underwear of flannelette, and sewed buttons, and
mended my shirts and my old overcoat, which last,
however, I declined to take with me. She filled several
jars with jam for me and one or two with some of her
far-famed pickles. In the evening when we were alone
together she would make me sit on her footstool, and
while her deft fingers manipulated the knitting-needles
she would gaze into my eyes as if she tried to absorb
enough of me to last her for the coming months of
absence. "You will write us, dear?" she kept asking
continually. "You won't forget your old father and
mother when the Lord blesses you with riches. You
won't, will you? Promise me again, my son. And
if I should die when you are gone, you will remember
me in your prayers, oh, my *kadish*, my male child."
Once or twice she gave way to passionate sobs: "I have
borne you, my boy, and brought you into the world in
pain, and I have nurtured you, and prayed over your
cradle in the night, oh, my joy and my solace." At
such times I tried to comfort her by promises of daily
letters, by calling her silly for imagining dreadful things,

and by assuring her again and again that it was only a matter of a little time before we should be once more united.

Throughout those days of preparation father was silent with that pregnant silence which he always maintained when his heart was breaking. Only on the day before my departure he betrayed himself. He had apparently been worrying all the time about that incident at the swimming-hole, when I had come dangerously near drowning, and he had resolved that he would impress me with the seriousness of it so that I should never again imperil my life. On that memorable Saturday night, therefore, after the beautiful home service with its candles and songs was over, he took me around to the house of the rabbi and made me take part in a scene which still lingers in my memory as one of the most solemn experiences of my life. Even at the time I remember comparing it with that impressive incident in the Bible when Jacob calls his son Joseph to his death-bed. As we entered the rabbi arose and shook hands with me. Then, still holding my hand in one of his, he placed his other hand on my head and pronounced a blessing in Hebrew. When he had finished that he asked me to promise him by the love I bore my father and mother that I would never again bathe in open water. "That was an omen from above," he said. "The Lord of the universe has spared you. But you must not tempt Him again. Promise me that you will not. Be a good son of Israel." Then

he bade me a cheerful good-by and a successful journey.

When at last my preparations were completed the last and greatest obstacle to my migration had to be faced. By this time the second Vaslui group was approaching the city of Galatz on the Danube, which is about two hundred miles from Vaslui. Father was using his influence as a member of the committee to get me admitted into the group at that point. But the leaders of the organization would not hear of it. To begin with, they argued, it was against the constitution and the by-laws, and, besides, it would set a bad precedent. Why should any one care to walk at all and endure all the hardships after this, if he could come in at the last moment and reap all the advantages? They had wandered about over the whole country, had once or twice been attacked by brigands, and had exposed themselves to sickness and every variety of danger. And now, just as their difficult journey was drawing to an end, a member of the committee was trying to foist a raw recruit upon them. But father was determined, and after endless dickerings and pleadings and debatings he won his point.

It had developed, you see, that the walking was not to be continued all the way to New York, after all. The home committee—the general staff, as it had come, appropriately enough, to be called—had apparently decided that at the outset. But the captains and the other leaders of the groups themselves had found the

tramping too jolly—in spite of their occasional complaints to the contrary—and threatened to rebel. Not until they were convinced that without the support of the committee they could not march a step, would they listen to reason. So they agreed to walk only as far as Galatz, and there board a Danube River steamer for Vienna. Once out of Rumania, they would be out of the jurisdiction of the national committee and would be taken charge of by the Jüdische Allianz zu Wien. From Vienna they would journey by rail through Germany as far as Rotterdam, at the expense and under the guidance of the Verband der Deutschen Juden and the Alliance Israélite, and from Rotterdam they would sail for New York. That was the route that the group, and I along with them, actually followed.

It was not until Sunday morning that I knew whether I was going or not. As soon as the good word reached me I proceeded to put the finishing touches to my packing and to attend to the inevitable farewells. All that day I went around shaking hands with what was left of the community—most of them people I had never spoken to before—and every one asked me to deliver his regards to some relative in New York, and to urge him to send a steamer ticket to this one or that one. During the early part of the evening mother and I walked up and down in the front yard, my hand in hers, talking of the past and the future, and carefully avoiding any reference to the present. Just before train-time she put the gold-clasped prayer-book into

my grip which father had given her on their betrothal, and sewed two gold napoleons into the lining of my waistcoat. She seemed calm and resigned. But when the train drew into the station she lost control of her feelings. As she embraced me for the last time her sobs became violent and father had to separate us. There was a despair in her way of clinging to me which I could not then understand. I understand it now. I never saw her again.

For several hours I sat stark and stiff on a wooden bench in my railway carriage, unaware of the other passengers, mechanically guarding with one hand the fortune in my waistcoat, as father had repeatedly urged me to do. I did not even try to collect my thoughts. I could only see a blurred vision of my mother going home from the station, and kept vaguely wondering whether America, with all her prizes, could be worth that.

Toward morning my mind cleared and I could see things a little more in their true relations. As the train approached Galatz I looked out and beheld the wide expanse of the Danube with the rosy hues of dawn reflected on its placid surface. There were ships along the wharves, both on the Rumanian and on the Bulgarian side. My heart leaped up at the beautiful sight. I had never seen a real ship before. Here was the gate of the great world opening up before me, with its long open roads radiating in all directions. It was but an earnest of the nobler destiny ahead of me. In a very

few days I should be out of Rumania. And then in two weeks more New York would no longer be a vision, but an inspiring reality. I could no longer doubt that my sacrifice was worth while. And I turned my face to the West.

PART II
THE ALIEN ABROAD

VI

IT seems to be assumed by the self-complacent native that we immigrants are at once and overwhelmingly captivated by America and all things American. The mere sight of this new world, he fancies, should fill our hearts with the joy of dreams realized and leave us in a state of surfeited contentment, empty of all further desire. Why, he would ask, if the doubt were ever to occur to him—why should we not be happy? Have we not left our own country because we were in one way or another discontented there? And if we have chosen America, it is quite clear that we must have been attracted by what she offered us in substitution. Besides, no man with eyes could fail to see right off the superiority of this great Republic to every other country on the face of the earth. Witness how the tide of immigration is forever flowing— and always in one direction. If the alien were dissatisfied with America, would he not be taking the first steamer back instead of inviting his friends and family to follow him?

And yet, in spite of logic and appearances, the truth

remains that the immigrant is almost invariably disappointed in America. At any rate, of this much I am certain: I myself was very bitterly disappointed in America. And, unless observation has been altogether astray with me, I think I am justified in the generalization that nearly all other new-comers are at least as disappointed as I was. It was not that this land of my aspirations had failed to come up to my dream of it, although in a measure it did fall short there. Neither was my disillusionment due to the dreariness, the sordidness, and the drudgery of immigrant life, although this, too, may have entered into the equation. All these things came only later. I am writing of the first impact of America—or of that small fraction of it which was America to me—of the initial shock that came to me when I first set foot on American soil. And I say that long before I had had time to find out what my own fate would be in this new world, I experienced a revulsion of feeling of the most distressful sort.

What were the reasons for it? Well, there were a variety of them: To begin with, the alien who comes here from Europe is not the raw material that Americans suppose him to be. He is not a blank sheet to be written on as you see fit. He has not sprung out of nowhere. Quite the contrary. He brings with him a deep-rooted tradition, a system of culture and tastes and habits—a point of view which is as ancient as his national experience and which has been engendered in him by his race and his

environment. And it is this thing—this entire Old World soul of his—that comes in conflict with America as soon as he has landed.   Not, I beg you to observe, with America of the Americans; not, at any rate, immediately. Of that greater and remoter world in which the native resides we immigrants are for a long time hardly aware. What rare flashes of it do come within range of our blurred vision reveal a planet so alien and far removed from our experience that they strike us as merely comical or fantastic— a set of phenomena so odd that we can only smile over them but never be greatly concerned with them.

I needed sadly to readjust myself when I arrived in New York. But the incredible thing is that my problem was to fit myself in with the people of Vaslui and Rumania, my erstwhile fellow-townsmen and my fellow-countrymen. It was not America in the large sense, but the East Side Ghetto that upset all my calculations, reversed all my values, and set my head swimming. New York at first sight was, after all, not so very unlike many other large cities that I had traveled through. I viewed it from the upper deck as my steamer plowed into the harbor and up the river, and was not the least bewildered by the sight. I cannot remember whether I thought it was ugly or beautiful. What did it matter? From the pier I was hustled with hundreds of others of my kind into a smaller boat and taken to Ellis Island. There I was put through a lot of meaningless manœuvers by uniformed, rough officials. I was jostled and dragged and shoved and shouted at.

I took it philosophically. I had been through the performance many times before—at the Hungarian border, at Vienna, in Germany, in Holland. It did not touch me, and I have forgotten all about it.

But I have not forgotten and I never can forget that first pungent breath of the slums which were to become my home for the next five years. I landed early one Sunday morning in December, 1900; and no sooner did I touch firm ground than I dug into one of my bundles and produced the one precious thing that formed the link for me between my old home and my new. It was a crumpled bit of wrapping-paper which I had brought all the way from Vaslui and on which was scribbled in his own handwriting Couza's address in New York. Do you remember Couza? Ah, well, he was to be my first disappointment in a series of heartaches and disillusionments. With what hopeful enthusiasm I approached a policeman at the Battery and dumbly shoved my document into his face! And with what a sinking of the heart I peered through the frosty windows of that jangling, rickety horse-car as it bounced and wound through one shabby alley after another on its way to Attorney Street, where my millionaire kinsman held court!

The mansion, when at last I reached it, presented an imposing enough front. And though the weather was very sharp I passed up and down a long time before that marble portico with its brass railings and its tall cans of garbage and cinders lined up at the door, before

I could summon the courage to ring the bell and enter. The interior was even more impressive. I was marshaled through a large room in which there were a number of sewing-machines littered with quantities of textile materials, and into the parlor. There I found the table set for breakfast, and a magnificent display it was, with its German-silver coffee-urn and pressed-glass bowl, and silver-plated spoons and white linen. After a somewhat unceremonious introduction to Mrs. Couza—a lank, prematurely aged person—handshaking with Couza himself and my little girl cousin whom he had brought back with him from Vaslui, and after one or two perfunctory questions about my people and my journey, I was invited to partake of a cup of coffee with cake. I was amazed. Cake for breakfast! If I had been offered swan's eggs or steak or broiled pigeons, or almost any other thing, I should have kept my self-possession. But the very notion of serving cake for breakfast struck me as an extravagant fancy of which only millionaires were capable.

And there was Couza himself, the magnificence of him as I had seen him in Vaslui apparently quite undimmed. And yet, with all the splendor of that scene before me, I could not help wondering, vaguely, as I thought of the revolting misery I had seen from the horse-car, whether there was not a worm somewhere at the heart of this brilliant appearance. In Vaslui, as you may remember, there had been many who doubted and openly slandered Couza as a sham, while the rest of

the town worshiped him as a millionaire and (by his own confession) an ambassador, and hailed him as a savior. Now, without anything in particular having happened, I found myself, with a kind of terror, sinking into agreement with those doubters and knockers. Yes, there was Couza in his customary frock-coat and his customary newspaper spread before him, but with some terrible new vision I seemed to see through all this. I knew that no one had been expecting me here, but I had an insane feeling that this whole *décor* had been set against my coming. And I ended up by wanting to cry out that I had been cheated, that Couza and the New York he had lured me to were miserable frauds, that I wanted to go back to Vaslui.

My depression was increased after breakfast. I do not know just what I had been expecting that my kinsman would do for me, but I must have been entertaining some vague hope that he would at once set me to making money in one of his factories, or, at least, that he would use his great influence with the American Government to find me a comfortable place worthy of my family and my genteel bringing up. I made some timid advances on that score, but Couza merely grunted in his familiar bass voice and declared that he would see. Mrs. Couza looked puzzled, and intimated that in America there were no such things as relatives; that money was a man's best friend, and that the wisest course to pursue was to depend on oneself. And then, without any kind of warning, my youthful cousin spoke

up and asked me to accompany her to her mother's home on Rivington Street, where I would take up my temporary lodgings until I found work.

Of Couza I was to see a great deal more. He had evidently not been found out by the other Rumanians, for he had the air of keeping the entire colony he had, as it were, brought into being, under his spacious protecting wing. On Sundays he paid us his weekly visit. Dressed in his frock-coat and chimney-pipe hat, he would walk from Attorney to Rivington Street and be greeted deferentially by all who passed him on the way. He always had matters of great moment to talk over with his sister-in-law, and some time during his stay the two would mysteriously disappear into one of the bedrooms, whence their earnest whispers would be heard by us outside. Mrs. Segal, my cousin and landlady, entertained a pathetic respect for Couza, whom she always addressed as "Brother-in-law" and never by his christian name. Before departing, Couza always distributed largess of the nickel denomination among the children, and a quantity of advice on how to become Americanized and successful among the elders. Once I had the distinction of sitting at the same table with him at one of those elaborate East Side weddings, where the hard-earned savings of years of toil of both bride and groom are lavishly wasted, and it made my eyes pop to see him hand the waiter a five-dollar bill in return for a toothpick! He was continually bestowing praise on those young men and women

who showed a tendency to become "Americanized."
I tried for a long time to find out just what he meant
by the word, and never succeeded—beyond the obvious
definition of becoming like himself. But I know that
he frowned upon me and a few others who betrayed an
inclination to mingle with the radical and intellectual
life of the quarter. That bent, he thought, was sure
to ruin our chances for success in America, and make us
personæ non gratæ with the best people.

That walk from Couza's residence, with my bundles,
to Rivington Street was a nightmare. I know that the
idea prevalent among Americans is that the alien
imports his slums with him to the detriment of his
adopted country, that the squalor and the misery and
the filth of the foreign quarters in the large cities of the
United States are characteristic of the native life of the
peoples who live in those quarters. But that is an
error and a slander. The slums are emphatically not
of our making. So far is the immigrant from being
accustomed to such living conditions that the first thing
that repels him on his arrival in New York is the
realization of the dreadful level of life to which his
fellows have sunk. And when by sheer use he comes to
accept these conditions himself, it is with something
of a fatalistic resignation to the idea that such is
America.

I shall never forget how depressed my heart became
as I trudged through those littered streets, with the
rows of pushcarts lining the sidewalks and the centers

of the thoroughfares, the ill-smelling merchandise, and the deafening noise. My pretty little cousin, elegant in her American tailored suit, was stepping along beside me, apparently oblivious to the horrible milieu that was sickening me well-nigh unto fainting. So this was America, I kept thinking. This was the boasted American freedom and opportunity—the freedom for respectable citizens to sell cabbages from hideous carts, the opportunity to live in those monstrous, dirty caves that shut out the sunshine. And when we got beyond Grand Street and entered the Rumanian section my cousin pointed out to me several of our former fellow-townspeople—men of worth and standing they had been in Vaslui—bargaining vociferously at one kind of stand or another, clad in an absurd medley of Rumanian sheep-pelts and American red sweaters. Here was Jonah Gershon, who had been the chairman of the hospital committee in Vaslui and a prominent grain-merchant. He was dispensing soda-water and selling lollypops on the corner of Essex Street. This was Shloma Lobel, a descendant of rabbis and himself a learned scholar. In America he had attained to a basket of shoe-strings and matches and candles. I myself recognized young Layvis, whose father kept the great drug-store in Vaslui, and who, after two years of training in medicine at the University of Bucharest, was enjoying the blessings of American liberty by selling newspapers on the streets.

Here and there were women, too, once neighbors of

ours, mothers of sons, and mistresses of respectable households. And what were they doing here in this diabolical country? Well, here was one selling pickles from a double row of buckets placed on a square cart, yelling herself hoarse to an insensible world in a jargon of Yiddish and "English," and warming her hands by snatches over an outlandish contraption filled with glowing coals. Farther on I came upon another, laboriously pushing a metal box on wheels and offering baked potatoes and hot *knishes* to the hungry, cold-bitten passers-by. And all the while there was the dainty little figure of Cousin Betty walking airily beside me, unaware of the huge tragedy of it all. She had herself arrived no more than a year before, but how callous America had already made her! I asked myself whether I, too, would harden and forget the better days I had known, and I fervently hoped not.

VII

THE IMMIGRANT'S AMERICA

A S I look back over my transition from the alien to the American state I cannot help wondering at the incredible changes of it. I see a curious row of figures, as in a haze, struggling to some uncertain goal, and with a shock it comes upon me that I am all this motley crew. There is the awkward, unkempt, timid youth of sixteen, with the inevitable bundles, dumbly inquiring his way from the Battery to the slums. A little farther on, shivering in the December drizzle with a tray in his gloveless hand, the vender of unsellable candies dreams of Christmas far away by his Rumanian fireside. A tap-boy in an East Side barroom follows next; his hair parted in the middle, his gift-breeches fitting a little snugly on his well-groomed young carcass, he hums to himself over his tub of glassware. Then the sewing-machine operative, now in his sweat-shop assiduously at work, now at his anarchist meetings scheming to reform the world. And then the student in school and college, with his new struggles and problems piled high over the old, old worries about bread and bed. And then—and then the picture gets

too near for a good perspective, and anyhow the tale is all but told. The alien is become the self-made American.

What a fortunate thing it was for me that I got to New York just before Christmas! Fortunate, that is, as immigrant's luck goes. If I had got here after Christmas I would, without a doubt, have starved as well as frozen. You know, of course, why I froze— because I did not obey my mother, which is simply saying that it served me right. Mother, it will be remembered, had insisted that I take with me the old overcoat which she had herself recreated out of a garment once worn by my well-to-do uncle Pincus; and I had refused because, to begin with, I already had too much to lug, and because I could see no sense in carrying old clothes to a country where I would at once become rich enough to buy new ones. That I did not starve, in spite of my landing with the proverbial fifteen cents in my pocket, was due not only to the fact that I tumbled right into the midst of the prosperity of the Christmas shopping season, but to a further piece of good fortune.

What I would have done if little Cousin Betty had not had the foresight to bring over her folks, is more than I can tell. To be sure, the family had arrived only about three months before, but three months is a long time in the evolution of Americans. And so there they were, the whole seven of them—mother and son

and five daughters—on the tunefully named Rivington Street, already keeping house and talking English, and the oldest young lady receiving callers, and Betty, her next of age, declaring that she would not go without pince-nez glasses when all the fashionables, including her own sister, possessed and wore them. Betty and her modish sister, being old enough to work, did consequently work at men's neckties, while the remaining four children went to school or kindergarten, or danced on the street to the music of the grind-organ, or stayed at home to be rocked in the cradle, according to their varying tastes and years. Yes, there they were, quite Americanized, happy in their five rooms, three of which faced on Allen Street and joined their window-sills right on to the beams of the Elevated trestle. They were still happy, because neckwear was a genteel trade that could be worked at in the home until any hour of the night with the whole family lending a hand, and because Cousin Jacob, the father and tyrant of the household, had been left in Rumania "to settle affairs," because the business of cooking with gas and turning a faucet when you wanted water was an exciting novelty and because keeping roomers was a romantic undertaking. They lived on the third floor, which was something to be proud of, since back home in Vaslui none but the rich could afford to live up-stairs; and of course "up-stairs" in Vaslui was only a beggarly second floor.

I never contrived to find out just how many people

did share those five rooms. During the day my relative kept up the interesting fiction of an apartment with specialized divisions. Here was the parlor with its sofa and mirror and American rocking-chairs; then came the dining-room with another sofa called a lounge, a round table, and innumerable chairs; then the kitchen with its luxurious fittings in porcelain and metal; then the young ladies' room, in which there was a bureau covered with quantities of odoriferous bottles and powder-boxes and other mysteries; and, last of all, Mrs. Segal's and the children's room. I remember how overwhelmed I was with this impressive luxury when I arrived. But between nine and ten o'clock in the evening this imposing structure suddenly crumbled away in the most amazing fashion. The apartment suddenly became a camp. The sofas opened up and revealed their true character. The bureau lengthened out shamelessly, careless of its daylight pretensions. Even the wash-tubs, it turned out, were a miserable sham. The carved dining-room chairs arranged themselves into two rows that faced each other like dancers in a cotillion. So that I began to ask myself whether there was, after all, anything in that whole surprising apartment but beds.

The two young ladies' room was not, I learned, a young ladies' room at all; it was a female dormitory. The sofa in the parlor alone held four sleepers, of whom I was one. We were ranged broadside, with the rocking-chairs at the foot to insure the proper length.

And the floor was by no means exempt. I counted no fewer than nine male inmates in that parlor alone one night. Mrs. Segal with one baby slept on the wash-tubs, while the rest of the youngsters held the kitchen floor. The pretended children's room was occupied by a man and his family of four, whom he had recently brought over, although he, with ambitions for a camp of his own, did not remain long.

Getting in late after the others had retired was an enterprise requiring all a man's courage and circum-spection, for it involved the rousing of an alarmed, overworked, grumbling landlady to unbolt the door; the exchange in stage whispers of a complicated system of challenges and passwords through the keyhole; the squeezing through cracks in intermediate doors, which were rendered stationary by the presence of beds on both sides; much cautious high-stepping over a vast field of sprawling, unconscious bodies; and lastly, the gentle but firm compressing and condensing of one's relaxed bedmates in order to make room for oneself. It was on such occasions as these also that one first became aware of how heavy the air was with the reek of food and strong breath and fermenting perspiration, the windows being, of course, hermetically sealed with putty and a species of padding imported from home which was tacked around all real and imaginary cracks.

In the morning one was awakened by the puffing of steam-engines and the clatter of wheels outside the

windows, and then the turmoil of American existence began in real earnest. First, the furniture must be reconstructed and restored to its decorative character, and then the scattered disorder of feather-bedding must be cleared from the floors and whisked away into cupboards and trunks. The men-folks had to fly into their clothes before the ladies emerged from their quarters, so that the latter might pass through the parlor on their way to the kitchen. In spite of all the precautions taken the night before, some one invariably missed one portion or another of his costume, which he promptly proceeded to search for with a great deal of wailing and complaining against his own fate in particular and the intolerable anarchy of Columbus's country in general. Then followed a furious scramble for the sink, because the towel had a way of getting unmanageably wet toward the end; and this made it necessary for Mrs. Segal, who slept in the kitchen, to be up before every one else. By the time the camp had once more become an elegant apartment, the coffee was already steaming on the round table in the dining-room, and the whole colony sat down to partake of it before scattering to its various labors, breakfast and laundry being, of course, included in the rent.

The first two days Mrs. Segal would not hear of my going out to look for work. She insisted that I must rest up from the journey, look around a bit, and in general play the guest. "A guest is a guest even in America," she said. "And don't worry," she added;

"you'll have time enough to make the money." After which she smiled in a peculiar manner. So I stayed home alone with her, and feeling that I owed her something in return for her hospitality, I tried to make myself useful to her by helping with the housework. The army of roomers had no sooner dispersed than she packed the youngsters off and threw herself into the task with enthusiasm. "Housekeeping," said she, "is wonderfully easy in America."

I had to agree that it was wonderful, but I myself at least could hardly say that I found it easy. It certainly was an extravagant way of doing things. The first thing we were going to do, she told me, was to scrub the kitchen. "Very well," I said. "Where do you keep the sand?" "Sand!" she exclaimed. "This is not Vaslui," and proceeded to take the neatly printed wrapper off a cake of soap which back home would have been thought too good to wash clothes with. For the floor she employed a pretty, white powder out of a metal can and a brush with which I had the night before cleaned my clothes. Moreover, she kept the light burning all the time we were in the kitchen, which was criminal wastefulness even if the room was a bit dark. She herself would certainly not have done such a thing at home.

About ten o'clock she started off to market. If she had not told me where she was going, and if it had not been a week-day, I would have believed she was on her way to temple. There she stood in her taffeta gown (it was the very one mother had once told me had come

from her wedding) and all the jewelry I used to see on her at the services in Vaslui, and a pair of brand-new patent-leather pumps. As soon as she was out of the house I took the opportunity to blow out the gas in the kitchen, only, however, to be scolded for my pains when she re-entered and to be informed that greenhorns must keep their eyes open and their hands off. I could see nothing wrong in what I had done, but she kept saying over and over again that I had narrowly escaped death or blowing up the building.

The things she brought back from market! Egg-plant in midwinter, and tomatoes, and a yellow fruit which had the shape of a cucumber and the taste of a muskmelon. I had never seen such huge eggplants in all my life. And here was another thing which was entirely strange, but which inquiry revealed was cauli-flower—an article father had once eaten at the home of my cousin, the doctor, in Bucharest and had never ceased talking about. Could there be anything in it, after all? I repeatedly asked myself during that day. Was I doing Couza an injustice? Oh, if the Lord would only grant that I should turn out to have been mistaken! Yes, but how about the boarders? If the Segals had actually made their million in these three months, why did they share their fine apartment with strangers? Who but the very lowest of people kept roomers in Vaslui? I could not figure it out. America was surely a land of contradictions.

Mrs. Segal and I had meat in the middle of the day,

and then about six, when the two girls got home, there was meat again. I remember writing home about it the next day and telling the folks that they might think I was exaggerating, but that it was literally true, all the same, that in New York every night was Friday night and every day was Saturday, as far as food went, anyway. Why, they even had twists instead of plain rye bread, to say nothing of rice-and-raisins (which is properly a Purim dish) and liver paste and black radish. And then about eight in the evening two young gentlemen called on Cousin Rose and capped the climax of the whole day by insisting on bringing in some beer in a pitcher from the corner saloon. There I was! I could say all I wanted to about America being a sham, but no one would believe a word of it until I could prove that Segals and Abners and Schneers indulged in such luxuries as beer at home—a thing which no one could prove because it was not so.

VIII

"how do you like america?"

NO, my first impression of America was right, and
no mistake. With every day that passed I became
more and more overwhelmed at the degeneration of my
fellow-countrymen in this new home of theirs. Even
their names had become emasculated and devoid of
either character or meaning. Mordecai—a name full
of romantic association—had been changed to the
insipid monosyllable Max. Rebecca—mother of the
race—was in America Becky. Samuel had been shorn
to Sam, Abraham to Abe, Israel to Izzy. The surprising dearth of the precious words betrayed a most
lamentable lack of imagination. Whole battalions of
people were called Joe; the Harrys alone could have
repopulated Vaslui; and of Morrises there was no end.
With the women-folks matters went even worse. It did
not seem to matter at all what one had been called at
home. The first step toward Americanization was to
fall into one or the other of the two great tribes of
Rosies and Annies.

This distressing transformation, I discovered before
long, went very much deeper than occupation and the

externals of fashion. It pervaded every chamber of their life. Cut adrift suddenly from their ancient moorings, they were floundering in a sort of moral void. Good manners and good conduct, reverence and religion, had all gone by the board, and the reason was that these things were not American. A grossness of behavior, a loudness of speech, a certain repellent "American" smartness in intercourse, were thought necessary, if one did not want to be taken for a greenhorn or a boor. The ancient racial respect for elders had completely disappeared. Everybody was alike addressed as "thou" and "say"; and the worst of it was that when one contemplated American old age one was compelled to admit that there was a good deal of justification for slighting it. It had forfeited its claim to deference because it had thrown away its dignity. Tottering grandfathers, with one foot in the grave, had snipped off their white beards and laid aside their skull-caps and their snuff-boxes and paraded around the streets of a Saturday afternoon with cigarettes in their mouths, when they should have been lamenting the loss of the Holy City in the study-room adjoining the synagogue. And old women with crinkled faces had doffed their peruques and their cashmere kerchiefs and donned the sleeveless frocks of their daughters and adopted the frivolities of the powder-puff and the lip-stick.

The younger folk, in particular, had undergone an intolerable metamorphosis. As they succeeded in picking up English more speedily than their elders, they

assumed a defiant attitude toward their parents, which the latter found themselves impotent to restrain and, in too many cases, secretly approved as a step toward the emancipation of their offspring. Parents, indeed, were altogether helpless under the domination of their own children. There prevailed a superstition in the quarter to the effect that the laws of America gave the father no power over the son, and that the police stood ready to interfere in behalf of the youngsters, if any attempt to carry out the barbarous European notion of family relations were made.

Thus the younger generation was master of the situation, and kept the older in wholesome terror of itself. Mere slips of boys and girls went around together and called it love after the American fashion. The dance-halls were thronged with them. The parks saw them on the benches in pairs until all hours of the morning, and they ran things in their parents' homes to suit themselves, particularly when their families were partially dependent on them for support. Darker things than these were happening. These were the shameful days when Allen Street, in the heart of Little Rumania, was honeycombed with houses of evil repute, and the ignorant, untamed daughters of immigrants furnished the not always unwilling victims. And for the first time in history Jewish young men by the score were drifting into the ranks of the criminal.

The young, however, were not the only offenders.

The strong wine of American freedom was going to the heads of all ages alike. The newspapers of the Ghetto were continually publishing advertisements and offering rewards for the arrest of men who had deserted their wives and children. Hundreds of husbands who had parted from their families in Europe with tears in their eyes, and had promised, quite sincerely, to send for them as soon as they had saved up enough money, were masquerading as bachelors and offering themselves in wedlock to younger women for love or for money. Very often the entanglement reached that screaming stage which lies on the borderland of tragedy and farce, when the European wife, having been secretly and hurriedly sent for by her American relatives, appeared on the scene and dragged the culprit before the rabbi or the law-court.

Whence had my countrymen got their sickening habits of carelessness and downright filthiness? It was impossible to pass through the streets after dark without being hit from above by a parcel of garbage or a pail of dirty water. Where was the good of dressing the children in expensive white clothes and white kid shoes and, apparently, never washing their poor little shrunken pale faces? A new pest of scurrying creatures unheard of at home had made their appearance here, which shared the dwellings of my friends and got into their food and their beds; and the amazing part of it was that no one seemed to mind them beyond making jokes about them and using the word by which they were

called as a nickname for one's neighbors or even as a pet-name for one's own offspring.

Ah, the blessed life we had left behind! And for what? To chase after a phantom raised by Couza the fanatic and the humbug. To follow a will-o'-the-wisp and sink in the quagmire of this repulsive Gehenna. Back there at home the houses were low and made of mud, and instead of hardwood floors the ground was plastered with fresh clay—mixed with manure to give it solidity—which had to be renewed every Friday. A family occupied but one room, or two at the most; but the houses were individual and sufficient, and the yard was spacious and green in summer, filled with trees and flowers to delight the senses. Business men scarcely earned in a week what a peddler or an operator made here in a day, but they were free men and had a standing in the community, and with God's help they supported their families in decency. They were not unattached, drifting nobodies, as every one was here. Life ran along smoothly on an unpretentious plane. There was no ambition for extravagance, and therefore no unhappiness through the lack of luxuries. Homes in Vaslui were not furnished with parlor sets of velvet, and the women-folks did not wear diamonds to market; but, on the other hand, they did not have to endure the insolence of the instalment agent, who made a fearful scene whenever he failed to receive his weekly payment. No one was envious because his neighbor's wife had finer clothes and costlier jewels than his own had. The

pride of a family was in its godliness and in its respected forebears. Such luxury as there was consisted in heavy copper utensils and silver candelabra, which were passed on as heirlooms from generation to generation—solid, substantial things, not the fleeting vanities of dress and upholstery.

The prices of things in America were extortionate. The rental per month for a dark, noisome "apartment" on Rivington Street would have paid for a dwelling in Vaslui for an entire year. A shave cost ten cents, which was half a franc; if we had had to pay that much for it in Vaslui the whole community would have turned barbers. When I asked my cousin landlady how much my room-rent would come to, she told me that every one paid fifty cents a week. Two francs fifty! I tried to calculate all the possible things that my parents could buy for that vast sum at home if I were to desist from the extravagance of living in a house, and I resolved that as soon as I found work I would try to devise some substitute, and send the money home where it could be put to some sane use.

My Americanized compatriots were not happy, by their own confession. As long as they kept at work or prospered at peddling, they affected a hollow gaiety and delighted in producing a roll of paper dollars (which they always carried loose in their pockets, instead of keeping them securely in purses as at home) on the least provocation, and frequented the coffee-houses, and indulged in high talk about their abilities

and their prosperity, and patronizingly inquired of the greenhorn how he liked America, and smiled in a knowing way when the greenhorn replied by cursing Columbus. But no sooner did he lose his job or fail in the business of peddling than he changed his tune and sighed for the fleshpots of his native home, and hung his head when asked how he was getting on, and anathematized America, and became interested in socialism. At such times it was quite apparent that America's hold on his affections was very precarious— a thing that needed constant reinforcing by means of very definite, material adhesives to keep it from ignominious collapse.

How feeble his attachment to his adoptive land was, and how easily his sentiments shifted from adoration to indifference or contempt, was strikingly illustrated by the various and contrasting names he had for America. Now it was gratefully termed the home of freedom and then, with a shade of irony in the tone, he referred to it as the land of gold. If he brought home a satisfactory bargain from the pushcart merchant he beamed and sang the praises of the "all-right country," and the next moment if the article turned out to be discolored or rotten or otherwise defective he fussed and fumed and swore that there never had been such a stronghold of fakes in all the world as this same America. His fondest hope was to become a "citisnik" of the Republic, but the merest scratching of the surface showed beyond a doubt that his desire for naturalization

did not have its roots in any conversion to the principles of democratic self-government, but rather in certain eminently human motives. Abe Sussman, for instance, entertained an ambition to become a street-cleaner because he hated peddling and because his brother-in-law, Joel, who had come here before him, was in that service. Jake Field had a crippled mother at home who had once before been brought over at ruinous expense, only to be excluded by the despots of Ellis Island. He was certain that the American Government would think twice before rejecting the parent of a full-fledged voter. Joe Katchke was perfectly frank in telling you that if he only had a pull with the district leader—which, of course, he could not have as long as he had no papers—he could get a letter from him to the street-car company's superintendent which, added to his fine command of English, would at once get him a job as a conductor. Harry Heller's ambitions were not quite so soaring. He, too, craved a pull with the governing powers, but only for the modest purpose of making the renewal of his peddler's license less trouble-some and of assuaging the rapacity of the policeman.

As a greenhorn I got my share of the ridicule and the condescension and the bullying that fell to the lot of my kind. In my cousin's house I was constantly meeting Americanized young men who came to call on the girls, and invariably I must submit to the ever-lasting question and its concomitant, the idle grin: "How do you like America?" Well, after what I have

given you of my impressions, you may readily guess that I did not like America; that, indeed, I very emphatically hated America. In my most courageous moments, which usually came to me when my young gentleman questioner was particularly insistent and particularly stupid, I declared so openly and with great stress, which declaration of mine was regularly met with loud peals of superior laughter, interspersed with phrases of that miserable gibberish which the Americanized of the foreign colony fondly regard as English, and which, even in those first days, I recognized for the sham it was. After such encounters I came away hating America more than ever.

Yes, I hated America very earnestly on my first acquaintance with her. And yet I must confess here and now that for a whole year every letter that came from my parents in Vaslui was an offer to return home, and that I steadily refused to accept it. Those letters, by the by, added their very considerable share to the tragic burden of my readjustment, for my parents suggested that, if I liked America well enough to remain there, they would endeavor to raise the money and join me. And to this I was constrained to reply, "Vaslui is not for me, and America is not for you, dear parents mine." These words were obviously a confession that our separation must remain indefinite. I did not want my parents to come to America, because I could not endure the thought of father as a match-peddler on Orchard Street; and since he was neither a

shoemaker nor a woman's tailor nor a master of any
of the other profitable professions in America, and since
I was as yet far from equal to the task of supporting the
family, there was nothing for us to do but to rest apart.
But the odd thing was that I declined the alternative
offer. Somehow, even in those dark days of greenhorn-
hood, an occasional ray would penetrate through the
gloom and reveal another America than that of the
slums.

And in the mean time the East Side Ghetto *was* my
America, a theater within a theater, as it were. No, it
was even more circumscribed than that. The outsider
may imagine that the Ghetto is a unified, homogeneous
country, but a little more intimate acquaintance will
rectify that mistake. There are in it strata and sub-
strata, each with a culture, a tradition, and a method of
life peculiar to itself. The East Side is not a colony;
it is a miniature federation of semi-independent, allied
states. To be sure, it is a highly compact union,
territorially. One traverses a square, and lo! he finds
himself in a new polity. The leap in civilization from
Ridge Street to Madison Street is a much wider one
than that between Philadelphia and Seattle. The line
of demarkation is drawn sharply even to the point of
language—the most obvious of national distinctions.
Though both speak Yiddish, the Jew from Austrian
Poland will at first hardly understand his coreligionist
from Lithuania. Their dialects differ enormously in
accent and intonation and very appreciably in vocabu-

lary. And each separate group entertains a humorous, kindly contempt for the speech and the manners and the foibles of all the others.

As I had come from Vaslui, it was my lot to settle in that odd bit of world which I have referred to as Little Rumania. It was bounded on the east by Clinton Street, with Little Galicia extending on the other side to the East River; by Grand Street on the south, with the Russians and Lithuanians beyond; and on the north lay the untracked wilds surrounding Tompkins Square Park, which to me was the vast dark continent of the "real Americans."

Even as far back as 1900 this Little Rumania was beginning to assume a character of its own. Already it had more restaurants than the Russian quarter—establishments with signs in English and Rumanian, and platters of liver paste, chopped eggplant, and other distinctive edibles in the windows. On Rivington Street and on Allen Street the Rumanian delicatessen-store was making its appearance, with its goose-pastrama and kegs of ripe olives and tubs of salted vine-leaves (which, when wrapped around ground meat, make a most delicious dish), and the moon-shaped cash caval cheese made of sheep's milk, and, most important of all, the figure of an impossible American version of a Rumanian shepherd in holiday costume, with a flute at his waxen lips, standing erect in the window. Unlike the other groups of the Ghetto, the Rumanian is a *bon vivant* and a pleasure-lover; therefore he did not long delay

to establish the pastry-shop (while his Russian neighbor was establishing the lecture platform), whither of a Saturday afternoon, after his nap, he would betake himself with his friends and his ladies and consume dozens of dainty confections with ice-cold water.

He it was, also, who, out of a complex desire to serve his stomach and his faith, brought forth an institution which has now become universal in America—the dairy lunch-room—which, owing to the exigencies of religion, was originally just what it is called, a place where nothing but the most palatable dishes built out of milk and milk products were to be had, and where no morsel that had been in the vicinity of meat could be obtained for love or money. And, most characteristic of all, he transplanted that unique near-Eastern affair, the *kazín*, or coffee-house, which is a place of congregation for the socially-minded, and where the drinking of fragrant, pasty Turkish coffee is merely incidental to a game of cards, or billiards, or dominoes.

This was America, and for this we had walked here— a gay Rumanian city framed in the stench and the squalor and the oppressive, noisy tenements of New York's dingiest slums. As I have already intimated, of the broader life and the cleaner air of that vast theater within which this miniature stage was set I was hardly aware. What I knew of it came to me vaguely by hearsay in occasional allusions to a hazy, remote world called variously "up-town" and "the South," to which the more venturesome of my fellows now and then

resorted, only to find their spunk failing them and to return forthwith. In addition, there was the policeman, who made life miserable for the peddler, while accepting his bribe. He was a representative of "up-town," for as soon as his tyrannical day's work was over he vanished into the mysteries of that uncharted region. There was, likewise, the school-teacher, with her neat figure and sweet smile, and a bevy of admiring little children always clinging to her skirts as she tried to make her way from the corner of Eldridge Street "up-town." Now and then in my search for work I wandered into Broadway and across Fifth Avenue, and stared at the extravagant displays in the shop windows and the obvious wealth (judging from their clothes) of the passers-by. But altogether I remained untouched by the life of greater America. It merely brushed me in passing, but it was too far removed from my sphere to affect me one way or the other.

IX

TO return to my cousin's camp and the order of events.

The two days allotted to a guest being over, I was given broadly to understand that I must enter the race for American dollars. During the remainder of that week and throughout the entire week following I went about "trying." Early in the morning I would go down-stairs to buy a *World*, and after breakfast I would get one of the children to translate the want advertisements for me. When I glanced at the length and the number of those columns, I saw that I would not be long in getting rich. There were hundreds of shops and factories and offices, it seemed, that wanted my help. They literally implored me to come. They promised me high wages, and regular pay, and fine working conditions. And then I would go and blunder around for hours, trying to find where they were, stand in line with a hundred other applicants, approach timidly when my turn came, and be passed up with a significant glance at my appearance. Now and then, in a sweat-shop, I would get a hearing; and then the proposition

was that if I would work without pay for two weeks, and give ten dollars for instruction, I would be taught to be a presser or an operator. The thing baffled me. I could not bridge the gulf between the advertised appeals for help and this arrogant indifference of the employing superintendent.

Half the time I had not the remotest idea of what was wanted. I had been told what a butcher was and what was meant by a grocery-store. But what were shipping clerks, and stock clerks, and bill clerks, and all the other scores of varieties of clerk that were so eagerly sought? However, I did not let trifles discourage me. There was only one way to succeed in America, my friends continually told me, and that was by constant, tireless, undiscriminating trying. If you failed in one place, or in ten places, or in a hundred places, you must not give up. Keep on trying and you are bound to be taken somewhere. Moreover, American occupations were so flimsy, they required so little skill or experience, that a fellow with a little intelligence and the normal amount of daring could bluff his way into almost any job. The main thing was to say "yes" whenever you were asked whether you could do this or that. That was the way everybody got work. The employer never knew the difference. So I followed the counsel of the wise, in so far as my limited spunk permitted, and knocked at every door in sight. Time and time again I applied, at department stores in need of floor-walkers (that, I thought, could certainly require no special gifts), at

offices where stenographers were wanted, at factories
demanding foremen. But my friends' predictions
appeared to be only half-true. Of failure there was,
indeed, no end, but that ultimate inevitable success
which I had been promised did not come. There was
nothing to do but change my tactics.

Then there was the problem of distances. I could
not dream of paying car fares everywhere I went.
Even if I had had the nickel, the mere thought of
spending twenty-five *bani* at every turn would have
seemed an appalling extravagance. And, somehow, the
jobs that I supposed I had a fair chance of getting were
always at the ends of creation. An errand-boy was
wanted in Long Island City, and a grocer was looking
for an assistant in Hoboken. By the time I had reached
one place and had had my services refused, I was too
late in getting to the others. And always I was
refused. Why? At last one morning a butcher in the
upper Eighties gave me the answer with pungent
frankness. I had got to the spot before any one else,
and when I saw it in his eye that he was about to pass
me up, I gathered all the pluck that was in me and
demanded the reason. He looked me over from head
to foot, and then, with a contemptuous glance at my
shabby foreign shoes (the alien's shoes are his Judas),
he asked me whether I supposed he wanted a greenhorn
in his store. I pondered that query for a long time.
Here, I thought, was indeed new light on America.
Her road to success was a vicious circle, and no mistake.

In order to have a job one must have American clothes, and the only way to get American clothes was to find a job and earn the price. Altogether a desperate situation.

Then my relative suggested peddling. Here I was occupying part of a bed that could bring fifty cents a week, and paying nothing for it. Moreover, she was giving me meals. This was America. Everybody hustled, and nearly everybody peddled. If I had some money I might start right off on the grand scale with a pushcart. But there were other ways. There were lots of young fellows from Vaslui, of just as good family as mine, who sold pretzels in a basket, or mantles from a hand-bag—anything they could find—and paid for their board, and bought clothes for themselves, and even saved money. Here, for instance, was Louis Carniol, whom everybody at home had considered a ne'er-do-well—a *schlim-mezalnik*. Did I notice how nicely he was dressed? Did I know that he had money in the bank? Yes, I need not look incredulous, for only the week before he had sent home fifty francs. And there was Rose Marculescu, a mere girl, and in three months she had nearly paid for the steamer ticket her brother had sent her. Of course the lucky ones and the clever ones got jobs. But what could a body do? In the land of Columbus one did what one could, and there was no disgrace in doing anything. A shoemaker was just as good in America as a doctor, as long as he worked and made money and paid for everything.

I denied the imputation that I was ashamed, and asked her what she proposed that I should do, considering that my fifteen cents had gone for ferry rides. She answered that she proposed to lend me the money for a start, and irrelevantly quoted the Rumanian adage about when thousands are lost hundreds don't count. So I accepted her dollar, and let her lend me a small brass tray she had brought from home; and in the afternoon I went around to Orchard Street and invested my borrowed capital in two boxes of chocolates. Monday morning you might have seen me at the hour of seven standing at the corner of Fourteenth Street and Fifth Avenue, inviting the crowds that rushed by to work to partake of my wares. I was very enthusiastic in spite of the nipping cold. But, oddly enough, no one in that whole rolling sea of humanity seemed to be fond of chocolates. Moreover, the policeman took a strange dislike to me and chased me from one corner to another. Once a young American humorist flipped my tray in passing, and nearly succeeded in spilling my entire stock under the feet of the hurrying throng.

However, late in the day my affairs took a turn for the better. Toward nine o'clock the whole army of peddlers came forth into the daylight, and the winter air grew suddenly warm with friendly babbling and mutual offerings of assistance. The mere sight of them, with their variegated equipages and their motley goods, was reassuring. There were peddlers with push-

carts and peddlers with boxes, peddlers with movable stands and peddlers with baskets, peddlers with bundles, with pails, with satchels and suit-cases and trunks, with an infinite assortment of contrivances designed to display the merchandise and to enthrall the eye. Some of the carts were ornamented with bunting and colored paper edging and Christmas bells and sprays of holly; others carried glass show-cases and feather dusters; a great number were provided with tops built of lumber and oilcloth. They came pouring in from all directions— men with patriarchal faces and white beards, old women draped in fantastic shawls out of the *Arabian Nights*, boys with piping voices, young mothers with babes in their arms. On they came, scurrying through the congested traffic, dodging vehicles, trudging with their burdens, laboriously wheeling their heavy-laden carts— these representatives of all the nations of the earth making for their appointed posts in the international exposition that stretched along Fourteenth Street and up Sixth Avenue as far as Twenty-third Street. It seemed to me, as I looked out upon this vast itinerant commerce, whose stocks were drawn from the treasures of the East and the industries of the West, that I was no mere detached trafficker engaged in a despised trade. I was a member of a great and honored mercantile guild.

I found myself surrounded by friends. An elderly man with a telescope case set up camp beside me and proceeded to remove therefrom, in the manner of a

conjurer, endless packages of Oriental spreads and table-cloths. As he drew one forth, he shook it gently out of its folds, held it up to view with a pleased expression, made some queer passes with his hands, like an acrobat about to ascend a tight-rope, and placed it affectionately on his shoulder. I glanced up at him and shied away. His head was swathed in a white turban, and with those laces hanging down his person he had the air of some barbarous Eastern priest. The effect was heightened by his swarthy face and grizzly black beard. I was somewhat alarmed, and was about to move on, when he suddenly spoke up to me in my native tongue.

"How is business?" he inquired.

I confessed timidly that I had not yet made a sale. Then, in an access of boldness and with a sinking suspicion of occult powers at his command, I asked him how he had recognized me for a Rumanian. His eyes twinkled with amusement as they looked meaningly at my shoes.

"From Vaslui, for a guess," he went on. "I am from Berlad myself. My family is still there. Can't get enough together to bring them over. I am an old peddler—know the game—have been here once before, years ago, when I was a boy. Ah, times are hard. America is not what it used to be—played out. Too many in the business. They pamper the customer and ruin the trade. God! if I had not been such a fool, to go back and waste all those good years in Rumania,

serving the Wallachian with a gun and a bayonet, I
could have had a store on Fifth Avenue by now. But
you are a youngster. It's your America. I wish I
were in your shoes.—Nice Syrian laces, lady?"

All this went over my head. I was as yet too fresh
from the steerage to grasp its significance. But when,
his persuasive arts having failed, he informed his
customer that those Syrian laces were meant for people
with money and not for dickering paupers, he came
back to me with more definite counsel.

"You'll learn, all right. Never fear. How much do
you sell those chocolates for? All right, here is my
penny for a starter—a *saftia*. But that is too cheap.
You'll do more business if you ask five cents. Your
American likes to be charged a stiff price; otherwise he
thinks you are selling him trash. Move along; elbow
your way through the crowds in front of the stores, seek
out the women with kids; shove your tray into their
faces. Don't be timid. America likes the nervy ones.
This is the land where modesty starves. And yell,
never stop yelling. Advertising sells the goods. Here
is a formula to begin on: 'Candy, ladies! Finest in
America. Only a nickel, a half-a-dime, five cents.'
Go on, now; try it."

I did, reluctantly and with some misgiving. What
would I do if those elegantly dressed ladies should
resent my aggressiveness and call the dreaded policeman? Moreover, there were altogether too many
mischievous youngsters in the throng who seemed bent

on adventure, and I wished no disaster to befall me. So I moved along cautiously, applying my friend's advice only by degrees. But it astonished and delighted me to see how magically it worked. I was really making sales. Incredible as it seemed, these people actually paid five cents for every piece that cost me less than two-thirds of one cent. Once a customer—a man—gave me a dime and refused to take change, and I began to wonder whether I could not raise the price to ten cents—whether, as a matter of fact, there was any limit to the gullibility of my customers.

One thing, indeed, that impressed me right early in my contact with the world outside the Ghetto was the almost ludicrous liberality of American life. Every one was sufficiently dressed in the streets of New York. At home people who were thought of as in comfortable circumstances usually wore their clothes and shoes away past the patch stage and thought nothing of it. In America nobody, except the newly landed and a certain recognizable type styled a bum, wore patched garments. Then, again, in Vaslui none but young ladies of marriageable age wore gloves; for any one else the article would have been regarded as silly dandyism. Of course, most of us wore worsted mittens, home-knitted, in cold weather. But I am talking of gloves, a very different thing in appearance as well as spiritual significance. In New York it amused me not a little to observe that even teamsters and street laborers wore gloves at their work, to preserve, I supposed, their

dainty hands. Indeed, one of the most curious things in America was the fact that, if you went merely by their dress, you could not tell a bank president from his office-boy.

In the mean time my first day's peddling made one thing certain: I was a successful business man. "Trying" was a thing of the past. I began to hold my head high. And that evening I had the satisfaction of going to a Rumanian restaurant on Allen Street and ordering the first meal I had ever paid for in America. It consisted of a dish of chopped eggplant with olive-oil, and a bit of pot-roast with mashed potato and gravy. It did cost ten cents; but I was in an extravagant mood that night. I had a right to be, for while I dined I reckoned up my earnings for the day and found that they were no less than seventy cents, not counting the chocolates I had eaten myself.

Thenceforth I returned to my restaurant every night. It was a great comfort, after a day spent out in the cold, to go into a cozy room, and have a warm meal, and hear my native Rumanian spoken. Now and then a musician would wander in and gladden our hearts with a touching melody of home, and we would all join in until the tears drowned our voices. I began to make acquaintances; and after the meal we would sit around at the tables, discussing America with her queer people and her queer language. Those of us who worked at the building trades and those who sold fruits and vegetables up-town brought back with them the most

amazing stories of their adventures in exile. The American, it appeared, was a spendthrift and a finick. His home had the most luxurious appointments, and his pantry was loaded with fabulous edibles. He affected a curious liking for hushed whispers and silent footsteps. His women-folks were meticulous cranks. His language was a corrupted jargon of Yiddish and Rumanian. From the oddities of the native's life we would come back to things that touched us nearer. We sighed or bragged over our business ventures, bestowed admiration or advice; and when the clock that hung over the display of victuals on the counter struck midnight we found that our talk had drifted back to where it had started—to gossip about the latest arrivals and the recent news from home.

In the course of my adventures as a man of business I was frequently brought in touch with school-boys, and the encounter always left me wistful and envious. Fortunate youths! Here they were, at such tender years, and they already talked a very "high" order of English—it was "high" enough to go over my head for the most part—and studying profound things out of profound books whose very titles were an unfathomable mystery to me. What was in those great stacks of books that they always carried around with them? I tried to draw them into talk in an effort to find out; and as the colloquy progressed I grew bold enough to ask the one great question that lay nearest my heart. Were they all going to be doctors? To which they

answered with great shouts of laughter and called me
"greeny." Only once I managed to draw a young
gentleman out of his reserve. "A doctor!" he sneered.
"Lord! no. Who on earth wants to go to school half
his life and then fool around sick people for the rest of
it? Not me. I am going to high school because mother
is silly and because I ain't old enough yet to get my
working-papers. But just you wait until next year,
and see how quick I chuck it and go to business."
This was a tremendous revelation. How any one with
the chance of becoming a doctor could dream of wanting
to do something else was something I could not get
through my head at all. Oh, if only I had their luck!

With my royal ambition constantly before me, and
the demands of my business, learning English was
becoming a necessity. I felt, besides, that going on
living in America without knowing the American's
language was stupid. But the East Side offered few
facilities and plenty of hindrances for the study. The
abominations of English orthography I mastered early
enough, so that I could spell hundreds of words without
knowing their meaning. But the practical use of the
language was another matter. A greenhorn on Rivington Street did not dare open his mouth in English unless
he wanted to bring down upon himself a whole torrent
of ridicule and critical assistance. The mere fact that
he had arrived in America a week later than a fellow-
alien seemed to justify the assumption that he knew
less of the language, and East Side etiquette demanded

that he should defer to the "Americanized" and accept
their corrections without question.

At first I was inclined to be meek and let myself be
taught by my elders and betters. I even let them
laugh at me when I spoke in my native tongue. In
America, it appeared, it was against the rules of good
breeding to call things by their right names. Certain
articles must always be referred to in English, irrespec-
tive of whether one was talking Yiddish or Rumanian.
But as soon as I saw through their flimsy pretensions—
which did not require very long, nor any special talents
—I revolted. Indeed, I turned the tables on my critics,
and started to do some laughing myself. There was no
scarcity of occasion. My friends were finding English
contemptibly easy. That notion of theirs that it was
a mixture of Yiddish and Rumanian, although partly
justified, was yielding some astonishing results. Little
Rumania was in the throes of evolving a new tongue—a
crazy-quilt whose prevailing patches were, sure enough,
Yiddish and Rumanian, with here and there a sprinkling
of denatured English. They felt no compunction
against pulling up an ancient idiom by the roots and
transplanting it bodily into the new soil. One heard
such phrases as "I am going on a marriage," "I should
live so," "a milky dinner." They called a cucumber a
"pickle" and an eggplant a "blue tomato" because in
Rumanian a pickle was a sour cucumber and tomatoes
and eggplants were distinguished from one another
merely by their color. All balconies were designated

as fire-escapes because the nearest thing to a fire-escape known at home was a second-floor balcony.

I found the language of America much harder than that. One of the first purchases I made out of my peddler's earnings was a copy of Harkavy's Dictionary. As it was my purpose to learn the whole English language and nothing less, I meant to start at the letter A and proceed alphabetically right through to the end. That appeared to me the surest way of not missing anything. But when I beheld that bulky volume, and found on the title-page something about thirty thousand words, my enthusiasm got a little chilled. I had never realized that Americans were so loquacious. Why, even if I were to learn a hundred words every day, I could hardly hope to master enough vocabulary for an intelligent conversation in less than three years, to say nothing of studying medicine. Moreover, experience had already taught me that words, even when perfectly memorized and pronounced, had an exasperating way of turning into nonsense as soon as they were put to the practical test. Supposing you did know what "give" meant, or "turn," and had managed, in addition, to discover the meaning of such particles as "up," "down," "in," and the like, you were still at sea as to the connotations of such phrases as "give in," "give up," "give way," "turn off," "turn out," and no end of others. No more helpful was the dictionary in your search for the sense of such bewildering oddities as "that will do" (which sounded like "dadldoo"),

"rushing the growler," "inc." (seen on signs in the street), and "Dr." (obviously having nothing to do with the thing you wanted to be). There must be some magic glue outside the dictionary that held them together. So I added a Bible to my library and studied the English version side by side with the Hebrew original. I read the signs on the streets and the legends in the shop windows, and in the evening hunted up whatever words I could remember in my dictionary. Now and then I made an incursion into the *Evening Journal.* But it required a gigantic effort of the will to keep up the grind. The very fact that I could read the news in two or three other languages was a handicap.

In my adventures with the outer world I made another discovery. Bargaining was discouraged. I stopped in front of a grocery-store to buy a basket of what I thought were plums of a species I particularly liked. The man asked ten cents; I offered him six, and he calmly put the basket back in its place and proceeded to walk into the store. I called him back and suggested splitting the difference. Whereupon his face assumed a threatening shade and I handed over my dime. When I reached home I discovered that my plums were tomatoes. I set to work to prepare a long and convincing speech which opened in the petitionary vein and ended in menace. Then I marched back to the store with my heart thumping. I had scarcely opened my mouth when the salesman, divining my

mission, took the package out of my hand and handed me back my ten cents.

This was something more than the liberality I had observed before. It was a peculiar generous trustfulness, of which I was to see more and more as I went on living in America. My old friend Yankel Bachman, for instance, was employed for a brief period as assistant to a milk-driver, and it made me marvel to hear him tell how his customers left bottles with money in them at the doors, where anybody could have taken them, and how he in turn left the milk in the same places. Somehow they never were taken—or at least he never heard of it. Imagine, I used to say to myself—imagine doing business after that fashion in Vaslui. Once a newspaper-wagon sped by and dropped a bundle of magazines right at my feet. I picked it up and was walking away with it when a man emerged from a stationery-shop and politely, though smilingly, informed me that it belonged to him. I gave it up, of course, in confusion, but I thought that if that had happened at home the case would have gone to the courts before the owner could have proved his right to the goods. And we were honest people in Vaslui; only our ideas were different. This undiscriminating confidence in God and man was a distinctly American peculiarity.

On one occasion, however, the confidence I had come to feel in American people was cruelly abused. I had had an unprofitable day on Fourteenth Street and had remained out till late in the night. To forget my

troubles I stopped on the way home at one of the "penny arcades" on the Bowery, and amused myself by looking into those forerunners of the movies which showed a single still-life picture free of charge and a dramatic performance as soon as a cent was deposited in the slot. A somewhat shabby-looking but decidedly friendly individual approached my machine and, much to my surprise, started it going with a penny of his own for my benefit. I asked him to share the pleasure with me by applying an eye to one of the two openings, but he declined on the ground that he had already seen everything in that place. This led up to his inviting me to a much finer place farther down the street where the pictures were of a superior character. As we walked along he suddenly bent down and picked up a purse. "See that fat woman there turning into Houston Street?" he asked me. "She dropped it." I could not see her, but that was of no consequence. Then my friend proceeded to give me a rapid account of his misfortunes—his dismissal without cause from a place he had held for ten years, his sick wife and dying little boy—and ended by thanking the Lord, before he had any idea whether there was anything in the purse to be thankful for, because He had rescued us—he could see that I, too, was poor—from our poverty. Finally he opened the wallet, and found in one pocket a bunch of keys and in the other a nickel and an Elevated ticket. With trembling hands and dilated nostrils he now turned to unlock the center compartment, and he

heaved an "Ah" of relief as he drew forth a crumpled
twenty-dollar bill. But at the sight of the tremendous
find his reason seemed all at once to have deserted him;
for the first thing he said, as soon as he got back his
breath, was, "It is not right, and it is dangerous. Let
us go to the police station and give it up."

I had a dreadful time, with my scanty English and
my excited nerves, to persuade him not to do such a
foolish thing. "It's ours, is it not?" I cried. "Besides
the woman looked rich; she would not miss it, and we
could make good use of it." Only when we got in
front of the Bleecker Street station did he come to his
senses. "All right," he said. "We'll go over to my
sister's house and I'll get ten dollars for your share.
She lives up on Seventh Street." "Why not go into
a store," I asked, "and get it changed?" "It's dangerous, I tell you; we'll get caught," he insisted. "Say,"
he cried with a sudden inspiration, "you say you are a
peddler. Give me ten dollars and you keep the bill."
But I did not have ten dollars. I only had seventy-
five cents. He looked incredulous. As we approached
his sister's house he began to run off. "Wait a minute,"
I yelled. "I can't let you take the money with you.
How do I know you'll come back?" He gave me an
injured glance, and quite justly asked me why he
should trust me when I had no faith in his integrity. I
might at least let him have my seventy-five cents as
partial security. But to this I answered with a laugh
that if he could trust me with nine dollars and a quarter

he might as well trust me with ten dollars. My logic seemed to carry conviction. He turned over the bill to me (but not the keys and the rest of the find) and set off on a dash for the sisterly home. I waited half an hour, but he never came. The next day being Sunday, I mysteriously informed my cousin that I was going to Coney Island. She looked astonished and I grinned. "I thought you complained about business being poor," she asked. Then I waved the bill in her face and told her the whole story. "You had better wait," she advised; "it may be one of those American fakes." About ten o'clock "brother-in-law" Couza arrived on his weekly visit, and she asked him into the children's room for an important conference. My heart sank as I heard his deep laugh through the keyhole. It was a Confederate bill.

After two weeks of chocolates I turned to toys. Success begets greed, and even a dollar a day will lose some of its first glamour by monotonous repetition. Besides, the holiday rush was fast drawing to a close. If I was to save up anything toward a better day, I must deal in some article that would not tempt my palate. And, as the man who sold me the new merchandise pointed out, toys had various other advantages over candies. They went at a superior price; the profit was greater; and, whereas chocolates spoiled when kept overnight, toys could be returned if not disposed of. Nevertheless, when the season was over and I was left with some eight dollars' worth of sheet-metal acrobats, I discovered

that my man had changed his address and was nowhere to be found. That was the beginning of my American disasters and simultaneously of my American education. For that eight dollars represented all my savings for the season, not counting my canceled debt to Mrs. Segal, and I was left to starve and "try" until I got my first job, or from Christmas to the end of January. Of course, I could have gone back to my relatives, now that my credit had proved good, but my pride told me that it was better to walk the streets after the tea-houses were closed than to be lectured.

X

PURIFICATIONS

NO doubt this was proper pride, but in the month and a half that followed I often had good reason to feel that the price I was made to pay for it was a trifle extortionate. I had come to New York in search of riches and adventure. Well, now, here at least was adventure a-plenty, even if the riches were a bit scarce. To be sure, the adventures I had most craved were of quite another sort. But, having neglected to specify in advance, it was not my place to complain against Destiny when she chose to put the broad interpretation on my order and supplied me with an ample stock of all the varieties in her shop. All the same, I could not for the life of me see any fun in the thing, not, at any rate, while it lasted. Think of me as devoid of imagination all you please, the fact remains that, with the best intentions in the world, I never succeeded in tapping the romance of my experiences. Going without meals two-thirds of the time was just as dull as it could be; tramping through the slushy, wind-swept streets while the rest of the world snuggled and snored under its warm covers was monstrously nasty; and the callousness, the indifference, the smugness of employers and

acquaintances alike were both dull and nasty, and soul-destroying to boot. No, I got precious little poetry out of my adventures. Wisdom, perhaps—of the toughening kind. By the time my trials were over I had ceased to be a boy. I had become a man, with the disillusionment, the wiliness, and, I fear, the cynicism of a man.

I had thought that that first week preceding my peddling ventures had exhausted all America's possibilities of hardship and disheartening failure. But that was because I was a greenhorn, unversed in the ways of Columbus's land. It was only now that I was to get my American baptism—that cleansing of the spirit by suffering which every one of us immigrants must pass through to prove himself worthy of his adoption. The population of Little Rumania was made up of two classes, the greens and the yellows. They were not stationary castes; every yellow had once been a green, and every green was striving and hoping to become a yellow some day. But in order to effect this coveted change of color and class there was but one thing for the new-comer to do—he must be purified. Purification —that was what, with telling aptness, the East Side called the period of struggle, starvation, and disappointment in America, which was the lot of the green. If a fellow-townsman of mine chanced to ask my cousin and former landlady whether she had seen me and how I was getting on, she answered apathetically and as if it were only what one might expect, "Oh, he

is bleaching out—getting purified, you know." People who had known my family in Vaslui would now and then pass me in the street or run into me in a tea-house, and the dialogue that then ensued was after this fashion:

"Working?"

"No, not yet."

"Um, getting properly purified. Oh, well, wait until you are a yellow. You'll be all right in America yet."

And my friend would suddenly discover that he had important business in hand and bid me a breathless good-by.

Happily I was not alone in my misery. A large percentage of those who had come to America on foot were, in a twofold sense, in the same shoes as I was, in spite of all the efforts of the newly formed Rumanian American Society to provide for the comfort and self-support of their compatriots. The dingy hotels on the Bowery were filled with them, and the communal kitchen on Broome Street saw scores of such of them as were willing to submit to charity, stand in line every day for their meal tickets. The "labor agencies" did a thriving business by finding jobs for them somewhere in "the South," which, however, turned out exceedingly short-lived, as those who managed to get back reported. With the help of some of my fellow-sufferers I picked up a variety of scraps of industrial information; but my extreme youth and my unconquerable timidity

prevented me from making any use of them. There was Ascher Gold, for instance, who for two entire weeks earned two-fifty a day by replacing a certain boiler-maker who had suddenly taken it into his head to refuse to work because he thought two-fifty a day not enough! Then there was the office on Second Avenue which sent people wherever they wanted to go and even got places for them; but one had to know how to get friendly with its secretary, and buy him a cigar or a dish of ice-cream, before one stood any chance of even getting inside. Yankel, however, came and told me that after spending thirty cents on that unapproachable gentleman the best that he offered to do for him was to send him to work in a mine at the other end of the country.

One of the objections that father had had to my going to America was that I was too young to be exposed to the dangers of a strange large city, and at the time I had laughed at his fears. But my enforced idleness, I found, was leading me into worse things than physical discomfort. For one thing, the persistent failure to find work has a curious effect on the mind. The victim begins by doubting whether he ever can be employed and ends up by fearing that he might! I used to approach a prospective employer with a kind of sinking dread lest he should take me; and in the morning as I set out on my daily round I would say, devoutly, "I am going to look for a job; Lord prevent that I should find one." In the solitude of the night, while lingering

in the shelter of a doorway, I would take stock of my
fix and steel my heart with resolution. "How long,"
I would ask myself, reproachfully, "can this state of
affairs go on? I cannot live without meals forever.
My shoes—those traitor shoes from home—will no
longer keep out the snow. Sooner or later the folks
in Vaslui are bound to guess or hear why I am ignoring
their requests for help. And the more I put off getting a
job the farther recedes the realization of my ambition."

The coffee-houses I frequented were a continual bait.
On the East Side respectability mingled freely with the
underworld. These elegant resorts where well-dressed
shopkeepers brought their bejeweled wives and treated
them to fat suppers, became, toward midnight, the
haunts of the pickpocket and the street-walker. Every
now and then a young gentleman with piercing, restless
eyes, faultlessly attired in modish clothes, high collar,
and patent-leather boots, generously invited me to share
a bite with him, and in the course of the meal painted
me a dark picture of the fate of the fool who thought
he could succeed in America with the antiquated notions he had brought with him from the old country. If
I really wanted to make money and bring my family
to America, he would show me how, just as he had
shown others. It was quite easy, and the partnership
basis was half-and-half. The landlord of the place
made me a different proposal. An ambitious young
fellow could get a girl to support him. He did not
really have to marry her; he would only pose as her

husband at a pinch. But as I was either too stupid
or too scrupulous or too timid to avail myself of
these opportunities, I went on getting purified, until
the day came when I was left without the price of the
indispensable *World*. Then once—but just once—I
was sorely tempted to beg the penny of a likely-
looking stranger, only to be arrested by a paralyzing
shame at the thought.

My parents did, surely enough, get wind of the actual
state of things before long, and the minute detail with
which they wrote about it made me suspect that the guess
had been inspired from this side. During the first month
after my arrival father never omitted to give me an
account of the situation at home, and to urge me to be
saving, because mother and he were only waiting for
Paul's discharge from the army to follow me to New
York. He suggested that I either put my money in
the savings-bank, or purchase the steamer tickets one
by one as funds accumulated. That, he felt, was the
surest way to avoid temptations of extravagance. "Do
not waste your resources," he advised once, "on silly
things like jewelry. There will be time enough for
luxuries later on. At present your only thought should
be for the reunion of us all. I hope that we may be
with you by Easter. Your mother is not likely to
stand your absence very much longer." Then followed
solicitous warnings against the pitfalls of the city:
"Remember that the tavern-keeper loves the drunkard,
but never gives him his daughter for a wife."

PURIFICATIONS

Yet now, in spite of all my cheering prevarications, father suddenly adopted an entirely new tone. Times had unaccountably changed for the better in Vaslui. Grain was booming. He could find use for my services in various ways. It was a mistake, as he had felt from the start, to let me go away at all. He and mother were getting too old to undertake such a lengthy journey. Besides, Harry had got a new place in Constantza; he was virtually the head salesman, and he had it in his power to create a vacancy for me. Even Aunt Rebecca had repented of her unkindness. She now was not only willing to have me in Uncle Pincus's store, she was even ready to advance me the money for the return trip—*if I needed any.*

I replied proudly that I wanted nobody's money or patronage. It was true, I wrote, that thus far I had not succeeded in saving a great deal, but that was because I could not yet speak English and had not learned a trade. Nevertheless, I was amply capable of taking care of myself. I was gradually making my way. America was exactly as Couza had pictured it. It was all right. They need not worry.

In a consultation with my boyhood friend Yankel I confessed that I was tempted to accept the offers from home. I read him one of father's letters, and it made his eyes and his mouth water. "My! you are lucky," he exclaimed. His folks, too, it seemed, had divined that all was not well with him. But Monish was a stern father, and what *he* had written was something to

this effect: "My dear son, you have wanted fun. Very well, be a man; stick where you are, and maybe you'll get it, after all. There is no milk and honey flowing here, either."

Yankel thought there was. Distance co-operating with hunger cast a glowing spell over the past, and my friend, falling into reminiscence, summoned up a picture of home that set both our hearts aching. He was thinking only the other day, he said, how jolly it would be to be back in Vaslui at this very season, just for a little while. In this miserable New York one was losing track even of the calendar. Did I know that last week was the Feast of the Maccabees? How could any one know it in America? In a land where every day was some kind of a denatured holiday—where you could eat Sabbath twists on Wednesday, and matzoths on New-Year's—the holidays themselves became meaningless and dull. Besides, the little things that made the joy of a feast at home you could not get here at all. The bee's-wax tapers and the *dredlach* ("tops" made of metal), where were they? How, he wondered, would they keep Tabernacles in a tenement? Where was the yard to put up the structure? Where was the brook with the rushes growing on its banks to make the roof out of? And the Feast of Weeks, you could not celebrate that without fresh green twigs. There was no spring on Rivington Street. There was not even any real cow's cheese to make the prescribed pastries with.

PURIFICATIONS

And now Purim was coming. Back there the boys
who had not been such fools as to walk to America were
getting the costumes ready to re-enact for the thousandth
time the mask of Joseph and Pharaoh and the spectacle
of Esther and Ahasuerus. Welvel Tseenes was probably at that very moment climbing up into the garret
and unearthing his mother's old purple wrapper, which
in another week would be turned into the royal robe of
the King of the Medes and the Persians; while the
handy Yossel Beyles was undoubtedly neglecting his
father's shop on the Ring and designing a cardboard
sword for his majesty and a colored-paper head-dress
for Esther the queen. Now that I was in exile, it would
be interesting to know who was composing the words
and coaching the performers. Every mother in town
was now breaking walnuts by the thousand and crushing the kernels in the big brass mortar and making
them into crisp strudels that crumble in your mouth.
Whole jars of plum-butter are being emptied into a
maple bowl and put in small dabs into the three-cornered
Haman-pockets. And every youngster who is not too
awkward to be intrusted with fine glassware will soon
be going about delivering gifts of confectionery and
red wine to his parents' relatives and friends, in accordance with the injunction contained at the end of the
Book of Esther.

Did I remember how last year he and I decided to
depart from the traditional masques and to make the
gang sit up and take notice by pulling off an entirely

new stunt? How we stole into the parlor of his home
and ransacked his eldest brother's cabinet until we
found the two pistols that Judah always carried with
him when he went about the country; and how I
found difficulty in cocking the larger one, so that he
tried it with all his might, and the trigger flew back
with a deafening noise (happily all the windows were
shut and no one heard it) and he thought he had shot
me, and made a careful examination of my person, which
resulted in the discovery that he had merely blown
away half the left skirt of my new coat; and I had to
go about the rest of that Saturday with my left hand in
my breeches pocket to cover up the disaster, and that
evening insisted on putting my Sabbath costume into
the clothes-chest myself, and on the following Saturday
raised an unblushing cry that the rats had got into my
things.

Four weeks after Purim was the Feast of Matzoths;
and although this was only midwinter there must
already be a Paschal note in the air of Vaslui. The
fatted geese were being killed to furnish forth the
shortening for the glorious rich puddings and the fat
for the fried matzoths and the innumerable pancakes.
He could almost see in his mind's eye the cheerful
activity: Early in the morning his little brother was
driving the team with the roan down to the butcher's,
a dozen or so of the heavy, snow-white birds lying with
their feet tied in the back of the cart; as soon as he
returned his mother and sisters flew into their aprons

and proceeded to fill two separate sacks with feathers
and down, which were to be turned later into cushions—
important additions to the girls' trousseaux; then the
carcasses were dressed and hung in the chimney to be
cured into pastrama; and for the rest of the month an
unending succession of palatable goose-liver patties and
dumplings created out of the driblets and giblets.

Ah, that week before the Passover! Was there
anything in America with all her wealth and freedom
to match that? Particularly if one was a boy. Who
could enumerate all its joys, even from this appalling
distance? The busy hum of house-cleaning; the
bringing in of the huge bale of crisp, new, unleavened
cakes; the putting up of the all-year's dishes and the
unpacking of the holiday dishes out of the box where
they had remained since the last time; the rediscovery
of half-forgotten pet cups and glasses; the cleansing
with red-hot stones and scalding water of the silverware, a task always performed by the boys in a pit dug
somewhere in the back yard; the shaking out of all
pockets lest a crumb of leavened bread should inad-
vertently undo an entire month's work; the last meal
at noon on the day before the festive week, which must
be eaten out of doors; the ceremonial sweeping away
of the last traces of non-paschal food; and lastly the
brief service at the temple attended only by father and
sons, the welcoming by the women-folks dressed in
spotless white; the very lengthy home service alternating with the courses of the banquet, the symbolism

of the Four Questions, the Invitation to the Poor and Hungry, and the Glass for Elijah—Yankel smacked his lips and sighed as he pictured it all.

He found a romantic word even for the heathen customs of the peasantry, and discovered a hitherto unseen bright side in the very tyranny of the Rumanian Government. He recalled that we had just recently left behind the first of January, and reminded me of the huge ice cross which always appeared on that morning in the principal square of Vaslui, to which the peasants bowed and kneeled when they came in from the country while the regimental band played beautiful, solemn airs. The Christian Easter, if it did not come at the same time as the Passover, was almost like a feast of our own. To be sure, we were not allowed to eat the colored eggs, but we could still play "touch" with them; and as for the cake called cozonac no amount of prohibition sufficed to prevent us from sharing it with our young neighbors. Was not the search for the cross in the churchyards on the night before Easter a beautiful ceremony, after all? And the joyous ringing of bells when it was at last found by the priest who had hidden it? And the Easter swing which even our mothers enjoyed riding in? He used to resent it bitterly when the police came and closed our private schools in midsummer; but now as he looked back to it he could see that it was really a kindness, at least to us boys. It enabled us to enjoy the adventure of being taught secretly in his father's or my father's shed; and, what

is more, the lessons had necessarily to be shortened, which gave us time to go swimming and to take the calf out to pasture.

So Yankel advised me not to be a fool a second time and take a good thing when it was offered me. I was debating whether he was right, and asking myself whether, after living in the large world for a little time, I could again feel at home in a place which had no street cars, when suddenly—it was now the last week in January—my nightmare cleared and I got my first job. For that, thanks to Couza. Couza had hitherto shown no inclination to interest himself in my behalf, in spite of the fact that it was his preaching and example that had brought me to New York. When, however, word reached him of my purifications his heart was touched, and within a day or two he left word at my old Rivington Street address that he had found me a place in a barroom on Division Street. I have since that day received telegrams notifying me of university appointments, and I have been very glad to get them, too, but no message of that kind has ever since struck me dumb with joy. The news of that first job, back in 1901, did.

XI

THE ETHICS OF THE BAR

THEY took me. There were a number of regulation questions—about my family, how long I had been in America, what I had done before—and then Mr. and Mrs. Weiss exchanged an approving glance, and Mr. Weiss told me that I would do. He at once asked me to remove my coat and get into a white apron. Then he conducted me behind the beautiful oak counter—which I was soon to be informed was called a bar—and initiated me into the mysteries of the beer-taps. "Read this," he said, suddenly, and held up a bottle. "Fine! Did you say you have been here less than two months?" he asked, incredulously. I could see that I had made an impression, that he was getting more and more pleased with me.

For my own part, I found the saloon a paradise, at least for a time. I got three meals every day and a clean bed every night, and three dollars a month, just like that, if you please, to do what I liked with. It was oppressive to have so much money. During the middle of the afternoon, after I got through washing the windows, and polishing the brass fittings, and preparing the free lunch, and there was nothing to do

but to wait for the evening trade, I would sit down at the far end of the bar next to the window and do intricate problems in fractions, in an effort to calculate by just how much my fortune had increased since the day before. Then the figures would puff and swell into fantastic sums as I went on to multiply them by five in order to obtain their equivalents in Rumanian francs and *bani*. You may laugh at this if you like, but it was I who had a new suit and new shoes and a derby hat when Easter came. The derby was my first, and it played queer tricks with my face; but I was proud of it, all the same, because it made me look like a man.

My employers, being a childless couple, in a manner adopted me and father-and-mothered me. Mrs. Weiss —"The Mrs.," as I was taught to call her—gave me some good clothes which her brother had cast off, and fed me on the choicest. In leisure moments she took occasion to continue my education by little hints on the importance of courtesy in America, on the most effective style of dressing the hair for a young gentleman in my position, on the wisdom of thrift, and, in general, on how to pass from the green into the yellow state in the shortest possible time.

Mr. Weiss, too, was kind and helpful, except when he was in his cups, which, fortunately, happened regularly on Saturday nights only, so that an observant young man need not be too much in the way when his master was irritable. From him I first learned that honesty, particularly with an employer, is the best policy, that

bar-men never drink (except at a customer's invitation, which is another story and is governed by a special ethical rule), and that patience with a liberally spending customer, even when he says and does unpleasant things, is a virtue that is its own reward. He advised me to let him keep my wages for me instead of exposing them to the risks of pickpockets and loss, and assured me that I need not worry over the trifling sum in such well-to-do hands as his, and that I could have the whole amount owing to me at any time when I should need it or wish to quit his employ. He invariably paid my bath and hair-cutting bill out of his own pocket. On Sunday mornings he let me sleep until seven and opened the shop himself. He even offered me assistance in English, but of this I did not avail myself because I noticed that he always referred to Mrs. Weiss as "he."

But I was an ungrateful soul, for I soon began to detect the flaws in my paradise. Just before the Passover my employer filled his windows with announcements to the effect that he had received a large stock of kosher liquids for the holiday, but shortly afterward the goods arrived from the distillery and I lent a hand in mixing them, and discovered to my horror that the chief ingredient was grain-alcohol, which was, ritually speaking, poison. Several times I was humiliated by a ridiculous fashion they had of testing my honesty, which consisted in leaving a quarter or half a dollar near my bed, and then watching the next day to see whether I would return it. The pair quarreled scandal-

ously and interminably; and when their squabbles began to degenerate into downright brawls, I hoped and prayed that I might find another job.

The saloon also offered ample opportunity for an adolescent, impressionable youth to go to the dogs, and I had to hold on very tenaciously to my parents' trust in me to dodge them successfully. The "Family Entrance" admitted a constant stream of shady female characters to whose thirst I must minister, and who, if they had not inspired me with a physical repulsion, might have become a degrading temptation. The treating system was a more immediate danger. My employer constantly impressed it upon me that it was my duty to his firm to accept every treat that was offered me. It pleased the customer, he explained, and it increased the sales. But I had not yet learned to like beer—at home the commonalty drank wine and only the elegant rich indulged in beer—and I detested whisky. Therefore, when a certain German bricklayer foreman, who was running up a big bill in our place by treating every one in sight, insisted on my participating in all his revels, I suggested to him one day that I would appreciate his generosity in some more solid form. He said, "All right," and reported my suggestion to Mr. Weiss. Thereupon followed a terrific fuss, in which Mrs. Weiss took sides with me, declaring, in the customer's face, that she would not allow any one to corrupt a young boy intrusted to her care by filling him with liquor that no one was paying for. I

thought Mrs. Weiss was a brick, and told her so re-spectfully.

And yet, for all its shortcomings and unpleasantness and dangers, I would not have you carry away the impression that the part played by the saloon in my evolution was merely harmful or negative. Quite the contrary. The lessons I learned while standing behind the bar or while pouring out miscellaneous drinks to the people at the card-tables have instilled into me more of the rich wisdom of life than I got out of all the labeled and classified knowledge imparted to me afterward in my three universities—and this is no dubious praise for the universities. For if a young fellow will go to perdition at the mere sight of evil, the probabilities are that there was not very much worth saving in him to begin with. But if he holds himself erect and comes through the mire unsoiled, I warrant you that he will prove the better for his experience. Many a man more fortunately surrounded (as the phrase goes) in his youth than I was has, in later life, sought to round out his knowledge of mankind and to deepen his sympathies by a voluntary descent into the maelstrom of the slums. I hope that such efforts are properly rewarded, but I confess to a mistrust in the efficacy of the method. The palpitating facts of life cannot, I am afraid, be got at through the resolves of middle age. Youth is the time for adventuring, and chance necessity is a better cicerone through the ins and outs and the ups and downs of existence than deliberate intent. What a young

man learns by hard knocks in his teens will quicken his senses and enrich his heart to better purpose than any amount of shrewd jottings in a slummer's note-book.

A barroom—even an East Side barroom—is not, as some good people suppose, a mere hang-out for the indolent and the degenerate. It is, whether you like it or not, one of the central meeting-places of humanity. It is an institution where all the classes congregate in all their moods—the bestial and the generous, the morose and the convivial. Thither the laborer may escape from his shrewish wife when she makes his home unbearable; but thither also the merchant will resort with his customer when both are jovial over a particularly satisfactory bargain. A bum will shuffle in to dry his rags by the stove or to snatch a morsel from the free-lunch counter, and before departing will give you an invaluable glimpse into his sad history and his cheerful philosophy. The next moment a surgeon, returning from a successful operation, will toss you a quarter for a glass of vichy, and leave you gaping in idle wonderment at the incalculable wealth that a man who can so lightly do such a thing must have in reserve. At the noon-hour, a gang of workmen from a near-by "job" will trudge in in their heavy boots and grimy overalls to devour a plate of free soup and innumerable hunks of bread with their schooner of beer, and to teach you the wholesome moral that good digestion attends on honest toil. And if your mind is built to receive

impressions, and if your heart is attuned to beat in harmony with other human hearts, your apprenticeship in a saloon will serve for as good a start toward a well-rounded education as you could desire.

It was in the saloon—or, at least, in what I might call the extension department of it—that my eyes were first opened to the true meaning of American democracy and to my own opportunity in the midst of it. I should blush for my ingratitude if I did not, in recounting the influences that helped to make me an American, allude, at least *en masse*, to the hundreds of my nameless friends who assisted me forward in the general direction of my goal. In particular I must mention the wife of a physician in the Bronx to whom my employer one night sent me to deliver an order. She fell into conversation with me, and then, without warning, looked up at me and exclaimed:

"Why, my dear boy, this is no occupation for you. You must look for something better."

I ought to have been flattered, but in my confusion I could only pluck nervously at my cap: "It's all right. I like my work, and it pays fine."

"Yes," she insisted, "but haven't you any higher ambition?"

"Of course," I blurted out; "I want to be a doctor."

"I thought so," she said, with satisfaction. "They all do. Well, *you* will be," she added, with the air of a divinity granting a mortal's wish, "I know. My husband was a poor immigrant boy once, and now he is a

THE ETHICS OF THE BAR

doctor. Do you know why? Because he was ambitious and discontented."

These were strange and inspiring words. Hitherto I had been piously following my parents' injunction to obey my master and to be thankful for whatever God gave me. I had not thought of discontent as a virtue. Now suddenly it dawned upon me that if I was ever to realize my father's dream I must follow a course directly opposed to the one he had outlined for me. As I looked about me I became aware that discontent with fortune's favors was the order of life and the rule of progress. On the East Side, I observed, there were no classes. Men were engaged in given lines of work or business. But their occupations were not permanent things. They did not chain them down to any definite place in the scheme of existence. What a man did in no way determined his worth or circumscribed his ambitions. Peddling and hawking and the sewing-machine were just so many rungs in the ladder. A dingy apartment in the tenement was merely a stage in the march toward a home in Brownsville or a shop in the Bronx. The earth was young and fresh from the hand of the Maker, and as yet undivided among His children. That was another distinctive superiority of America over Rumania.

From that night on my hope to get into other work turned into determination, and at Easter an incident occurred which promised to open the way. In the three months that I had been in the saloon I had never had

131

a day to myself. I had been too well contented to ask for it. But when my new clothes came I must go and show them to my friends. Mrs. Weiss thought so, too; and between us we persuaded Mr. Weiss to let me off for the afternoon and evening of Easter Day. Among the relatives and friends whom I visited that day I met a cousin of mine who worked at shirts as a collar-maker. He opened my eyes to the lay of things. Here I was working day and night for three dollars a month, while he was earning six and often seven dollars in a single week, and he had his evenings to go to the Rumanian restaurants and tea-houses. I wondered whether I could become a shirt-maker. My cousin thought so, and promised to watch for an opening.

I passed a restless and discontented month before my opportunity came. Then a firm on Walker Street offered to teach me sleeving, on condition that I work for two weeks without pay. I had a month's wages coming to me, so I felt that I could manage it; but when I timidly announced my purpose to Mr. Weiss—in my excitement I forgot that it was the fateful Saturday night—he flew off the handle and refused to pay up. Even Mrs. Weiss was against me this time. She declared me a fool for leaving a good home to go to the sweat-shop (the very argument I have since employed with domestic servants), and revealed an ambition she had been cherishing for some time of setting me up in a saloon of my own when I had become sufficiently Americanized. She prophesied that if I did not come

to my senses at the very first sight of a shop, I would never leave it at all. "Once an operator always an operator," she reminded me. Grocers' assistants worked their way up to grocery-stores, tap-boys became saloon-keepers, peddlers and clerks attained to businesses of their own, but a sweat-shop hand contracted consumption or socialism and never rose to anything better. The operative's lean years always swallowed up his fat ones. As long as I worked I might earn a little more than I was getting in the saloon—still, she was ready to give me a raise—but I would find saving quite impossible once I began to pay for every little thing out of my own pocket; and when the "slack" came I would starve as thoroughly as ever I did when I was a greenhorn and before she saved my life by taking me off the streets. No doubt I had forgotten those miserable days, now that prosperity had come to me through her; but she remembered very distinctly that first day when I gluttonously devoured potatoes like cheese dainties, and she was ashamed to let customers see me until she had found me some clothes.

My benefactor, Couza, happening to drop in, as he often did, Mr. and Mrs. Weiss at once appealed the case to him. Whereupon he settled himself into a chair by one of the tables and, while sipping a schooner of beer, proceeded to give me a sound lecture on my unethical conduct. My ingratitude to my employers and to him, he found, was simply monstrous. I ought to be ashamed for even asking them to pay me after the

return I was making them for their parental kindness. Was I aware that the very clothes I was wearing were theirs, and that they had tried to educate me into an American and a business man? As for the sweat-shop, he would not even discuss that. He could only think pityingly of my poor father and mother. They were decent, respectable people. If they had known that their favorite little son, on whom they were placing such high hopes, would ally himself with the outcast, the vulgar, the unambitious, the ungodly, they would never have consented to my emigration. And if they were to hear of it now—as they were certainly going to—it would break their hearts and they would disown me.

Heaven alone knows what they hoped to achieve by all this grilling, unless it was to do violence to my feelings, in which case they succeeded amply. But as far as gaining any result for themselves was concerned it could do no possible good. A month ago a raise of a dollar might have made me hesitate and consider. But now I had bettered Couza's own instruction. I had found the America he had seen in a dream. Even shirt-making with all its promise of freedom and money was but a stepping-stone. I was looking away beyond to my destiny dawning on the horizon—the golden destiny of my childhood. I had heard the tap of Opportunity on my door, and I was hurrying to answer the call.

PART III

THE EDUCATION OF AN AMERICAN

XII

SHIRTS AND PHILOSOPHY

O N the whole, I take it, the foreign colony in our
larger cities is a little unfavorably regarded by the
conventional enthusiasts for Americanization. These
kindly ladies and gentlemen appear to assume that the
trick of turning American is some kind of an affair of a
rubber stamp and an oath of allegiance and bath-tubs.
It is quite simple. You go down there, to the East
Side, or Little Italy, or Little Poland, and you establish
a settlement and deliver lectures and furnish them a
pointed example, and behold! the fog lifts, and before
your eyes stands the new-born American. The sooner
this effective performance is accomplished the better,
for it is quite clear that the immigrant invariably hails
from an inferior world, with queer notions about
manners and the use of soap and fresh air and constitu-
tions, and if he is long left to himself and his fellows he
will settle down to this pestiferous imported life of his
and never become one of us at all. He will become a
confirmed alien, a dangerous, disruptive element.

Into this complacent view the patent fact that
Americanism is a compromise does not enter. It is

quite overlooked that the adoptive American has always been and will always remain a composite American. My good friends are unwilling to see that the alien has as much to teach as to learn, that his readjustment is inevitably a matter of give and take, and that he only begins to feel at home in this new country when he has succeeded in blending his own culture and ideas and mode of life with those of the people that came here before him. Your self-complacent native takes stock of the Americanized alien and cries, delightedly, "See how America has changed him!" But I suppose he would be greatly astonished if the immigrant were to answer, with equal truth, "Look how I have changed America!" Americans can nowise be persuaded that, if there is to be any readjustment, it must come from this sort of mutual reaction; and they will simply laugh at you if you tell them that the foreign colony, far from being a danger, is about the only natural agency by which the process can be effected.

Now, if places like the East Side are looked at askance, how very little justice could one expect toward the institution of the sweat-shop? That, surely, is a veritable hotbed of un-Americanism. When my native friends, who never weary of the topic, ask me what influences I account as the most vital in making an American of me, and when, in a sincere endeavor to be enlightening, I answer them that it is a toss-up between the college and the sweat-shop, they smile and say that I am making paradoxes. Of course, they admit, in a

negative kind of way, the slums may perhaps arouse a craving for a broader and a fuller life, just as imprisonment develops a passionate love of freedom, or as a crabbed, bigoted religious parent may drive a youngster to atheism. But how such a place can possibly foster any idealism in a direct way, or itself become a bridge between ignorance and intelligence, between slavery and independence, in short between culture and stagnation, is more than they can understand. They think of the sweat-shop as all dark and poverty-ridden and brutalized.

The East Side itself, I may add—or, at any rate, the forward-looking, practical layer of it—holds no exaggerated opinion about the sewing-machine and the flat-iron, as Mrs. Weiss's convictions on the subject may serve to prove. Little Rumania, indeed, as a civilization, entertained an instinctive aversion to the industrial life. My former employers and their distinguished patron, the big-hearted Couza, whatever their ulterior motives might be in attempting to deter me from my course, really spoke from the depths of their souls when they denounced the sweat-shop. Almost everybody I knew warned me against it. Even my erstwhile landlady, Mrs. Segal, declared that she had never approved of Cousin Aby's collar-making, in spite of the fact that he came from the lesser branch of the family and had never received the fine schooling and home-training that we of the Vaslui clan had (Aby being a native of Galatz). What, she asked me, would

become of our splendid tradition as a family of merchants and professional men if we drifted one by one into the classes that worked with their hands? I could not answer that difficult question, but I reminded her that she herself had once long ago taught me that in America there was no such thing as high and low, and no shame in doing anything. Besides, her own daughters were earning their living at neckwear. Whereupon she invited my attention to the subtle fact that neckties were not shirts, and that I was now no longer a greenhorn, which altered the case entirely. But it was all right. I could go to the shop if I was determined to, and see for myself.

Well, I confess that there was more than a grain of truth in these gloomy predictions. The very walk to the shop that early morning with Cousin Aby, the collar-maker, was a depressing adventure. We were a little late, and I was being properly berated, as we hurried along, for my unindustrial habits. Canal Street west of the Bowery, with its cobblestones and clattering trucks, its bare, ugly sides and trudging throngs of unkempt men and girls, was not half so friendly as at its eastern extremity. And as we swung past Broadway and into Walker Street, the dreariness became almost intolerable. Here the thoroughfare was too cramped for normal traffic, and the stunted, grimy buildings seemed ludicrously undersized for their heavy tasks. All the same, the little alley was choked up with one-horse carts, its sidewalks were littered with bales

of unmade clothing, a pandemonium of rasping curses from drivers and half-awake, half-grown men with aprons, staggering under immense burdens, overtopped the rattling and the clanging from Broadway beyond.

And then we felt our way up two creaking flights of stairs, and my cousin opened a door, and we entered. We proceeded to the right toward an elongated counter, where I was introduced to the boss; my cousin removed his coat and collar, and disappeared into the wilderness beyond. I followed him with my eyes, and the sight did not cheer me. There were three endless tables running almost through the entire length of the loft in parallel lines. Each table was dotted with a row of machines, and in front of these sat the operatives like prisoners chained to their posts. Men and women they were, collarless, disheveled, bent into irregular curves; palpitating, twitching, as if they were so many pistons and levers in some huge, monstrous engine. On the nearer end, around a smaller square table, stood an old, white-bearded man, a young girl, and a boy, marking shirts with a pencil, pulling threads, folding, "finishing." The intermittent whirring of wheels, the gasping and sucking of the power-engine (somewhere out of sight), the dull murmur of voices, heightened the oppressive effect.

My first lesson, administered by a frowsy little man in shirt-sleeves and no collar, with his suspenders dangling loosely at his sides, was very bewildering. I had thought that I was to learn how to make shirts; but

now my instructor informed me with a smile that that would be a rather large order. No, I was to play only a very small part in the great performance. I was to be a sleever; and sleeving, it appeared, was as much as any one man could desire, for it involved a whole chain of skilful and delicate operations. The shirts were brought to you in two bundles, which you proceeded to place, each bundle in a separate box, one situated on the right side and the other on the left side of your machine. Then you suddenly discovered—sometimes a bit too late—that the bundles contained textiles of several designs and shades of color, and that you were expected to sew no green sleeves into brown shirts. The machine was of a kind that I had not even suspected to exist. It had two needles, and that implied two spools and two threadings and two bobbins. Just in front of the needles was an odd device called a "hemmer" which was designed to facilitate the work. But the whole contraption had a way of running away with you as soon as you pressed the power pedal, so that the material got twisted and bunched up in the hemmer, and usually broke both needles at once, and sometimes lodged one of them in your thumb, and invariably, at the least, tangled up the thread into a hopeless mess.

I sewed and ripped and sewed again for two weeks without pay, and I am afraid that the proceeds of my toil made but a poor return for the boss's patience and instruction. But if the bargain was unprofitable for him, it was well-nigh ruinous to me. My former

employers having declined (out of pure benevolence) to pay me the month's wages they owed me, my great problem was to survive the period of my apprenticeship. I had borrowed an amount equivalent to that reserve I had been counting on, and Mrs. Bernfeld, with whom I had taken up residence on Eldridge Street, was kind enough to let me pay her rent at the end of the month instead of in advance. But with all my skimping and economizing it was impossible to make three dollars last very much longer than two weeks. I had miscalculated somewhat. I had figured on getting some money when my instruction was over, forgetting entirely that while everything else had to be paid for as I went or beforehand, labor received its rewards only after it was done. I got nothing even when I had completed a week as a piece-worker. Payday was once in a fortnight, and I was in the shop for a month before my first envelope came around; and then I discovered that although I had sleeved a hundred and sixty dozens of shirts, which, at the rate of four cents per dozen, ought to have entitled me to very nearly six dollars and a half, my envelope contained only three dollars. One week's wages, it developed, was regularly held back. They said it was because it took that long to audit the accounts. But that was a euphemism. The truth was that that week's wages of the forty hands constituted the major part of the firm's operating capital.

For all that, I soon found myself very happy in my

new surroundings. Those novelists and sentimental-
ists who slander the sweat-shop and the tenement
should take notice. We certainly had a very much
more human time of it in the old days than we did
later on in the high-ceilinged, many-windowed, electric-
fanned, palatial prisons that conformed to the factory
laws. The reasons were these: In the sweat-shop the
hand and the boss belonged to the same class. That
made a big difference. There were no spying "fore-
ladies" and no rules, no peremptory calls to the office
and no threats of discharge. You did not have to
stand in line with hat in hand for the wages of your
toil. If we were hard up after a long, slack season, we
could get all our meals on credit from the old shop-
peddler, who sold baked liver by the slice, brandy,
bananas, and rolls, and sometimes lent us even a bit
of cash. The number of workers was small, so that
everybody knew everybody else. During the lunch-
hour we visited, and fell into violent arguments about
the labor movement and socialism and literature, and
mocked good-naturedly at the "capitalist" when he
ventured to put in a word (as he always did); and each
of us, except the girls, took his turn in going for the
can of beer. All this tended to preserve the human
dignity and the self-respect of the worker.

In spite of the fact that my firm was specializing in
the stiff black-and-white article intended for the
Southern negro, my earnings kept gradually rising,
until (with the standards of barroom wages still in

my mind) they attained dizzying heights. With softer materials, to be sure, I might have turned out more dozens per day, but I comforted myself with the thought that the work would be more "particular," so that the net results would probably be about the same. The "slack," indeed, was longer and more thorough-going than at the better lines. For the two whole months of January and February that temperamental gentleman in the South seemed to be dispensing with shirts. But while that meant going into debt and cutting down on luxuries, there were compensating circumstances even then, as we shall see. While work was rushing I got in touch with the instalment peddler and bought a solid-gold watch and chain on the basis of a dollar per week, and once in an access of extreme thriftiness I went the length of starting a savings account with the Bowery Bank, which, however, never went beyond the first deposit, for one thing because my fellow-workers got wind of the fact and poked fun at me and called me capitalist, and secondly because the slack fell upon us suddenly that year and I was forced to liquidate and the cashier told me in a coldly impersonal way that my patronage would not be desired again. The jewelry, on the other hand, was as good as a solid estate and much better than money in the bank, because at a pinch it was not necessary to wait thirty days to cash in. All I had to do was to take the things to "the uncle," or, as you would call it, the pawn-shop, and get thirty dollars all at once, which sufficed

to keep the peddler pacified with regular payments as well as to make me comfortable until prosperity was mine again. There was no denying that, for all its good things to eat and drink, and its lazy afternoon hours, and educational opportunities, the saloon could not hold a candle to the two-needle machine.

Indeed, the sweat-shop was for me the cradle of liberty. It was more—it was my first university. I was not long there before I discovered that there were better things I could do with my free evenings than to frequent the cozy hang-outs of my fellow-countrymen. When I overheard a dispute between the young buttonhole-maker and the cadaverous, curly-haired closer, on the respective merits of the stories of Tchekhov and Maupassant; and when, another day, the little black-eyed Russian girl who was receiving two cents per dozen shirts as a finisher boldly asserted that evolution pointed the way to anarchism and not to socialism, and cited the fact that Spencer himself was an anarchist, my eyes were opened and I felt ashamed of my ignorance. I had been rather inclined hitherto to feel superior to my surroundings, and to regard the shop and the whole East Side as but a temporary halt in my progress. With my career looming on the horizon, and my inherited tendency to look down upon mechanical trades, I had at first barely given a tolerant eye to the sordid men and girls who worked beside me. I had not realized that this grimy, toil-worn, airless Ghetto had a soul and a mind under its shabby exterior.

SHIRTS AND PHILOSOPHY

It knew everything and talked about everything. Nothing in the way of thought-interest was too big or too heavy for this *intelligenzia* of the slums.

I made an effort to listen attentively in the hope that I might get some hint as to where my fellow-operatives got all their knowledge. I observed that nearly all of them brought books with them to work—Yiddish, Russian, German, and even English books. During the lunch-hour, if the disputatious mood was not on them, the entire lot of them had their heads buried in their volumes or their papers, so that the littered, unswept loft had the air of having been miraculously turned into a library. While waiting for my next bundle of shirts, or just before leaving the shop, I would stealthily glance at a title, or open a pamphlet and snatch a word or two. I was too timid to inquire openly. Once a girl caught me by the wardrobe examining her book, and asked me whether I liked books and whether I went to the lectures. I became confused and murmured a negative. "You know," she said, "Gorky is going to speak to-night," and held out a newspaper to show me the announcement.

So they were going to lectures! I began to buy newspapers and watch for the notices. I took to reading books and attending meetings and theaters. There were scores of lectures every week, I found, and I went to as many as I could. One night it was Darwin, and the next it might be the principles of air-pressure. On a Saturday night there were sometimes

two meetings so arranged that both could be attended by the same audience. I remember going once to a meeting at Cooper Union to protest against the use of the militia in breaking a strike somewhere in the West, and then retiring with a crowd of others to the anarchist reading-room on Eldridge Street to hear an informal discussion on "Hamlet *versus* Don Quixote." It did not matter to us what the subject was. There was a peculiar, intoxicating joy in just sitting there and drinking in the words of the speakers, which to us were echoes from a higher world than ours. Quite likely most of us could not have passed an examination in any of the subjects we heard discussed. It was something more valuable than information that we were after. Our poor, cramped souls were yearning to be inspired and uplifted. Never in all my experience since, though I have been in colleges and learned societies, have I seen such earnest, responsive audiences as were those collarless men and hatless girls of the sweat-shops.

The East Side theater was another educational institution. It was seldom that an attempt was made to entertain us there, and whenever it was made we expressed our resentment by hooting. We did not go to the theater for amusement any more than we read books or listened to lectures for amusement. It was art and the truthful representation of actual life and the element of culture that we demanded, and the playwrights who satisfied us we rewarded by our

homage and our devotion. No American dramatist
was ever worshiped by his public as Jacob Gordin was.
I remember that when a reactionary newspaper tried
to stab him in the back by raising a cry of immorality
against one of his plays, the whole progressive element
in the Ghetto came as a unit to his support by packing
his theater and clamoring for his appearance. The
sheet that dared attack him was nearly boycotted out
of existence. And when, some years later, Gordin died,
every shop was closed on the East Side and a hundred
thousand followed his hearse in genuine mourning.
There is no parallel, I think, in the whole history of the
American drama to this testimonial of popular devotion
to an intellectual leader.

Nor was Gordin the only divinity on our dramatic
Olympus. There were younger men like Libin and
Kobrin, who, while they might be said to have been
members of Gordin's realistic school, had made some
interesting departures in subject-matter by laying
emphasis on the humor and pathos of life in the New
World as affecting the immigrant. These two had for
a long time been principally occupied with fiction, but
had turned to the stage because of the greater educational possibilities of the drama. The Russians, too,
kept in touch with their exiled brethren and saw to it
that our souls did not starve for lack of spiritual
sustenance. Not only did the Canal Street publishers
bring out the beautiful humorous tales of Sholom
Aleichem and Mendele Mocher Sforim and the poetry

of Frug and Peretz, several amateur organizations—precursors of the numerous "advanced" playhouses now fashionable everywhere—were formed for the purpose of producing the poetic dramas of Hirshbein and Peretz and the symbolic plays of Asch and Pinsky, which, owing to their extreme literary character, were not adapted to the regular theaters. Notably the Progressive Dramatic Club conducted readings and performances of choice tragedies "from home," which, although they were intended for the elect, were attended by as large audiences as ever went to the Thalia and People's theaters.

I saw more good literature on the stage in those days while I was sewing sleeves into shirts than I saw in all my subsequent career. When the original playwrights could not fill the demand, the lack was supplied by the translators. While Broadway was giving Ibsen the cold shoulder, the East Side was acclaiming him with wild enthusiasm. I saw "Monna Vanna" on the Bowery before the Broadway type of theater-goer had ever heard the name of Maeterlinck. Many foreign writers—Hauptmann, Sudermann, Gorky, Andreiyev, Tolstoy—had their *premières* in the Ghetto. The same was true of actors; I saw Nazimova in "Ghosts" before she could speak English. And I made my first acquaintance with Greek tragedy when I had not yet learned how to speak English.

XIII

THE SOUL OF THE GHETTO

I DID not for a long time perceive the drift of all this feverish intellectual activity. I was too busy reading and listening to care about the ultimate purpose of it all. Gordin was giving his brilliant talks on the Evolution of the Drama, and running a series of suggestive articles on the topic in *Die Zukunft*. A group of young writers had just begun the publication of *Die Freie Stunde* (The Idle Hour), which was devoted only to what was best in belles-lettres. The war between the radical and the reactionary press, always raging, was just now assuming a most violent character. The anarchist *Freie Arbeiter Stimme* was bringing out the journal of a Catholic priest who had attained to atheism, and publishing column upon column of letters in which the merits of religion and free-thought were discussed by the public, a certain well-known agnostic taking up the defense of religion for argument's sake. Within the progressive circle there were continual debates between socialists and anarchists, which sometimes rose to passionate fury, but always remained enlightening. My mind was eagerly absorbing all these new impressions and all these wonderful ideas. A new

world was unfolding itself before me, with endless, magnificent vistas extending in all directions.

The "slack," that bugbear of the factory hand, was losing its terror for me. A time arrived when I would start to the shop in the morning in hopes that I might find the power turned off and the boss explaining that work was "slow." On such days I would keep my coat and collar right on and take myself off to the nearest library, despite the boss's protests and assurance that he was expecting the bundles from the manufacturer to arrive any moment. There was so much for me to do. There were whole stacks of Norwegian dramatists, and Russian novelists, and Yiddish poets that I had as yet barely touched. In my room there was a collection of the Reclam editions of Zola and Maupassant, and an assortment of plays of all nations which had been suggested to me by Gordin's lectures which I had not yet found time to touch at all. Besides, I was trying to become a writer myself. The *Forward* had accepted and published some aphorisms of mine under the pen-name of "Max the Sleever," which my friends at the shop had greatly admired. I was devoting whole nights to a novel in the manner of *The Kreutzer Sonata*. Above all, I delighted in lingering outside the literary coffee-houses on Canal Street, where every now and then I would catch a glimpse of Gordin and his circle.

With my mind so busy, then, it was not surprising that I should remain somewhat indifferent to what was going on in my soul. My ancient religion had, under

American skies, vanished long ago; but I was scarcely aware that a burning new faith had taken its place with me, as it had done with thousands of others. I cannot now say whether I was taking it for granted or did not know it. I continually heard people in the shop, and in the quarter generally, referred to as "clodpates" and "intelligents," and I knew that an intelligent was a person who went to lectures and read books, and preferred tragedy to vaudeville, and looked upon America as a place which afforded one an opportunity to acquire and express ideas, while a clodpate cared more for dollars than for ideas, and worked hard so that some day he might have others work for him, and in the evening he went to a dance-hall or to the Atlantic Garden or to Miner's or to a card-party, and kept himself scrupulously respectable so that some day, when he could afford it, he might rise to be the president of the synagogue or the lodge, and read (when he read at all) the *Tageblatt* and the joke-books. All this I knew, and, in addition, that I was already being classed as an intelligent among the hands at the shop.

It never occurred to me, however, to attach any ulterior meaning to the word. It was obvious enough; I could have seen it if I had only looked. But somehow I did not look—until one day the thing struck me and I had to look. It was an idle day at the shop. The boss had persuaded us to wait for the work, and we were lounging about on the machine-tables and on the ends of cases. Some of us had been to a reading of

Ibsen's symbolic drama, "When We Dead Awaken,"
the night before, and were, of course, discussing it. I
said that I liked it. Then the girl who had the year
before put me on the intellectual track spoke up and
asked me, in a tone of pained astonishment:

"Why, aren't you a radical?"

"Yes, of course," I said, a little uncertainly. "Who
is not?"

"Who is not? The clodpates are not."

"But what has this got to do with literature?"

"Well," she answered, "it has this to do with it.
This symbolism business is reactionary. It has always
been. It's churchy."

Then I suddenly realized that everybody I knew was
either a socialist or an anarchist. It came to me in a
flash that this social idealism was the soul that stirred
within everything that was going on about and within
me. I remembered that all our meetings and lectures
were colored by it. And I understood that every
intelligent was an atheist partly because every clodpate was a believer and partly because the established
creeds were cluttering the road to social and spiritual
progress. When I asked myself why we studied the
abstruse principles of physics, the answer was that it
helped us to disprove the arguments of the religious.
Our enthusiasm for evolution, I saw, was due to that
doctrine's implied denial of the biblical story of creation.
And if we loved the poets, it was because they seemed to
us to be pervaded by a lofty discontent with the existing

order of things. In short, I perceived that we were moved by a very vital religion of our own; although, of course, we would have scorned to call it by that hated name.

I imagine that one of the things that had misled me was the absence of every trace of sect exclusiveness in the movement, at least on its intellectual side. Bitter as we were against the ruling class, we took no exception to its books. In our little radical libraries Burke rubbed elbows with Rousseau and the works of the imperialist Kipling touched sides with those of the revolutionary Kropotkin. Some of our leaders were as assiduously translating Machiavelli as Oscar Wilde. At Warschauer's Russian tea-house—the principal labor resort—I often heard Bacon mentioned respectfully as a philosopher alongside of Spencer. Of course, it was hard for us to see how a man who had the mental and emotional equipment of a great author could be blind to the justice of our cause, and we naturally did favor the insurgent writers. But art is art, we held, and the value of a good book is not changed by the fact that its author is wrong about the rights of women or the referendum. The only kind of writing we scorned was the stupid and the fraudulent. Toward genuine literature we were as friendly as the medieval monks who saved the literary treasures of paganism from destruction.

Yes, our radicalism had all the nobility and all the weaknesses of a young faith. We were no mere parlor

socialists, we toilers of the slums. Our atheism was no affectation; our anarchism was not a fad to make conversation with over the tea-cups. Nor were we concerned with the improvement of our own material condition merely. We were engaged in the regeneration of society, and we were prepared to take up arms in the great social revolution which we saw daily drawing nearer. We were all missionaries, and some of us were quite genuine bigots. On the Day of Atonement, when all the conservative people of the quarter fasted and repented and knelt in prayer, we ostentatiously went about with big cigars in our mouths and bags of food in our pockets; and in the afternoon we met in the public square and marched off in a body with flags and trumpets to the atheist picnic somewhere in Brooklyn. Similarly, during the Passover, we gave an entertainment and ball, where we consumed more forbidden food and drink than was good for us. No doubt this was foolish—perhaps it was even vulgar—but to us it was propaganda for our faith among the unconverted.

I recall a lean devotee I used to see at the anarchist meetings. He never missed one, and he never failed to occupy a seat right in front of the speaker's stand. During the address he would lean forward and glue his eyes on the speaker, as if he were determined that not a word should escape him. And then, somehow, it appeared that he always did miss something very essential, after all. When the floor was thrown open for general discussion he was invariably the first to

arise. Whereupon he would begin with, "Thinkers and comrades," and proceed to make a few irrelevant remarks which showed at once that he had understood nothing at all of the lecture. Some of the audience would smile at him and some would murmur impatiently until he would grow confused and sink back into his seat. But these ignominious exhibitions never prevented him from heading each contribution list with some extravagant sum. Occasionally I would run across him at a little restaurant in the rear of a saloon on Eldridge Street, where one could get a tolerable meal for thirteen cents, and it puzzled me to reconcile that open-handedness at the meetings with this skimping on food. I understood it only when I became a devotee myself.

I have often since looked back with a melancholy regret to those splendid days, and have tried to reconstruct them in my memory and to find a parallel for them somewhere. From this distance they seem to me comparable to nothing else so much as to those early times when Christianity was still the faith of the despised and the lowly. There was in us that apostolic simplicity of speech and manners, that disregard of externals, that contempt of the world and its prizes, that hatred of shams, that love of the essential, that intolerance for the unbeliever, which only they who feed on a living ideal can know. In our social relations it was the sincere intention, the rigid adherence to the truth as we saw it, that counted. In an argument it

was your duty to be frank and honest; if your opponent was offended, so much the worse for him. You could come to a meeting, to a play, or to a gathering in the house of a friend in your working clothes and unshaven if you chose. The man and not the costume was the thing. A woman was but a human being in petticoats; therefore if you happened to want company at Warschauer's, or felt the need of giving play to your opinions at the theater, you need not hesitate to address the first girl that came your way; therefore, also, you need not spare her in a battle of ideas; but therefore, also, you need not expect to be looked up to as a superior creature with a whole chain of exploded privileges and immunities. She was in every way your human equal and counterpart, whatever the animal differences between you might be. Your business in life was to labor for the things that you devoured, to cultivate your mind, and to serve the ideals of your class. Beside these, the sordid concerns of the bodily existence were a secondary matter. Wherefore the American heathen with his wealth and his show, his worldliness and his materialism and his sporting page, was an object worthy of your profoundest contempt.

What else could it be, if it was not this ancient dream of the prophets revitalized and recast into a modern mold, that had the magic power to transfigure the rotting slums into an oasis of spiritual luxuriance, and the gloomy, dust-laden factory into a house of light and hope? The mere human thirst for knowledge, the

purely selfish craving for personal advancement, is
hardly strong enough to have made us sit up night after
night and listen to abstract discussions about monkeys
and men or the basis of religious belief, when our worn-
out bodies were eminently entitled to rest and light
entertainment. And surely nothing but this attachment to the uplifting promise of a noble future for
mankind, this devotion to something outside of our
unwashed selves and above our grimy surroundings,
could have rendered us so heartlessly indifferent to the
bleeding hearts of our poor bewildered elders. How the
wretched graybeards and peruqued grandmothers
suffered at the disaffection of their young! For even
in the most advanced households it was a rare thing if
the two generations were in spiritual accord; and in
the greater part of them clodpate and intelligent dined
at the same table and clashed continually—the parents
enduring violent agonies over the children's disloyalty
to the ancient faith, their sacrilegious mockery of the
Law and its practices, their adherence to an abhorred
creed, their oblivion to the ambitions that father and
mother had so long entertained for them; while the
youth thought of nothing but the progress of the cause
and flaunted the red flag in the faces of their beloved
parents in the hope of convincing them of its honesty
by the simple device of getting them used to it. It
needed just that element of tragedy to add to East
Side radicalism the cup of martyrdom without which no
religion is quite genuine.

XIV

THE TRAGEDY OF READJUSTMENT

I MYSELF was in the meantime moving in two separate worlds. Nominally, at least, my home was still in Little Rumania among my own respectable relatives from Vaslui. Time and again I resolved to find a lodging somewhere south of Grand Street, where the majority of my comrades in spirit lived and where all my interests lay. But I never did it. Of friction there was enough between us. They were very outspoken, were my kinsfolk, in their disapproval of me. They found fault with my impiety, my socialism (or anarchism—they did not know just which it was), my indifference to dress and the social proprieties, my ragamuffin argumentative associates. Mrs. Segal, who still attempted to hold a protecting wing over me, took me to task often for not dropping in to her Sunday afternoon "at homes," which were the rendezvous of the gilded youth of our home town, and especially for neglecting to assist at the betrothal-party of her oldest daughter. Others of my blood observed that despite my aptness in picking up English, I was unpardonably slow in getting Americanized and doing nothing toward be-

coming a doctor. I was making quite a lot of money, too, but not only did I send very little of it home, I did not even have a bank account. Cousin Aby, who, though he was still making shirt-collars, had never become a radical, kept eternally at me for smoking on the Sabbath instead of going to the services. I, for my part, had my own opinions of their superficial Americanism, their indifference to the seething intellectual life about them, their blindness to the fine merits of the labor cause, and missed no opportunity to express my views. And yet some curious bond held us together. I had a strange feeling that I would miss them, that I would feel lonely without them, and I knew that they would take it as the final insult if I were to draw away from them altogether.

These strained relations with my Old World kin, as well as the tragic experiences of my fellow-radicals, often made me pause and wonder how I should get on with my own parents if I were ever to succeed in bringing them over. Father, to be sure, was not, as I remembered, what one could call fanatically religious, and mother had implicit confidence in me to do the right thing. But they were both, after all, to the last degree old-fashioned and rigidly conservative. They had a horror of the very word "socialist." I recalled how shocked they had been once—I was a mere child at the time—when mother's nephew Herschel came back from a long sojourn in Vienna and declared himself a socialist. He caused a most painful sensation, and

my parents declined to have him come to our house lest he should contaminate it, and his own mother treated him as an apostate and offered up candles at the synagogue for the reclaiming of his soul. Of course, America was a different story; and they would be coming into my world and not I into theirs. But it was difficult to imagine mother accepting me, her *kaddish*, in the rôle of an unbeliever, and father going off alone to temple on the morning of the Day of Atonement while I prepared for the F. A. S. picnic. I wanted them, however, very much to come. Conditions were now somewhat favorable. It was my third year at the trade and I was now an expert sleever. I was employed at the very best line; I was turning out forty and often fifty dozen a day; my rate (thanks, in part, to the union) had risen to five and a half cents, and when the material was silk, as it often was, I got as much as twenty cents per dozen. I had paid every penny on my watch and chain, and the instalment man was eternally asking me when I was going to give him another "show." Didn't I want a diamond ring or a steamer ticket for some one? Or something? Yes, I did want more than one steamer ticket, and later on I would want, very likely, quite a lot of house-furnishings. But—I was revolving the problem in my head, when suddenly Destiny stepped in and solved it for me in her own summary fashion.

Early in the spring of 1903 I wrote to my brother Harry, who was still at his big job in Constantza, to get

his advice—not, of course, on the *real* difficulty, but on the general situation. He answered that, owing to the commercial depression in Rumania, he was himself thinking quite seriously of going to America. His suggestion was that I should send a steamer ticket to Paul; and then, when the three of us were together, we would manage by our joint efforts to bring over the old folks. Paul had met with hard luck at his trade ever since his discharge from the army, so that he had no money of his own to make the trip. I hunted up my peddler at once, gave him a deposit of five dollars on a direct Vaslui-New York second-class ticket, and sent it off to Paul. A little more than a month later I heard from Harry again, this time from Vaslui. He wrote that their preparations for the journey were completed, and that he meant to sail with Paul from Bremen about the 1st of June. I watched the ship news for the next four months. Several times I went down to the offices of the Lloyd to inquire. I haunted the piers. I even telephoned to Ellis Island, thinking that perhaps my guests had been detained there in spite of their superior mode of travel. But not a sign of any brothers. Not even a word of explanation. I was nearly out of my wits with apprehension. I bombarded Harry and father and everybody I could think of with anxious letters, without results. At last—it was autumn now— it occurred to me to make inquiries at my former address. My former landlady, Mrs. Bernfeld, appeared ill at ease at my unexpected visit, contrary to her

habitual pleasure on seeing me. When I told her what I had come for she asked me nervously what made me think that she would not forward my mail. With my suspicions and fears aroused by her manner, I insisted that there must be something for me. Then she yielded it up. It was a postal card, written in the hand of the rabbi, advising me that father had died in August and urging me to perform the religious duties expected of a son in the circumstances. Some days later a second card in the same hand informed me that mother had caught cold at father's funeral, pneumonia had developed, and she had died in less than a fortnight.

My brothers did not get to New York until February. When I met them at Hoboken we kissed and wept together, and I got the details of my parents' death. Harry, being a man of business, was bent on going at once into an account of the disposition of the estate. He began by observing that since he had had to stand the expense of the illnesses and the funerals, it was no more than just that he should inherit the feather-bedding and the brass things. As for the remainder— but I waved the topic aside, assuring him that there was time enough for that. On the ferry-boat across the river I observed that he was taking me in critically. No sooner had we seated ourselves in an Elevated car than he turned upon me and, without preface or introduction, demanded to know whether I was doing my duty by the dead. My first impulse was to tell him

the unpalatable truth without delay; on second thought I decided to spare him. This was no time for propaganda; it would merely pain him; he would not understand my position offhand like this. So I begged again for time. Brother Paul, who had thus far merely sat there holding my hand and devouring me with his eyes but saying nothing, agreed that a public vehicle was no place for family conferences. But Harry insisted. Surely I could answer a plain question: Did I say *kaddish*—yes or no? Well, it was yes and no. The truth was that at the first shock of the terrible news I had compromised with my conscience and had attended services, mornings before going to work and evenings after returning. I had kept it up for ten days. Then I had rebelled. I simply could not endure the sham of it and the self-deception. The lickspittle, mercenary air of the beadles had disgusted me. He had better wait before he judged me. America, he would find, would change his ideas, as she had changed mine. It could not be helped. Father and mother would forgive me. They, too, would have understood if they had lived and come here. Harry regarded me with a pitying look and turned away. He refused to speak to me for the next twenty-four hours.

My brother Paul had been a spirited youngster and had objected to the rigid methods of education at home, with the consequence that he was a bit backward in bookish things. He found now that he had to pay the price of his youthful escapades. He experienced great

difficulties in finding his way about, in reading street names, and in handling foreign money. Nevertheless, thanks to his mechanical occupation, he was not long in getting work. In fact, he got his first job several weeks before Harry got his, and immediately offered to take over the payments on his ticket. Harry was thoroughly scandalized by everything American. He found every one, from Mrs. Schlesinger (our landlady) down to his prospective employers and his own brother, coarsened and vulgarized. The children were too smart and forward; the women were loud and over-dressed and ill-mannered; above all, the shops were dingy and ill-kept and inelegant. From these last he had expected a great deal. He had thought of New York as a kind of magnified Bucharest—a great, refined, luxurious city, with beautiful stores where it would be a proud joy to work. That was one of the things that had induced him to come to America. In Rumania he had always been employed in the haberdasheries— *magazins de gallanterie* they were called—of the small Black Sea port-towns, and he had for years dreamed of getting a situation at one of the brilliant shops of the capital. His longing had never been fulfilled, and he had emigrated to America with a feeling that here he would better his own aspiration. And what did he find? Of course, the department stores on Fourteenth Street and on Sixth Avenue, which he sallied forth to look over with wistful eyes on the very day following his arrival, were inexpressibly wonderful; but they

were, for the time being, at least, out of his reach. He had learned to speak Greek and Italian and Turkish in Constantza, but all these languages were of no earthly use in New York without English. The only places that were open to him were the unspeakably shabby holes in the Italian quarter or on Hester Street. They were, for the most part, in gloomy basements; their owners were rough, unkempt Polish and Russian ex-peddlers with fat, noisy wives (in one of them he had actually found the whole family lunching on the counter); the customers, instead of the sea-captains and naval officers and refined Greek ladies and suave Ottoman traders he had been accustomed to, were crude Sicilian peasants whose harsh dialects he scarcely understood, or East Side fishwomen. It made him very unhappy.

I suggested that, since he had brought quite a bit of money with him, he could easily learn to be a cutter at cloaks. That, surely, was elegant enough for any taste. It was universally considered the next best thing to a doctor. The very first families in Little Rumania thought a "cotter" an excellent catch for their marriageable daughters. All the best young men in the quarter who had a sense of what was "classy" were saving their pennies toward that end. Cousin Aby was dreaming of exchanging the machine for the knife as soon as he had enough money for the instruction fee and the wageless month of apprenticeship. But Harry cried out that my suggestion was an insult. Was that

AN AMERICAN IN THE MAKING

what he had clerked for all his life, and economized, and learned refined manners from his aristocratic customers in Constantza? Was that what he had come across seas to America for—to become a woman's tailor? No, thank God he had enough money left to go back to Rumania, where character and ability and gentlemanly qualities still counted for something. Curse Columbus and his country. He was going back. But he did not; because before he had time to buy his ticket he found a job in a basement store on Mulberry Street and got eight dollars a week, which he estimated to be nearly twice as many francs as he had ever received in the most elegant shop on the shores of the Black Sea.

While Harry was idle he amused himself by rummaging among my books and papers—when he was not, that is, making excursions through the department stores. One evening—it was during the first week after his arrival—he picked up a copy of the *Zukunft* and regarded it dubiously. Then, with a sudden inspiration lighting up his puzzled face, he looked me squarely in the eye and charged me point-blank with being a socialist. I could not help marveling at his sharpness, because there was nothing on the cover of the publication to betray me. His next sally enlightened me: "Young men who are respectable and mind their business," he said in a voice shaken with emotion, "do not waste their time reading monthly magazines. Now I know why you sent home so little money and why you

do not attend to your *kaddish* and why, after three years in America, you are still an operator at shirts instead of having a business of your own. *Die Zukunft* (The Future)," he sneered, bitterly; "a fine future will come to you reading this sort of thing. Our poor parents would die again if they knew what has become of the promising son of their old age." When the April holidays came and I made no pretense of keeping them, he suffered keenly. He tried to reason with me and to bring me to a conviction of sin. He was older, he argued, and he knew better. He by no means meant to have me a bigot in religious matters, but my behavior was treason to everything that had from time immemorial been sacred to our people.

In my own justification I must say that I did everything I could, short of betraying my convictions, to lessen his suffering. I went to my meetings secretly and did all my reading at the library. I avoided argument, even at the cost of losing a possible convert. I even kept all my radical friends away from our room, fearing that their zeal might get the better of their discretion. But I did not have to keep up this religious regimen very long. Harry had scarcely been in New York three months before I began to notice that he was rapidly undergoing a change. He began to funk in his prayers for the dead, offering at first the excuse that his long hours of employment made it impossible for him to go to daily services. After a time he openly began to smoke cigarettes on the Sabbath. I asked

him about it, and he answered that he was not the simpleton I took him for. In fact, he admitted, he had never been able to see anything in the old-fashioned faith. It was all well enough for unintelligent, unemancipated people, but he was a modern man. His profession of enlightenment could have furnished me with lessons in blasphemy. But when I invited him to accompany me to a lecture on a Sunday evening he told me that he was too tired and that he needed recreation. It was as impossible now to get him interested in radicalism as when he had landed. The ancient faith had gone, but nothing had come to take its place.

All the same, it was Harry who brought me my first and most successful proselyte. For it was through him that I met my excellent friend Esther. Harry had no sooner got a job and opened a bank account and settled down to his place in the American scheme of existence than he invested his surplus income in some first-class clothes and furnishings and plunged into the social whirl. Unlike myself, he regularly attended Mrs. Segal's *salon* and sought out the most desirable people. He saw that with his knowledge of Italian it would not take him long to have a shop of his own, and he was frankly looking about for a gentle partner to share his future prosperity with him. On a Sunday afternoon as soon as his store was closed he would hurry home and clean up and get into his best shoes and neckwear, to say nothing of suits, and bolt forth on his round of calls.

Now and then he would persuade Paul and me to go with him, and it was on one of the first of those occasions that I fell in with Esther.

Something about her hearty, almost masculine handshake and her unaffected manner arrested my attention. Her plain way of dressing and tying her hair, the straightforward tone of her speech, her reserve—all these told me that she was not the customary Rumanian girl. I got into talk with her, and found that she was reading quite a lot, and by no means the conventional books for young ladies. She had been in America no longer than I had, but (partly because of her unfamiliarity with Yiddish) she was managing to get on with English print. We compared notes, and found that our history as well as our leanings had much in common. She, too, had had her purifications. She had run the gamut of occupations, from cash-girl in an East Side department store to the factory, but now she was a trimmer at millinery and earning enough. Nevertheless, she was discontented. She had a vague feeling that she wanted to "do" something with herself and with the world.

We became fast friends. I read things to her from the *Zukunft* and from the other radical publications, and she drank in everything with wide eyes. This was a new and splendid world of ideas and ideals, she told me. In some remote way she had been thinking similar things. Then I offered to take her to a lecture. She went and came away radiant. She was furious with

her folks for not having been taught the humble mother tongue, as her brothers had been. She had never dreamed of its literary treasures and of the things that were reported in its press. I undertook to teach her to read Yiddish; and before long she abandoned her English fiction and devoured Peretz and Gordin.

She bettered my instruction. Although a little sentimental, her devotion to the radical faith was far more intense from the start than mine. She would not let me miss anything. In the hottest weather she would insist on going, and dragging me with her, to all sorts of out-of-the-way places, climbing endless flights of stairs, elbowing her way into jammed halls, and sweltering in the close air until the end. If I objected, she would look at me like Conscience incarnate and ask me whether I was not backsliding and whether I was not becoming a bourgeois "again"! At such times I would tell her that I wished I had bit off my tongue before talking to her about the Movement. But in the depths of my heart I was very proud of her. She was such a soul as any missionary might well be proud of having saved. And she was even a better friend than she was a disciple.

XV

THE TRIALS OF SCHOLARSHIP

MY radical interests had one salutary result immediately. I was not content to know at second-hand the great writers and thinkers whom I heard continually discussed. But in order to read them I must know English. I began my literary study of the language one memorable night by borrowing a one-volume edition of the complete works of Shakespeare from the Bond Street library. As soon as I got home I eagerly opened my treasure and turned to "Hamlet." To read "Hamlet" in the original had long been one of my most ambitious dreams. But, to my disappointment, I found that I could not get more than one word in ten, and of the sense nothing at all. Shakespeare as a first reader proved a total failure.

It was then I decided to go to school, although I should mention that my inspiration came in great part from Abe Wykoff, whom I had shortly before met at a lecture. The chap was a cloak-maker with ambitions similar to my own. As we came out of the building he said: "Comrade, I am going to throw up the machine. I am sick of cloaks. Three months in the year you

work overtime till midnight so that it nearly kills you intellectually and physically. And the rest of the time you are so hard up you have not a dime for the *Zukunft*. I am going to study dentistry. I had a little training at home, and I think I can pull through. Then liberty! Time to read and to think—to be a human being. I listened to Feigenbaum here the other night— did you hear him on 'Dominant Figures in World Literature?'—and it made my heart sick. Goethe, Calderon, Racine, Dante, what do I know about them? Hearsay, nothing more. I want to get into them, but, good Lord! where is the leisure? A professional man is different. I hear that Gordin and the others are getting together to start a progressive school for workmen. You and I ought to look into it. It is to be called the Educational League."

The new organization opened its doors toward the end of August, and Abe and I were among the first of its pupils. Tuition was entirely free, and there were no restrictions as to the choice of studies. All of the teachers gave their services without pay and with no lack of enthusiasm. Before a month had passed the place was filled—a student body made up of boys and girls in their teens, bearded men and middle-aged women, former gymnasium students from Russia and semi-illiterates from Galicia—all the ages and types of the diversified Ghetto. But the school turned out to be somewhat of a disappointment. Its fine liberal spirit tended to degenerate into a mere absence of

system and order. Pupils came in at all hours and interrupted the classes. Attendance was irregular, and those who were present one night were unable to follow the lesson because of what they had missed the night before. The program of the league, moreover, was an odd one. Its twelve rooms housed a course of study which began with elementary arithmetic and spelling and ended with university courses in evolution, the philosophy of Nietzsche, the history of the labor movement, Attic tragedy, and comparative religion; and teachers and students alike were too interested in the lectures and discussions on literary and social matters to give much attention to the exercises in orthography. By the latter part of September I took an inventory of my added stock of knowledge, and found that I had learned the names of some fourscore new books and authors as well as the difference in meaning between the English words "county" and "country" and "excellent" and "surpassing," of which latter I was far from certain.

Fortunately, there had lately begun to appear a whole crop of evening preparatory schools on East Broadway—largely, no doubt, a result of the league's experiment. They were usually owned and manned by young East-Siders who had recently graduated from the City College. I entered one of them simply in order to study English; but, once there, my ambitions expanded. I recalled my father's professional hopes for me, and conferred with my teachers about the possibility of

preparing for a medical college. They encouraged me, and I agreed to pay fifty dollars for the forty-eight-point Regents' course in monthly instalments of five dollars each.

The institution occupied the remodeled top flats of two buildings on both sides of the street. The ground floor of one of them was occupied by a second-hand bookstore, and the basement of the other housed a butcher shop. The class-rooms themselves were on off nights the meeting places of lodges and societies, and one of them did alternate duty as a chemical laboratory and a house of worship, as the brass candelabra and the paraphernalia on the east wall showed.

I used to travel across the street from algebra to English, and back again for German. The stoops and the halls and the stairways were always crowded with students, and during change of classes it was almost impossible to break through. I often wondered what would happen if there were a fire. At last the management rented a flat in a third building and turned it into a waiting-room and study-hall. The classes were overcrowded, so that, even with the best instructors, anything like a recitation was a practical impossibility.

The evening was divided into four periods, beginning at seven-fifteen and ending at eleven o'clock. As there were four Regents' examinations annually, our school year was arranged into four corresponding terms. Every course ran through a term. For instance, I took algebra three times a week for ten weeks and then went

THE TRIALS OF SCHOLARSHIP

up to the Grand Central Palace and passed the examination along with high-school pupils who had had the work five times a week for a year. I cannot tell you how we did it. I only remember that I would sit and puzzle over x's and y's from the time I got home at eleven o'clock until my eyes would give out; and at seven in the morning I would be back at the machine sewing shirts. I had registered late, and had missed the first two or three lessons. For a time the idea of algebra simply would not get through my head.

But even algebra was as nothing beside English. We were trying to cover the prescribed Regents' requirements, in spite of the fact that the majority of us could hardly speak a straight English sentence. The formal grammar, which was the bugbear of nearly everybody in the class, did not worry me. The terms were the same as in Rumanian, and I had been well trained at home. But the classics! We began, mind you, with Milton. The nights and the Sundays I spent on "L'Allegro" and "Il Penseroso," looking up words and classical allusions, if I had devoted them as earnestly to shirt-making, would have made me rich. And then I would go to class and the teacher would ask me whether I thought there were two separate persons in the poems, or just one person in two different moods. Bless my soul! I had not thought there were any persons in it at all. I had made up my mind that it was something about a three-headed dog that watched at the gate of Hades, whatever that was. So I would

go back and read those puzzling lines again and again, in a sort of blind hope that sheer repetition would somehow make me understand them, until I got them by heart. I can recite them yet.

As soon as I got straightened out a bit, I tried to take a little interest in the social life of my school. There was a socialist club, and a zionist society, and a chess club, and a debating club, and I don't remember how many others, that sent their representatives around with notices to the grammar class. One of the teachers was giving an unscheduled course in Greek between six and seven, and I joined it in the hope that it might enable me to read the dramas of Sophocles in the original. On Sunday nights the instructors took turns in lecturing in the study-hall on the other works of the authors we were studying in English and German, or on the colleges and universities of America, or on art, and I was drinking in a lot of things that the radical educators had omitted. In the debating society, too, the subjects were a little out of the usual. American politics and prohibition and the nature of the trusts touched elbows with such familiar things as the referendum and the initiative and the true Shakespearian conception of the character of Shylock; and what I particularly liked about the organization was that it gave greater opportunities for self-expression (and in English) than the regular lectures did.

My schooling brought a lot of new problems with it, and not all of them academic. Some of them were the

old, familiar ones with a new wrinkle. As a student
I could not work overtime, and many a row I had with
the boss about it. That meant a reduction in my
weekly envelope of about two dollars. There were the
monthly five-dollar payments, and several books every
quarter, which, however, one was not compelled to
buy, since the school itself supplied them at a nominal
rental of ten cents a month each. My room rent was
raised by fifty cents a month to pay for the midnight
gas I was burning. One had to dress a little better,
and shave oftener, and pay club dues.

But all this additional expense I could have endured.
It was the match-makers who made day and night
hideous for me. Being a prospective doctor had made
me quite a commodity in the marriage-market. One
of the men in the factory called my attention to the
fact that a certain pretty finisher had five hundred
dollars in the bank. An old woman of my acquaintance
hunted me up in my room one night after school to
make me a tempting offer. She knew of a rich jewelry-
peddler who was ready to finance me through college
on condition that I become engaged to his daughter.
"And he is a fellow-countryman of yours, too," she
added, "and of such a fine family! And the girl! A
jewel in the sight of God and man. Full of virtues.
Educated like a bookkeeper. Reads German—it is a
joy to hear her; and English, as if born to it." And all
this while I had a load of German and English of my
own to get through with before morning.

Not only among my own relatives, but in Little Rumania generally, I was causing an immense furore. My cousins and second cousins and aunts and uncles, to say nothing of my brothers, never ceased bragging about my change for the better. Even Couza, whom I had not seen since my barroom days, was pleased, and took occasion to remember that he was entitled to some of the credit because if it had not been for him I would still be in Vaslui. Cousin Jacob, who had in the mean time "settled affairs" in Rumania and followed his family, grinned with delight and forgave me my irreligious practices, and declared that he had always known that I would one of these days come to my senses. Next-door neighbors and fellow-townsmen beat a path to my hall bedroom to find out exactly what profession I meant to pursue and ventured an opinion as to which was the most profitable or the least irksome or the most elegant. I was set up as an arbiter on every variety of disputed question, linguistic, geographical, legal, and what not. Was Minneapolis in the South? If a chap had promised to marry a girl in Buzeu and now refused to marry her, could she sue him for breach of promise in New York? Was the dollar-mark derived from U. S.? Which was right, "myself" or "meself"? And if one, why not the other? Why could one say "yesterday" and not "yesternight"? If I confessed that I really did not know the answer to all these difficult questions, then I was told that pride goeth before a fall, and that I must not get so stuck on

myself, or else that I was a queer kind of a "college boy."

In January, at the end of my first three-month term, I took the examinations in English, algebra, and third-year German, and reaped five points. That left ten more between me and college. Unfortunately, it left something more besides, which even a conscientious student could not get by means of examinations. As we drew toward the end of our preparation, we "seniors," as we were called, had but one topic for discussion—how to get into and through college. I cannot enumerate half the schemes we cooked up. Some of us did more daring things than marry plutocrats' daughters. A great number became druggists, taking pharmacy as a stepping-stone to the higher ambition because it only required about one-fourth the number of counts and only one year in college. I knew several boys who became conductors and robbed the street-railway companies of nickels until they were caught and discharged, alas! too soon.

I myself, in company with Alfred (now Doctor) Goodman, chose another, more difficult, course. When September came, a year after I had entered school, I had enough credits to enter college on a condition, and, of course, no money even for the matriculation fee. Then Goodman heard of the State scholarships and came and told me about them. The stipend was good for four years' tuition at Cornell University, but the scholarships were open to none but high-school

pupils. I fretted at the loss of a year, but there was nothing for it but to go to high school and make myself eligible. I remember the afternoon when Goodman and I decided to go around to the nearest high school to find out what we had to do to get in. In our ignorance we wandered into a girls' institution somewhere on Thirteenth Street, and got laughed at at every turn, and as far as I can now recall never got as far as the principal's office at all. From a policeman on the street we learned that what we were looking for was the De Witt Clinton High School, which was a considerable distance up-town. There a warm-hearted old gentleman, whom I came later to know as Dr. Buchanan, the principal, took charge of us, and extracted from us our entire personal and family history, and gave us several score of cards to fill out, and conducted us about the building as if we were noted visitors, and introduced us to our teachers and commended us to their mercy because we "had never seen the inside of a public school."

We were admitted to the fifth form, and blushed with shame at finding ourselves in a class with mere youngsters. The English instructor was not much older than we were. On the very first test we were asked to write a hundred and fifty words on "School Spirit," and Alfred and I exchanged frightened glances and handed in blank papers. But the next day the teacher told us that we must not be bashful when we did not understand an assignment and allowed us to take our choice

of subjects and marked our substitute papers ninety-five and ninety-eight, respectively, and scribbled "excellent" on the margin for good measure. Things did not go quite so well, however, in the other classes. In the history-room the teacher was altogether helpless in the hands of his pupils, and in his misery he found fault with everything Goodman and I did, from the manner of our taking notes to our English intonation. How those boys could be so disrespectful to a learned man our European minds could not grasp at all. They threw chalk at him and at one another as soon as he turned his back to write on the blackboard, and cat-called him, and one fat youngster even went to the length of getting up and waltzing around the room in the middle of another boy's farcical recitation. And yet, as soon as they came into the physics-room, these same pupils became as meek as lambs and as attentive as a Clinton Hall audience.

We suffered so horribly under the discipline that at the end of a week Goodman gave up the effort and borrowed the money to go to a second-rate medical school where the tuition was comparatively cheap. At the evening school there had never been any insistence on getting exercises and themes into the hands of the teachers at any particular time. It was assumed that the work was done, as a matter of course. If a student could not or would not follow out assignments, he naturally dropped out altogether and devoted his money and his time to more pleasurable avocations

than going to school after a hard day's work in the sweat-shop. At Clinton, however, nothing was taken for granted; and I, who had fallen into the habit of doing lessons thoroughly enough, but by the method of inspiration, came into constant collision with the more conservative of my teachers, and was reported to my "guardian" for insubordination, and was kept in the detention room after classes when I should have been out earning my living, and was peremptorily sent down to see the principal, who did nothing more tyrannical, however, than to take me parentally by the arm and to tell me smilingly that he knew there were more ways than one to kill a cat, and that if I would not tell it "in Gath" he would confess to me that he thought my way as efficient as any, but that, nevertheless, I would find it beneficial to adopt in part, if I could, the ways of authority. I don't know how long my tormentors would have kept on worrying me if it had not gotten abroad that I had offered to join the penal class in higher spelling, of my own free will, which my task-masters accepted at once as a submission and as a stoic challenge to them to do their worst.

Going to day school necessitated giving up my shirts, which rendered the financial situation exceedingly tense. More than once I lacked the car fare to get to the school on 102d Street, and then I must either get up at five in the morning and walk, or invent some plausible but altogether untruthful excuse and compose a letter of explanation which must be signed by my

THE TRIALS OF SCHOLARSHIP

landlady—a process that, no doubt, appears simple enough to the uninitiated, but was, all the same, fraught with perils and difficulties because Mrs. Schlesinger had neglected to acquire the art of writing, and if I signed it myself with her name I made myself liable to the charge of forgery and the criminal punishments appertaining thereto. To make ends meet I attempted a return to the familiar occupation of peddling (on the grand scale, with a pushcart, this time, and the merchandise second-hand books instead of sweetmeats) but found it less congenial and less profitable—my wants having become extravagant—than in the old days. So I advertised myself, in Cousin Freedman's coffee-house window, as a private instructor in English and arithmetic. I charged twenty-five cents an hour, which would have brought me wealth enough if only the powers above had not cut the day to a skimpy twenty-four hours and if the desire for self-improvement in Little Rumania had not been so scarce. Time was particularly at a premium, inasmuch as my pupils were possessed with an excessive curiosity about the meanings of all sorts of words that I had not inquired into, so that if I prized my dignity and self-respect I must devote hour for hour to preparing my lessons; and also because the ancient problem of distances had still to be solved.

And then when the struggle was all over it turned out that I had labored and suffered in vain. Somehow I had never stopped to question my ability to win the

scholarship. Yet it required only a trifling accident to smash the hope on which I had staked everything. I scored ninety-six in English, and nearly as high in all the other subjects except one. In physics I was marked fifty. Out of four questions one was on the rainbow and another on some species of dynamo, neither of which topics had been touched on at all in the class. A month later I took the Regents' examination in that same subject, and, I believe, under the same examiners, and passed "with honor," which meant a percentage of over ninety. So decisive are examinations!

XVI

OFF TO COLLEGE

BUT to college I went that autumn, all the same. The examinations were no sooner over than I gave up my tutoring and my school and began to cast about for something real to do. I had entered the high school to attain a particular object. It had been defeated; but I had got something else in its stead. I had improved my English; I had acquired new and more regular methods of study; I had completed my entrance requirements, so that I need not worry now about working off "conditions" in college. Still, there was no sense in keeping up the grind, even though the authorities sent postal card after postal card to Mrs. Schlesinger, threatening me with the visitations of the truant officer. They were snail-slow in that city institution. The course was, to all intents and purposes, finished; but they were taking the entire month from the end of May to the last of June to review and "wind up." I could do better with those four weeks. Time was precious. If I got busy straight away, that very month might decide whether I should graduate in 1910 or 1911.

AN AMERICAN IN THE MAKING

In a financial sense I was no better off now than a year ago—rather worse, if anything. I had not only fallen behind by a year, so that if I entered college at all I would be a freshman when Goodman and a lot of others of my companions would be sophomores; I had missed the chance of laying up some money toward the lean years that were ahead of me. The failure to earn the State scholarship I had come to take philosophically. It merely prevented me from going to Cornell—the university I had set my heart on. But that prize would, after all, have paid only my tuition; my living expenses I must earn in any event. At one of the free out-of-town colleges, to be sure, it might prove harder to find work. But hadn't I tried this past year to combine study with business in New York? And with what results? Besides, college was not high school. By all accounts a medical student had practically no time left when his day in the lecture-room and the laboratory was over. In a small town there would at least be no wastage in traveling back and forth.

The road to follow was, therefore, plain: I must utilize every bit of the three or four months between now and the opening of college. How? that was the question. Ornstein and Stein—my former employers—had a vacancy at the double-needle machine. But a week's trial revealed the fact that shirts were going through one of their periodic slack seasons that summer. The union, too, had disintegrated, and piece prices were at their worst. Just when I was perfectly ready to work

overtime there was hardly enough to do during the day. A little figuring showed me that at the present rate I would not get enough together by September to pay even for my trip to college.

Fortunately my good cousin David was an electrician and was working as a lineman at the Pennsylvania Terminal, then building. I knew nothing about the trade beyond a few odd terms, such as "potential," "cathoids," "alternating current," and "Leyden jar," which I had picked up in my study of physics, and which David did not know and regarded as worse than useless. Nevertheless, he managed to get me taken on as his helper at a wage of one dollar and seventy-five cents a day. David was devoting his evenings to taking care of the tenement-house he was living in, and he insisted that I must come and take a room in his apartment. "You can save about twenty dollars," he urged, "and it will be no loss to me. We have more space than we can use, and I am not paying any rent." Once he got me up there he pointed out that there were no restaurants in the neighborhood (except American ones, which served food I could not eat), so that I must eat at his table. When the week was up and I asked Rose, his wife, to tell me how much I owed her, she sent me about my business, and added with a laugh that I could pay all in a bunch at the rate of ten dollars a week when I became a doctor, or I might reimburse her by treating her four children.

That David family saved the situation. Rose even

persisted, in spite of all my protests, to double the number of her husband's sandwiches, which she packed for him every morning along with a bottle of cold coffee; so that my lunch money went likewise to increase the great pile. David and I had an hour at noon; so I carried a book with me to work every day and employed the better part of the period in going over the English and American classics I had studied. Once one of the engineers on the job found my copy of Emerson's Essays in the supply-chest, and he asked David whose it was. My cousin pointed proudly at me. The gentleman, however, did not seem impressed. He threw me a sidelong glance and smiled superiorly. When he was gone, David burst out laughing. "That's a good one on him," he cried. "He doesn't know you could give him a few pointers. Why didn't you speak up, you big silly, and tell him that he wasn't the only college guy on the place?"

The whole world, however, is not made up of Davids and Roses, and my family was no exception to the rule. Looking ahead, I could see that the dollars I was saving would hardly suffice to carry me through. A friend (who, for reason of his own, must remain nameless) offered to lend me fifty dollars. But the attempt to persuade my two brothers to contribute each an equal amount met with only partial success. Indeed, my relatives, who had up to this time been very proud of my ambitions and my achievements, now held up their hands in solemn disapproval at my selfishness. It

was all very well, they declared, to become a doctor, but this business of borrowing money to get there was carrying matters to extremes. My cousin, the collar-maker, could not see why shirt-making was good enough for him and not for me. Another cousin thought I had enough education already. A third was convinced that I could persuade Mr. Rockefeller to lend me the money. Uncle Berl confessed quite frankly that he had his doubts about a fellow who could not win a paltry scholarship ever becoming a doctor, anyhow. Uncle Schmerl equally as frankly laid it before the whole assemblage that it was a foolish thing to encourage a poor boy to rise above his kind so that he might later put on airs and be ashamed of his own kindred. Brother Harry was not so philosophical as all that, but he was intending to go into business for himself. Might it not be best, he wanted to know, to wait another year and in the mean time earn the money at the machine? Only gentle Paul was silent at the family council—except to say that as long as he kept his job he would spare me his dollar a week. But all the advice and the censure was to no purpose. I had made up my mind. Money or no money, I was going. My earnings as an electrician would pay my fare. The Lord might do the worrying about the rest.

To my great astonishment, I discovered that even my radical associates were stanchly opposed to my plans and my ambitions. I had confidently expected that they, at least, would understand my longing for

emancipation and approve of it. It was from them, largely, that I had got the inspiration—the worship of learning, the ideal of culture, the dream for a higher plane of life. They had no illusions about the wretched, precarious existence of the working-man. They constantly lamented his lot, his oppression by the rulers and capitalists, his lack of opportunity to develop himself, his imprisonment in dingy lofts and airless tenements. Their newspapers and their lecturers never tired of insisting that the liberation of the working-class could only come by education, and that this education must come from within, from the conscious endeavor of the proletariat itself. Well, here I was carrying their theories into practice. I was going to get educated, to lift myself out of my class. I was going to make my fight for the freedom and the leisure and the opportunity to develop which they had taught me was the inalienable right of every man. Why should they not give me their most enthusiastic support?

I remember the stormy discussion at the anarchist reading-room that followed upon my announcement. Isidore Lipshitz, the cadaverous, curly-haired closer, who had befriended me in the days of my apprenticeship and had witnessed the beginning of my career, burst out into sarcastic, fiendish laughter; and Joe Shapiro, affectionately nicknamed the "red bull," jumped to his feet and launched into a passionate denunciation of my sacrilegious perversion of radical principles:

"The class-conscious proletariat is no longer good enough for you," he shouted. "You want to go to college, to become a gentleman and a bourgeois; to wear spats, I suppose, and silk gloves, quite like a little clodpate. All right, go, and the devil take you. But"—and here he waved a menacing finger in my face—"don't you come around here and pollute this place with your infernal sophistries. Did you hear that, Isidore? To our lecturers he compares himself. The cheek of the *nix!* Who ever told you that Feigenbaum and Hermalin and Liessin have gone to college? They started in the shop and they have developed by their own brains and the right kind of reading. But they have stuck to their class and have devoted themselves to the interests of the worker. They have not tried to climb in among the church-walkers and the capitalists and the oppressors. Traitor!"

In vain I tried to make myself heard and to explain that by getting a thorough education I was serving the best interests of my class. As a factory hand, I argued, all my energy and struggling against a complex system was doomed to be unavailing. They insisted that the emancipation of the worker could only come by the education of the body as a whole, not by the sporadic, selfish scrambling out of individuals into the ranks of the oppressors. My place was in the shop, among the men and women who were building up the movement with their blood and their brains. They predicted that no sooner would I enter college than my class-conscious-

ness would melt away and I would begin to feel myself as belonging in the camp of the enemy. My whole course was treason to the cause of labor. I smiled incredulously at their passionate presentiments; but the event, as you shall see, proved that they were not altogether wrong.

The only person I got any comfort out of was Esther. She admitted that theoretically there was, no doubt, something to be said for the point of view of our radical friends, but that in practice I was entirely right. She even found an element of the heroic in my undertaking. As long as the world was what it was there was nothing for the individual to do but to make the most of his own opportunities. Besides, I was not merely striving for economic betterment, if at all; and it was pure sentimental nonsense to raise objections against the aspirations of a hungry mind. About my financial difficulties she was equally encouraging. With my energy and my various abilities I ought to have no trouble at all in earning all I spent, to say nothing of my modest hope of making a dollar a week.

So, in the autumn of 1906, I started out on my great adventure. Throughout the summer I had been studying catalogues from all the ends of the country and making the rounds of all cut-rate ticket-offices in the city, in an effort to make my scant savings go as far as I could. The New York medical colleges, with their tuition rates of one hundred and fifty dollars and upward, were, of course, out of the question. Some of

the State universities, I found, charged no tuition fees; but a study of certain tables contained in the bulletin showed that the minimum expenditure for board and room per year was two hundred and fifty dollars. Heaven preserve me! One hundred was my limit, and I would have to earn the most of that. Therefore, even those schools that promised reasonable living expenses had to be passed up, as long as their catalogues said nothing about ways and means. Finally, after two months of figuring and comparing, I chose the University of Missouri. It appeared to combine all the advantages of economy with high academic standards. I calculated that by living at the dormitories and boarding at the University Dining Club I could make an appreciable cut in my first estimate. Perhaps I could skimp through the year on seventy-five dollars and pay my railroad fare with the remainder of the hundred. And the reports of the Y. M. C. A. made me feel certain that I could earn the better part of the outlay by doing odd jobs.

I did not start from New York until two weeks after the official opening of the university. My experience in the night school had taught me how to do a month's work in a week, so that I had no doubt of my ability to catch up with my classes. As long as I had a job, I felt that I ought to keep it as long as I could. Heaven alone knew when I would have another. So I worked at the Pennsylvania Terminal until one Friday late in September. On Saturday I packed my belongings,

bought the return half of an excursion ticket to St. Louis for three dollars less than the regular price, and went around to say good-by to my friends. Goodman gave me a pound of Russian tobacco and a case of five hundred cigarettes from his father's shop. Esther wanted to give me her fountain-pen, but I would not let her, and made her accept my two leather-bound quarto volumes of Dickens (left-overs from my book-selling venture) in gratitude for her confidence in me. On Sunday I was off. My brothers, my cousins, and a number of my schoolfellows came to the station. As I scrambled into the car with my telescope case and my big bundle of food for the journey, the women-folks burst into tears. "Poor Max!" they cried. "What will become of him out there in the wilderness, among strangers, cut off from the world?" I tried to smile encouragingly, but my heart was in my throat. I was to learn the reason for those kind, silly tears soon enough. I was going to the land of the "real Americans."

PART IV

AMERICA OF THE AMERICANS

XVII

IN THE MOLD

I AM sure that if the immigrant to America were ever to dream of the things that await him at his journey's end there would be no need for any laws to keep him out. He would prefer to eat grass and kiss the royal scepter and stay at home. Any man, I suppose, with a drop of vagabond's blood in his make-up and a family to support will, under the stress of necessity, fold his tent and move on to greener pastures; and no human soul will indefinitely endure the insolence of oppression without flaming into revolt. But there is, on the other hand, a generally accepted limit to the price of bread and freedom beyond which even a hungry and a weary voyager, if he retains a sense of value and of honor, will not go, purely as a matter of principle. One may be willing to submit, with a kind of grim cheerfulness, to train-robbers and steerage pirates, to seasickness and homesickness, to customs officials and—though this is really too much—even to Ellis Island inspectors; and count the whole thing—with the heart-wringing farewells thrown in—as a tolerably fair exchange for the right to live and the means of living. But no one, I

insist, would for a moment consider the transaction if he suspected that he must, before he is through, become an American into the bargain. Mortal man is ready for everything except spiritual experiences.

For I hardly need tell you that becoming an American is spiritual adventure of the most volcanic variety. I am not talking of taking out citizen's papers. It cannot be too often repeated that the shedding of one nationality and the assumption of another is something more than a matter of perfunctory formalities and solemn oaths to a flag and a constitution. Vowing allegiance to the state is one thing. But renouncing your priceless inherited identity and blending your individual soul with the soul of an alien people is quite another affair. And it is this staggering experience of the spirit—this slipping of his ancient ground from under the immigrant's feet, this commingling of souls toward a new birth, that I have in mind when I speak of becoming an American. To be born in one world and grow to manhood there, to be thrust then into the midst of another with all one's racial heritage, with one's likes and dislikes, aspirations and prejudices, and to be abandoned to the task of adjusting within one's own being the clash of opposed systems of culture, tradition, and social convention—if that is not heroic tragedy, I should like to be told what is.

I got to Columbia, Missouri, in the evening two days later. I had written to the president of the university

to tell him by what train I would arrive, and I was a little taken aback to find that he had not even sent any one to meet me. There were a lot of students at the station, but they paid no attention to me. They were making a great deal of noise and shaking hands in a boisterous sort of way with one or two decidedly rural-looking boys who had come in on the train with me. I began to feel very lonely. Yes, began was the word. It was to be continued.

My first thought was to make straight for the university and ask for the president. He was the only person who knew who I was. But inquiry revealed the fact that the campus was a good half-mile from the station, so I decided to wait until morning. There was a house not far away that looked like my own home in Vaslui, and it bore a sign with the word "Hotel" over its eaves. I went in and asked an old negro about a lodging for the night. He said the place was full, and conducted me across the street to what he called the annex. There I was given a room. In the morning I dressed and began to look for the kitchen. A little girl asked me whether I wanted breakfast. I said, "No; I'll have breakfast after I come back from the president's house. But where is the sink? I want to wash." It took her some time to understand me; then she grinned, and pointed to a pitcher and bowl on a little stand in my room.

At the university I learned that the president was out of town. But a clerk told me, with a twinkle in

her eye, that if I wanted to be registered she would show me where to go. At the registrar's office another clerk surprised me by saying that he remembered my name quite well, because he had got all the letters I had written to the president, and then astonished me still more by producing a folder which contained every one of them. He said, pleasantly, that my name was so unusual that he could not forget it, and added some other polite remarks about the fine city New York was and his hopes as to my happiness in Missouri.

Then we got down to business, and I felt my heart sinking as I watched my hard-earned funds melting away under his efficient pencil.

"Let's see, your incidental fee will be five dollars; biology lab., five again; you are going to take chemistry I—lab. fee, ten dollars."

I don't know just where I would have landed at this remorseless rate if I had not had enough presence of mind to interrupt him here.

"You will excuse me?" I asked. "I am afraid I shall have to wait a little, until I get some more money from New York, before I go any further."

"Yes?"

"You see, it is like this. I was hoping that I could earn something first. Is there not a Christian Association that gets work for students?"

"Yes. To your right, in the corridor, as you go out."

His courtesy made me bold. "You do not suppose

I could arrange to make my payments to the university more gradually, say a dollar a week?" I asked.

He did not know. He had never heard of its being done. But I might see the chairman of the Entrance Committee on the next floor.

"And I am sorry to tell you," he added, "that there is one other item which I omitted. Registration closed a week ago. There will be a late registration fee of five dollars." I could see he was completely desolated about my plight.

Did I have a room, he wanted to know next. If not, there was the Y. M. C. A. again, or the bulletin-board in Academic Hall. I would have no trouble in finding just what I wanted.

No, I had no room as yet, but how about Lathrop Hall? I should prefer to live in the dormitory.

He took me in with a sidelong glance. "I should not advise you to," he concluded. "You will find the boys a little jolly there."

"I do not mind that," I assured him, while my thoughts lingered anxiously on my resources.

Well, there was another difficulty. Not being a resident of the State, I was ineligible. But I could make my money go a long way at the University Dining Club, if I would buy a permit for twenty dollars. Twenty dollars! when I had seventeen in the whole world.

So I went around to the Y. M. C. A. and was told again that I was a little late. Most of the jobs had been

grabbed up weeks ago. Likewise, the chairman of the Entrance Committee saw no way of agreeing to my odd suggestion about easy payments. If I were a sophomore he might recommend me to the Loan Fund Committee. Anyhow, he would see that I got back my late registration fee if I filled out a blank stating the reasons for my tardiness. After wandering about in the buildings I came upon the bulletin-board and discovered scores of requests for roomers and room-mates and "baching partners." Here was a ray of hope. The majority of the rooms seemed to rent for six dollars a month, so that with a room-mate the expense would come to very little more than at the dormitory. But room-mates, as I was soon to learn, were a knottier problem than funds.

I jotted down a few addresses of boarding-houses, as well as the names of several students who announced that they had second-hand books for sale, and withdrew to the grounds to contemplate my situation. I walked across to the center of the quadrangle and sat down with my back against the base of one of the ivy-covered columns. Most likely they would wait with breakfast for me at the hotel; oh, well, let them wait. I was in no humor for food. My brain was in a turmoil. What I needed was air and the power to think straight. Now then, the first step was to clear out of that dollar-and-a-half house and take up lodgings, for the time being, in as inexpensive a place as might be found. Good economics told me that, in spite of the extortionate

price, the permit to the U. D. Club would prove a wise investment. Therefore the next step was to despatch a special-delivery letter to my friend in New York for the promised fifty dollars. And, above all things, I must not let the pessimism of the Y. M. C. A. office paralyze my spirit. Somehow I must see the thing through. If I cannot get German translations I shall wash dishes or clean shoes or peddle or—

But at this point my ruminations were rudely broken into, and I had my first set-to with the American reality. Two young gentlemen, emerging from the Engineering Building, were making their way toward me, earnestly conferring as they went. I glanced up at their faces, and told myself with some trepidation that I was in for it. There was an unmistakable bellicose light in their eyes. What had I done? Then I heard one whisper, "Go for him, Bud." My first impulse was to clear the field while there was yet time. But my curiosity got the better of me, and I waited in suspense to see what would happen. "Bud" advanced with one hand behind him.

"Freshman?" he asked, laconically, as he stopped in front of me.

A happy inspiration dashed the word "yes" from off my tongue, and I replied in the negative.

"Soph?" he persisted.

"Yes."

"Where from?"

"Cornell."

"Well, you'll have to get off the mound. Only juniors and seniors can sit by the columns."

As he walked away I saw that he carried a "paddle" in one hand. "Hazing"—a term I had occasionally heard in high school—flashed through my mind. I had saved the day, not perhaps by the approved method of open warfare, but at any rate by perfectly legitimate strategy.

During the remainder of that first week in Missouri I found out what it was to be a stranger in a foreign land; and as the year wore on I found out more and more. Columbia seemed a thousand times farther removed from New York than New York had been from Vaslui. Back there in the Ghetto everybody had thought me quite Americanized. Now I could not help seeing that Missouri was more genuinely American than the New York I had known; and against this native background I appeared greener than when I had landed. This new world I had suddenly dropped into was utterly without my experience and beyond my understanding, so that I could not even make up my mind whether I liked or hated it. I had to admire the heartiness, the genuineness, and the clean-cut manliness of it. But, on the other hand, it prided itself on a peculiar common sense, a cool-headedness, a practical indifference to things of the spirit, which the "intelligent" of the East Side in me revolted against.

Nevertheless, I tried very hard to make myself agreeable to my fellow-students. But I failed

miserably. In the first two months I had, and lost, a half-dozen room-mates. Do what I might, I could not make them stay with me. There were never any hard words; we always parted as "good friends." But almost from the first day they would hardly talk to me, and before the week was out they would find some excuse for moving or asking me to move. I spent many sleepless nights trying to figure out the thing. It wounded my self-esteem to find my society so offensive to everybody. Besides, it touched my poor purse. Every time I was left alone in a room I had to pay the full rent. But my predicament had its comic side, too. It got so that when I found a new room-mate I would take a perverse sort of pleasure in watching to see how soon he would begin to look the other way when I spoke to him. I never had to wait very long.

These broad intimations, so often repeated, should, I suppose, have convinced me that I lacked the stuff of which Missourians were made, and should have served to drive me back into my shell. Whatever their reasons and motives might be, it was quite clear that these fellows had no love for my presence; and common sense as well as a natural regard for my own sensibilities ought to have told me that the simplest way out of my scrape was to leave them alone. Besides, I may as well confess that this subtle distaste—this deep-lying repulsion of contrary temperaments—was by no means one-sided. Perhaps I liked my elusive room-mates a little better than they liked me. But I possessed

enough of self-esteem to tell myself that this was but a proof of my own superiority. If Missouri did not take to me, I argued, so much the worse for Missouri's powers of penetration and appreciation. It betrayed, at least, an extremely provincial state of mind. No doubt I had my share of damning imperfections, but even a college freshman, if he had eyes, could see that I was not altogether wanting in the virtues that make for grace. And if they should care to ask me, I could give these gentlemen a bill of particulars relative to their own shortcomings that would take as much of their conceit out of them as they avowedly persisted in trying to knock out of me.

All the same I did not leave them alone. I did the very opposite. How, in the first place, *was* I to avoid them? I was a lonely, deserted rock surrounded and buffeted by a vast ocean. Wherever I turned I must face them. If I wanted a job, I must work for and with them. The class-rooms, the library, the boarding-houses, the very streets swarmed and echoed with them. I had no choice but to walk with them, talk with them, and trade with them. Nay, my case was far worse than poor Shylock's: I must even eat with them and—at brief intervals—sleep with them. Think of it, an entire university, yes, a whole State, stretching over a hundred thousand square miles, filled with nothing but Missourians! Of course, there was one avenue of escape—I might go back to the Ghetto in New York; but I was not fool enough for that. Alive as I was from

the very start to his deficiencies and his foibles, I could see that the Missourian had something to teach me that I needed very badly to learn. In one of my earliest letters to Esther I wrote: "I am in an appalling mess, but it will be the making of me." The sheer conflict somehow appealed to me. It was not exactly any notion of valor, or any shame at the thought of failing to see a thing through. My bringing up had bred very little of the chivalrous in me. My friends would never dream of holding the failure against my character. I merely felt that the constant rubbing of shoulders with a body of people who were in nearly every way the opposite of myself was bound to do me good. Even if I acquired none of the enemy's virtues, the contact with him could do nothing less than throw light on my own all too numerous weaknesses.

And so I flung myself into the battle with an intense fury. I deliberately went out of my way to get stepped on. I attended chapel religiously, in spite of the fact that the speeches bored me and the prayers jarred on me. I was punctual at meal-time so as not to miss my usual portion of sidelong glances and grins and open ho-hos. Timid as I was, I let no opportunity slip to get into an argument at the cost of getting myself thoroughly disliked. I even went so far as to join the cadet corps, and was bawled at by the commandant (whose thundering bass voice reminded me of Couza), and was laughed at by the members of my platoon for my unsoldierly bearing, and was eternally posted for

soiled gloves or unpolished shoes or errors in executing
commands, and was made to write excuses (when I
would rather have read Heine or Huxley) for these
delinquencies and to rewrite them over and over again
until they conformed precisely to military etiquette,
and was haled before the adjutant and bawled at some
more when I revolted at the stupidity of it all, and was
punished with extra drilling in the awkward squad—
every bit of which was just what I deserved for betraying
my radical faith by getting into the silly business at
all. More than half the time—if you will pardon the
unmasculine confession—I was in the depths of the
blues, and during at least half of that I was contemplat-
ing suicide, which, however, I took no steps to commit,
beyond the penning of an exceedingly vivid portrayal
of the act, which was perpetrated with a vial of deadly
substances filched from the chemistry laboratory, and
the subsequent regrets of my fellow-students as they
reviewed the history of their uncharitable dealings
with me.

The worst of it was that all my heroic suffering seemed
to be going for naught, at least for a long time. For
the principal problem that I had set out to solve remained as obstinate as ever. Why would not those
boys room with me? To this puzzling question none
of my disagreeable adventures would furnish an answer.
Of course, it was quite clear they found me a queer,
unlikable animal. But I had known that all along.
Why did they not like me? None of my guesses satis-

fied me. At the boarding-house where I stayed while waiting for money from New York I heard a great many stories in an impossible dialect about Jews, and judging from the satisfaction with which they were received I thought at first that I was a victim of ancient prejudice. But I could not long hold on to that theory. There was not a trace of venom in the yarns. Why, these chaps had not the remotest idea what a Jew was like! Their picture of him was the stage caricature of a rather mild individual with mobile hands who sold clothing and spoke broken English. No one in Missouri knew that I had had Jewish parents until three years later, when, on the occasion of my graduation, the newspapers of St. Louis and Kansas City thought my career of sufficient interest to have me interviewed and I made some passing allusion to my origin. No more tenable was my surmise about class antagonism. Indeed, I was not long in Missouri before I was struck with the absence of every real class feeling, and I said to myself, exultingly, that however America might have broken faith with me in other ways, her promise of democratic equality she had scrupulously fulfilled. To be sure, there were the fraternities with their vague dream of building up an aristocracy on a foundation of first-rate tailoring and third-rate chorus-girls. But they hardly mattered. The genuine American recognized but one distinction in human society—the vital distinction between the strong, effectual, "real" man and the soft, pleasure-loving, unreliant failure. As far

as I could judge, the "real" men were chiefly "barbs" and the failures (at least on examinations) were for the most part "hellenes." If, then, my isolation rested neither on race prejudice nor on class exclusiveness, what did it rest on? My poor, bewildered brain was unable to answer.

XVIII

MY friend in New York, on whose liberality the financial success of my venture was entirely dependent, had not expected me to get into straits so soon, and it was nearly two weeks before help arrived. In the mean time I had canvassed the labor-market and had found it so discouraging that I informed Esther how unjustified her optimism had been. A lot of people had taken my name and address, but I could tell from the way they looked at me that my chances with them would be very slim even if they had not already got some one else. The soonest I could possibly expect to get employment was at the end of the semester, when a number of the present job-holders would be leaving the university on various missions. I had, also, caught up with my classes, and had succeeded, somehow, in impressing my teachers a little more favorably than my fellow-students. In particular, I was taking effective hold of the work in languages, so much so that my English instructor had twice read my themes to the class without (thank goodness!) divulging my name. My seventeen dollars had gone for books, incidentals,

entrance fee, and board; and I was now rapidly and ruinously running into debt, and anxiously inquiring at the post-office for mail.

When, at last, relief came in an envelope with yellow stamps, the first thing I did was to buy my permit to the University Dining Club and to secure myself against the future by paying for a month's keep in advance. The price for board, twenty-one meals, was one dollar and fifty cents; with the cost of the permit it amounted to about two dollars per week. There were between fifty and sixty tables in one vast room, and eight Missourians at each table. When the big gong rang there was a fierce scramble for places, followed by a scraping of chairs and a rattling of crockery and silverware. Usually during the noon meal the manager of the club would get up to make some announcement, and invariably he would be greeted by yells of, "Fire away," "Jack Horner," "We want butter," "Can the oleo." Before an athletic game, and particularly after a victory, the rooting and the yelling, the pounding on the tables and the miscellaneous racket were deafening. I thought I had wandered into a barbarous country. I confess I did not altogether disapprove of the barbarians. After a while I tried very hard to be one myself. But I did not know how.

Most of the conversation at the table and around the campus was about athletics. I wanted to talk about socialism, and found that these university men knew as little about it, and had as dark a dread of it, as the

clodpate on the East Side. Religion was taboo. They went to church because it made them feel good, as they put it; and there was an end. They took their Christianity as a sort of drug. Sex, too, was excluded from sane conversation, although there was no objection to it as material for funny stories. I went to one or two football and basket-ball games—I could not afford very many—and liked them. But I could not, for the life of me, say an intelligent word about them. The chatter around me about forward passes and goals and fumbles might just as well have been in a foreign language, for all I got out of it. When Missouri won a hard victory over Texas I caught the enthusiasm and joined in the shirt-tail parade, wondering, in the mean time, what my intellectual friends in New York would have thought if they had seen me in that outfit. But the hero worship bestowed on the overgrown animals who won the battle irritated me. I could not see what place this sort of thing had in a university. And it surprised and delighted me to find that some of the more sensible fellows, who loved the game, took the same view of the matter as I did.

I made heroic efforts to become an adept in sports, not so much because the subject interested me, but because I did not greatly relish being taken for a fool. There could be very little doubt but that my table-mates had made up their minds that I was one. No one else that they had ever seen or heard of could sit through a meal the way I did without opening his mouth, and

that while the calendar was crowded with "events" of every kind. Moreover, I knew but one way to make friends with people, and that was by the East Side method of discussion. There was no help for it; I was in the enemy's country and I must submit to his tradition and his customs or die. If he refused to talk about poetry and Nietzsche and the Russian revolution and the Scandinavian drama and the class struggle, I ought, at any rate, to be thankful that there was at least one topic he was interested in. It was not his fault that I had been sewing sleeves when I ought to have been playing ball, and that I had gone to the wrong kind of a school for my secondary training, where I had been made into a grind and a bore and a disputatious fanatic when I could just as well have learned to be a level-headed man among men. It was not yet too late, fortunately. The opportunities for rounding out my education were ample enough. I had but to bring my will into play.

Besides, the institution of sport had begun to interest me. No one but an intellectual snob could remain at Missouri for any length of time without perceiving that the enthusiasm of the ball-field was something more than a mere fad or a frivolous pastime. It was a highly developed cult, sprung out of the soil and the native spirit, and possessed of all the distinguishing characteristics of its type. It had a hierarchy and a liturgy and a symbolic ritual of its own. What was on first impression taken to be but an *argot* was in reality

a very exact sacred tongue, in a class with the choice Hebrew which my old rabbi's wife in Vaslui insisted on talking on Saturdays. A football match in full swing had all the solemnity and all the fervor and color of a great religious service. The band and the songs, the serpentine processions and the periodic risings, the mystic signals and the picturesque vestments, the obscure dramatic conflict with its sudden flights and hot pursuits, the transfigured faces of the populace, the intense silences alternating with violent outbursts of approving cheers and despondent groans—all this was plainly not a game but a significant national worship, something akin to the high mass and the festival of Dionysus.

What had deceived me about the true nature of this thing at first was that my Missourian professed devotion to an altogether different creed, a creed which was as alien to his Western clime as it was hostile to his temper and his aspirations. Six days in the week he labored at his field sports, and shouted from the house-tops his pagan maxim about a sane mind in a sane body, and looked upon the world as a fierce battle-ground in which every man must grapple with his fellows and in which the victor was not only the hero, but the saint as well, and resented the merest intimation of any contrary doctrine as an insult to human fortitude and a danger to civilization, and cultivated a strident, burly, rough masculinity, and despised the sensitive and the studious and the idealistic as morbid, effeminate, chicken-

livered weaklings; and then on the seventh day he suddenly turned his coat and changed his tune and denied this robust faith of his, and sighed about the materialism of the world and the folly of man's desires, and assented with bowed head and contrite heart to the assertion that the poor (which meant the weak) shall inherit the earth, and that men are brothers, and that God who feedeth the crow and clotheth the lily shall feed and clothe also him, and humbled himself before the gentle, impractical dreamer of Nazareth and sang hymns to Him and called Him Master. Who could under such circumstances fail to arrive at the opinion that if the Missourian was not a hypocrite he must at least be amazingly inconsistent?

Athletics, however, was not the only weak link in my chain. I was found wanting in the most unexpected places. In the class in literature I frequently attracted attention by displaying all sorts of scraps of curious knowledge, as when the instructor asked for a specimen of Hindu drama and I volunteered the play of "Sakuntala," or when, on another occasion, I pointed out that the German word *genial* was in no way related to the English word "genial." But when the boys in the house organized a 'coon hunt and asked me to join in it I had to admit that I did not know what a 'coon was, which gave Thompson, the wag of the crowd, an opportunity to tell me that 'coons were vegetables, and to inquire, in a tone of mock surprise, whether it were possible that I had never eaten 'possum and sweet

potatoes. In the work in biology and physics the things that both teachers and text-books were taking for granted as being matters of common knowledge were the very ones that puzzled me most. The entire lore of field and forest, of gun and workshop, was a sealed book to me. I could not drive a nail into a plank without hitting my fingers. What were persimmons? How was cider made? Where did the sorghum in the pewter pitchers that were always on the tables at the club come from? I had not the faintest idea. My familiarity with trees stopped at the oak; my acquaintance with flowers at the rose. I did not know how to swim or skate or harness a horse or milk a cow. It had never entered my head that not all clouds were rain-clouds; that a wind from the east brought one kind of weather and a southwester another; that gales, tornadoes, cyclones, and sand-storms were as distinguishable from one another as were hexameters from alexandrines and novellas from idyls. There were apparently more things in heaven and earth than were discussed at Warschauer's Russian tea-house or in the works of insurgent literati. Wherefore, I must at once revise my opinion of the heathen in Missouri and expand my notions as to what constituted a well-rounded education.

My fellow-students, having for the most part come to the university direct from the farm, were not slow in observing how ignorant I was of all things agricultural, nor in making the most of their discovery. They

found me a godsend for their ready wit and their native love of broad farce. They said I did not know the difference between a hoe and a threshing-machine; but that was an exaggeration. It was true, however, that I was not sure whether it was a pig or a sheep that bleated, whether clover was a plant and plover a bird, or the other way about, whether heifers and colts were both or neither of the genus bovine, and whether harrow and furrow were interchangeable names for the same object or were entirely separate things. I kept talking of sowing corn until I was told that "planting" was the word. In the Bible and in Shakespeare I had always read about the reaping of the grain; in Missouri they harvested the crops. I saw no connection between this gap in my education and my failure to make friends.

Then it dawned upon me that one reason why I could not get on with these fellows was that I did not speak their language. Why, I had thought that I was a wonder at English. Hadn't I got the highest mark in freshman composition? Hadn't Doctor Wilbur, of the English division, encouraged me to drop medicine on the ground that I was cut out for a professorship in that subject? Yes; but while I pronounced like a native and otherwise spoke and wrote with considerable freedom, my English was still the very grammatical and very clumsy book-English of the foreigner. I was weak in the colloquial idiom, and always had to resort to roundabout locutions to express the simplest idea.

THE AMERICAN AS HE IS

I had mastered the science of English speech; I had yet to acquire the art of it. My vocabulary ran to the Latin elements of the hybrid tongue, while what I needed worst were the common, every-day words. Of course, the professors understood me, and having somehow got hold of the outlines of my history, they even commended me. But the rank and file of the student body pricked up their ears when I talked and simply stared. Every time I tried to tell a story it fell flat because of some subtle shade of meaning that escaped me. My stock of words and phrases was not varied enough. I might know one word like "earth," whereas the Missourian had his choice of "ground" and "soil" and "sod" and half a dozen others which he could draw on with a sure hand.

These little difficulties in making myself perfectly understood had an evil tendency toward making me self-conscious and aggravating my timidity. I fell into the habit of studying out my sentences before intrusting them to the ears of my critical friends, with the consequence that they turned out more stilted than ever. As soon as I opened my mouth I would realize, of course, what a bad job I had made of them, and then my confidence would fail me, my throat would get parched and lumpy, and my interlocutor would cry, "What is it?" in such a way as to knock the bottom out of me altogether. After a number of experiences of this harrowing kind I determined that my voice was in need of cultivation and I joined the class in elocution, where

the instructor did most of the reading himself—he had once been an actor—and lectured interminably on deep breathing, and declared with much emphasis that a good delivery was essential to vivacious conversation, which was what I knew myself, and that it was largely a matter of intelligence, which was not true.   So that I dropped elocution and borrowed a volume of Mark Twain from the library and read pages and pages of it aloud to myself, as every one at M. S. U. who happened to be walking in the neighborhood of Hinkson Creek before breakfast can testify.   What is more, I bought a penny scrap-book and jotted down every word I overheard in my table-mates' conversation that was new to my foreign ear, and subsequently consulted the dictionaries to find out what it meant.

Unfortunately for me, the men of Missouri had command of a whole vast and varied vocabulary of which not a trace could be found in any dictionary, no matter how diligently I searched.   It did not take me long to lay hold of their peculiar trick of cutting words off at the end, and after a month or so I could myself refer to professors as "profs," to a course in literature as "lit," and to the quadrangle as the "quad."   I found that highly practical, like everything else in Missouri, and convenient.   But when a chap asked me to pass him "that stuff," and pointed one day to the potatoes and another day to a pile of typewritten notes I was mystified.   I could not easily perceive what quality it was the two commodities had in common that

made the same name applicable to both. Moreover, I observed that my friends expressed every variety of emotion—disappointment, enthusiasm, anger, elation—by the one word (or was it two?) "doggone." Food in general was called "grub," although gravies and sauces were sometimes distinguished as "goo"; while, on the other hand, money had a whole chain of names to itself; "rocks" and "mazuma" and "wheels" and, of course, "stuff." It was all very bewildering.

Perhaps the greatest stumbling-block in the way of my readjustment was the emphasis that my Missourian placed on what he called good manners. I was not quite so obtuse as to miss the rather frank curiosity with which certain details in my conduct at table were regarded. Well, I knew better; but it was part of my East Side religion not to be concerned with the externals of conduct. One was in peril of losing sight of the essential and of becoming insincere as soon as one began to worry about the correct thing and the polite word. Once or twice I succeeded in drawing an unwary freshman into an argument about religion or economics, and then I wished I had not. His good manners rendered him quite sterile as a debater. I could on no account get him to make a straightforward, flat-footed statement; and he exasperated me by a way he had of emasculating my own emphatic assertions with his eternal colorless conformity. He invariably introduced a remark with an "It seems to me," or an "It looks as if," or a "Don't you think?" And if I,

with my ill-breeding, shot back at him, as I usually did, "No, I *don't* think so at all; I disagree with you entirely," he looked grieved and surprised and visibly chilled, and crawfished out of the embarrassing situation by admitting that there were two sides to every question, and that no doubt I was right, too. And the next time he spied me on the street he suddenly developed a preference for the opposite side.

Did he have manners? My father would not have thought so. How many whacks over the fingers do you suppose I got at the family board at home for putting my elbows on the edge of the table, and for inclining the soup bowl away from myself while dipping the spoon into it backhand? It is painful even to recall. Yet that was precisely what they did in Missouri. As for using the fingers of the left hand to assist the fork in the right in the process of capturing an obstinate morsel, whacking, in my parent's opinion, was too good for that, and nothing but chasing the offender from the table would suffice. Yet that, again, was what they did in Missouri. I will say nothing about tossing biscuits across the dining-hall and suchlike violent business, because, in the first place, the good name of my college is precious to me, and, secondly, because that sort of thing was never the work of any but students of engineering or members of the Hannibal Club, and these two are not listed as civilized even in Missouri. But I will say something of the practice of parting with a companion in the street without wishing

him good-by, of resting one's legs on the table while reading, and of whistling incessantly inside the house; and what I will say is this: that what are good manners in one country are extremely bad manners in another.

The business of introductions was my chief abomination. In my little radical world in New York the institution hardly existed. If you liked a person, you went up to him and drew him into a discussion and became friends with him. If you did not like him, you paid no attention to him. In Missouri this queer formality was all over the shop. Everybody wanted to introduce you to everybody. They seemed to think I would take offense if I was not extended the dubious courtesy. The ritual of the performance would have been a rich source of entertainment to me if I had only had some one of my own kind to share it with. My gentleman would leap up, grab my hand violently, and, staring me right in the eye, exclaim, "Mighty glad to know you, man." And he expected me to answer him back in kind. But as a rule I was constrained to disappoint him there, because I was not at all glad to know him. I was wishing that I could meet him on Eldridge Street, where I was at home, and see how he would like that.

I suffered unendurably from hunger. It took me three years to get used to American cookery. At the club everything tasted flat. I missed the pickles and the fragrant soups and the highly seasoned fried things and the rich pastries made with sweet cheese that I had been brought up on. The breakfast hour was

outrageous. In New York I used to drink coffee in the morning, and then have breakfast at ten. Here I had to get down a full meal at seven o'clock in the morning or starve until one. The very order of the courses was topsy-turvy. At home we began the big meal of the day with radish or ripe olives or chopped liver or fish; then we had meat of one kind or another; then some vegetables cooked sweet or sour-sweet, and wound up with soup. The Missourian always began at the tail-end—started with soup (when he had any, which was all too rare); then piled his meat and potatoes (of potatoes he never tired) and vegetables in several heaps all on the same plate, devouring them all together; and concluded the performance with a muddy paste he called pumpkin pie and some powerful beverage that passed for coffee. Is it any wonder that I was so slow becoming an American when, as every one knows, nationality is principally a matter of diet, and it was this array that I must learn to cherish?

XIX

THE FRUITS OF SOLITUDE

MY expense account for 1906-07, which I still preserve, along with some choice compositions, a note-book or two, and a gratifying press-clipping about my maiden speech before the Cosmopolitan Club, as the precious mementoes of that incredible year, ought not to be allowed to perish in the dark. It should certainly prove of inestimable value to certain extravagant-minded members of the Committee on Student Budgets, by showing them what really are the possibilities of a minimum expenditure for young men in "moderate circumstances." They would learn, for instance, that the item of amusements and incidentals is capable of an amazing contraction from twenty dollars to very nearly nothing a year, or to be quite accurate, to two dollars and twelve cents, thus:

Two half-pecks of apples	30 cents
Twelve bananas	12 "
One football game	50 "
One basket-ball game	25 "
Two visits to the Nickelodeon	10 "
Smoking tobacco	80 "
One Christmas-dinner cigar	5 "

227

What a person of more modest tastes than mine could do still further to bring this elastic item toward the absolute zero is an interesting question. It is clearly not indispensable to the maintenance of life to go to moving-picture houses; and as long as the club table provides enough of bread and gravy, a consistently economical young man with a goal before him may conceivably eliminate such articles from his diet as bananas and apples.

Still, I admit that I was extravagant at times. Let the next item speak for itself. Here are stamps, postal cards, and correspondence stationery to the appalling amount of seven dollars and six cents! I hope no one will think me lacking in a sense of proportion, but the truth is that if I did not go oftener to the games and the shows it was in order to have more money for letters. It was the only way for me to keep my soul alive. I wrote to everybody I knew because I loved everybody now who was in New York. Sometimes it was business, but the greater part of the time it was untainted affection. I had to remind brother Harry several times how badly I needed those rubber shoes and socks he had promised me. Cousin Aby every now and then sent me a few of the radical papers, and I must express to him the genuine gratitude I felt for being kept in touch with the beloved world I had left behind.

But the bulk of my correspondence was with Esther and one or two others of my erstwhile fellow-students in the night school. It was to get their letters that I

regularly raced home to my room between the nine and the ten o'clock classes, and whether I was bright or stupid the rest of the day depended largely on what the mails had brought me from them. Esther was generous as to length when she did write, but no amount of urging could convince her that a daily letter was not too much. Perhaps if she had known how much such things meant to me she would have come around. But I did not want her to know. I was half-unconsciously putting the best face on my life in Missouri. I wanted her to follow me. I wanted everybody at the Manhattan school to come to Missouri. Was it a selfish craving for the society of my own kind? Or was it the peculiar psychology of the whipped dog longing for the sight of other whipped dogs? Perhaps. I do not hesitate to confess that I had developed a kind of passion for wanting to see all my school friends in my own scrape, but I think I am honest when I add that I was merely hoping that it would do them as much good as it was doing me. And so when Esther's resolution seemed to be on the breaking-point and she wrote me discouraged letters about the terrors of geometry and the heartlessness of examiners I assumed the schoolmasterly tone and scolded her for her lack of persistence and held out glowing pictures to her of the rewards that were awaiting her at the end of her struggles. And I was right, too—about Esther, at any rate. For the following autumn I had the satisfaction of seeing her in Missouri, where she still remains—as happy an Ameri-

can as ever came from Rumania. Of the three or four whom I succeeded in bringing out she was the only one who stuck it out; the others maintained that they could see no fun in the thing.

No, there was not much fun in being made into an American. I was painfully aware of that fact myself. Oh, the dreary loneliness of it! Particularly the Sundays. Of all the days in the week they were the hardest to live through. The very holiday tone in the air was suffocating me. Everybody else was busy and outrageously happy on Sunday. The boys in the house went to church in the morning, wrote letters in the afternoon, and went calling in the evening. I was left all alone. There was not even any mail. The library— the only place where I could still feel a sense of human contact—was closed. But there were whole seasons that, if anything could, surpassed even those intolerable Sundays. At Christmas nearly every fellow went home to his family, there was an exchange of presents and cheerful wishes, invitations were extended to "good chaps" to come and partake of turkey and mashed potatoes at the homes of their friends; and then for an entire fortnight the town looked deserted, and I was almost the only boarder left at the club.

I have an idea, for instance, that I was not particularly fond of the jams and the cakes and the fudge that a lot of the boys brought home with them from their week-end trips to the farm. If I recall aright, I had more than one taste of them; for those

queer fellows were absurdly generous in their own surprising way. First they would destroy my appetite for food by some thoughtless remark and the next moment they would ask me to partake of their dainties with a "Help yourself" which it was impossible to misunderstand. Ah, well, I had eaten better things in my day. And yet I envied them their "goodies." I often thought that it would be a jolly thing to have a mother on a farm somewhere and to have her bake and boil things and pack them into one's suit-case while one went out into the barn and inquired about the health of the newest calf or the old rheumatic dog.

And I sometimes even had an odd wish that I could be a "Christian." What did it matter, after all, that they took on faith so many unreasonable things, or said they did; and worshiped Jesus as a pale divinity while denying His fierce humanity; and coddled themselves into a belief in a second and much longer and rather emasculated existence? When one came right down to it, it was really immense for a religion—this Christianity, with its couples and its Easter bonnets, its socials and its watches, its clear-headed emphasis on the things of this world, its innocent, child-like hoydenism. If I had been born into any one of the many indistinguishable varieties of this faith, I often asked myself would I have turned against it? Possibly not; but all the same I did not often go to church.

And, of course, I did not go calling at all. Missouri is a coeducational university, but it might just as

well have been a monastery, for all the social good it did me. When my ways and my personality were finding so little favor with the men, my chances of making friends with the women were, as you may well imagine, very scant indeed. Now and then, in the course of a recitation, I might get a whispered distress call from a young lady whom fate, in the person of the professor, had surprised in the midst of other thoughts; occasionally in the library, too, such a one might, with a gracious smile, ask for assistance in the preparation of her English theme. But when she next saw me on the street or about the campus she betrayed no sign of recognition. Even those who had formally met me at the Deutscher Verein and had professed to be pleased to make my acquaintance, seemed unaccountably eager to sever that acquaintance as soon as the meeting was over. Their conduct toward me was a painful mystery. It struck me, with my East Side notion of frankness, as needlessly insincere. Why, I wondered, don't they come out openly and tell me when I displease them? And I wanted very much to be friends with them. Their interests were much finer than the men's, and their appreciation of literature was keener. I would have given a great deal for the privilege of calling on one of a few girls I had observed in class, to take a walk with her, and have a discussion in the good old style of East Broadway.

Yes, it was dreary, but it was far from dull. I had but to take a glance into myself to find excitement

a-plenty. Solitude had its compensations, like every-thing else. For one thing I was learning the valuable art of enjoying my own company. Back in the Ghetto there had come a time once when it was a positive tor-ment to remain alone. If there was not a gathering somewhere, if no one came to see me, I must at least run down into the teeming streets and mingle with the throngs and feel the pulse of people about me. If I could not see an "intelligent" I might walk into a *kazín* and have a chat with a fellow-Vasluiander. Here there was hardly any escape. The presence of the crowd was only a stimulant to my wistful thoughts. The gay laughter, the companionable groups, the beaming couples, only made me feel lonelier than ever.

In sheer self-defense I tried for a time to delude myself with a consolation picture of the Missourian as a cold, unsympathetic dog. I pounced on his intense anti-social individualism, his worship of the strong man, his devotion to the ideal of personal success at all costs, his sneering indifference to the unspeakable miseries of the black man in his midst, his lack of interest in inter-national matters, his snobbish disregard of the claims of the worker; and told myself that a fellow who walked about the world in that kind of thin shoes could hardly be expected to give much sentimental thought to the rather minor woes of a moping, hypersensitive individual who had chosen to thrust himself his way. It was a tremendous relief to think of him in this way, as a monstrous device of wood and steel, inasmuch as it

did away with the need of further thinking and removed the unpleasant business of self-criticism. But the picture would not hold its color, and kept gradually fading away before the light of facts. Willy-nilly, I must admit that there was an openness, a freedom, yes, even a delightful warmth and charm—a distinctive kind of pioneer neighborliness—in the social atmosphere of Missouri which was altogether unique in my experience. The very individualism of these people was in reality an emphasis on the happiness of the single life. They were far from unsympathetic among themselves, and anything but cold even toward the complete stranger. When I spent a day at the infirmary the whole crowd from the house and the table turned out to see me and poked fun at my grippe and (there was no escaping it) at myself. They made a religion of personal decency. No, it would not do. Unpalatable as the truth was, there was no evading the patent fact that if I was not taken in among the Missourians the fault was with me and not with them.

With this uncompromising confession came unexpected relief. I was floundering in the dark as you see, grappling with my obstinate problem like a miner without tools and without a lantern. But having made up my mind that I was not a victim, but an unconscious comedian, it behooved me to stand before the glass and enjoy, if I might, my own amusing antics. Once I admitted that I really was material for sport, the logical thing was to try and see some of it myself,

perhaps to do something in the way of toning it down a bit. And so there followed a pitiless dissecting of the internal man, a dragging out into the light of layer upon layer of incrusted self, a lining up for inspection of a whole vast procession of things—antiques from Syria, heirlooms from a long exile in Asia and Europe, shards and fragments of a proud and broken ancestry, warped bits of thin veneer from Rumania, heavy plate from the radical Ghetto, gems and rubbish without end. I took in the exhibition with mingled feelings, and asked myself incredulously whether all this was what I had been used to calling my simple self. The more I contemplated it the more I felt inclined to be struck with the oddity of it. If that was what my American neighbors had in mind when they talked of taking the conceit out of me, they were coming very near to accomplishing their purpose. Another glance and I would be grinning at the pile myself. I was being threatened with a novel thing for an East-Sider—a sense of humor.

Quite as novel, and as a further result of my solitude, was the opening of my eyes to the unsuspected miracles about me. Both in Rumania and in the Ghetto nature was looked upon as either vermin or vegetable, a thing to hold your nose at or to devour. As a child I had exhibited a fondness for animals; but when my father once found me playing with our neighbor's dog he took me into the house and made it very clear to me how un-Hebraic my conduct had been. Such things, he told me earnestly, were of the Gentile, and a good child

of our tribe should shun them. On the East Side people did frequently take excursions to the neighboring parks, but the real attractions were oftener the lecture that went with the picnic and the stores of assorted food than the loveliness of the landscape. So here again was a ragged edge to my training.

As the dreary months dragged on I took to wandering out into the country. At first my chief aim was to run away from the house and my own unpleasant thoughts. But it was impossible to roam over the pretty hills around Columbia for very long without falling under their spell. I walked for the most part at night, when my lessons for the next day were done, and I found myself becoming enchanted with its myriad mysteries. The fragrance of the damp earth, the rustle of the wind in the leaves, the murmur of brooks, the scintillating fires of innumerable glow-worms, the soothing feel of dew-filled cool grass, the sweep of clouds over the moon, the far-off voices of beasts and men—all these were filtering into my soul and making me into a new being.

My enforced exclusiveness served, also, to advance me in my studies. My professor of English has probably never found out why I was so prompt with my papers, when the majority of the class had to be urged and threatened and often penalized to make them bring theirs in on time. Well, what else was there for me to do when there were no girls to call up and no chums to come and drag me away to parties and things?

THE FRUITS OF SOLITUDE

Besides, I had for years looked forward to this opportunity when time and command of the language might
adhere to make extensive reading possible. On the
East Side literature had consisted almost entirely of
the insurgent moderns, interspersed with a few choice
English writers like Carlyle, Shelley, and Shakespeare,
whom we also regarded as "among our own." Now
with the aid of the courses I was coming upon whole
continents of undiscovered books, and I threw myself
with a navigator's zest into the joyous task of explora-
tion. I was filling note-books with exercises in style
based on Stevenson and Hazlitt; I was coming back to
my old enemy Milton and reveling in *Paradise Lost;*
and I was devouring the great critics in order to obtain
guidance for further voyages. Moreover, there was
German literature—a planet in itself. A class reference
had directed me to the hundred-and-thirty-odd-volume
collection of the Deutsche National Literatur, and I
actually undertook to go through the whole thing from
beginning to end.

On the whole, then, it looked as if I might yet
work out my salvation if only those barbarians would
leave me to myself. But it was not in them to do that.
They seemed to be determined on disturbing my peace
of mind. They were devoting, I honestly believe, all
their spare thoughts and all their inventive genius to
thinking up ways of making me uncomfortable. One
young gentleman, still reminiscent of my ignorance of
rural things, made up a tale of how I went to get a job

on a farm, and proceeded to relate it at the table. "The farmer gave Max a pail and a stool and sent him out to milk the cow. About an hour later, when the old boy failed to show up with the stuff, Reuben went out to see what was the trouble. He found his new assistant in a fierce pickle. His clothes were torn and his hands and face were bleeding horribly. 'What in heck is the matter?' asked the farmer. 'Oh, curse the old cow!' said Max, 'I can't make her sit on that stool.'" A burst of merriment greeted the climactic ending, although the yarn was a trifle musty; and the most painful part of it was that I must laugh at the silly thing myself.

It was not at all true, as one of my numerous room-mates tried to intimate, that I shunned baths. I was merely conservative in the matter. One day, however, he had the indelicacy to ask me the somewhat personal question whether I *ever* took a bath; and I told him, of course rather sullenly, that I did once in a while. Some time later I overheard him repeat the dialogue to the other men in the house and provoking shouts of laughter. It puzzled me to see where the joke was, until I learned that these fellows were taking a shower-bath at the gymnasium every day. It seemed to me that that was running a good thing into the ground. Again, I noticed that my room-mates were making a great show of their tooth-brushes. They used them after every meal and before retiring—as the advertisements say—and always with an unnecessary amount of splash

and clatter. At home I had been taught to keep my mouth and teeth clean without all this fuss. Nevertheless, I thought that I would get a brush and join in the drill. After that the other brushes became noticeably quiet.

And then, of course, there was the institution of the practical joke. On April 1st there was soap in the pie. If you got in late to a meal, it was wise to brush your chair and "pick your bites," if any bites were left. If not, there was no telling what you might swallow or sit on. More than once I tasted salt in my water and pepper in my biscuits. I seemed to have been marked from the first as a fit subject for these pranks.

On Hallowe'en a squad of cadets commanded by a corporal entered my room and ordered me to get into my uniform, shoulder my gun, and proceed to the gymnasium, which, according to the order read, the commandant assigned me to guard against stragglers. I guarded through a whole uneventful night. Toward morning the captain of the football team, who had a room in the gymnasium, returned from a party. I ordered him to halt and give the password. He smiled and tried to enter. I made a lunge for him, and would have run my bayonet through him if he had not begun to laugh. "Go on home, you poor boy," he said. "They pull that stunt off every year. Poor joke, I think." The next day my table-mates tried to jolly me about it. They said I would be court-martialed as a deserter from duty. I got angry, and

that made them all the more hilarious. Then a great, strapping fellow named Harvey spoke up. "Be still, you galoots," he said to them; and then to me, "For gosh sake, fellow, be human!" I tried a long time to figure out what he meant by "human," and for the rest of my college career I strove hard to follow his advice. It was the first real hint I had got on what America, through her representatives in Missouri, was expecting of me. Harvey became my first American friend.

XX

HARVEY

I WAS still at the stage where one American looked and acted exactly as every other, and it was a profound mystery to me how I had gained the favor of this very representative specimen of the type. I had not greatly changed, as far as I could judge, between September and February, unless it was for the worse. If I had only had one or two of my own people and had not been in such dire need of human fellowship, I doubt whether I should have been attracted to him, notwithstanding the fact that I owed him a debt of gratitude for having taken up the cudgels in my behalf. But he was a long way from being hard up for company. I walked home with him from the club that night, and I observed, with a feeling mingled of envy and admiration, that he was cordially greeted by almost every one that passed us, and during the half-hour that I remained in his room he must have had a dozen friends dropping in, who were as amazed to find him hobnobbing with me as I was myself.

My surprise at his unaccountable behavior toward me reached a climax when, a few days later, he asked me

to come and live with him. "Captain," he said, "you and I are pretty much in the same boat. If you want an old lady let's get together." I could scarcely believe my ears. What could he be up to? I wondered as soon as my first flush of joy at his offer had passed. Some new variety of practical joke that I had not yet experienced? Or was it really possible that I was "arriving" in Missouri? Be his scheme what it might, I felt a great temptation to accept. But, remembering my long record of failures as a room-mate, I hesitated lest my new-found friendship (if it was friendship) should go on the rocks. "I should like to," I said, "but I think I had better not."

Then Harvey told me some things about himself that opened my eyes and reassured me. I had thought that I was the only one at Missouri who did not know where his next week's board was coming from, and that every one else belonged, as they had warned me in the Ghetto, among the capitalists. But this fellow, who was in his own country, it turned out, was, if anything, poorer than I. He, too, had come to college from the ranks of the worker. He was toiling nights and vacations, and paying ten per cent. compound interest on periodic borrowings, to get an education which he, like myself, had been struggling for years to attain. That was what he had in mind when he said that we were in the same boat. In addition, we had various and sundry interests in common. As far as my observation could determine, he was the only freshman I had

run into who cared anything about reading as a recreation. He was intending ultimately to go into engineering, but he was taking courses in the languages—a rare procedure in Missouri. "Cultural value"—a phrase I had not often heard in the past five months—kept continually recurring in his remarks about studies. And, best of all, he confessed to a weakness for argument about religion and other matters which was as convincing as it was irresistible.

From the first our relations were those between master and disciple. Much as I had longed all these weary months for some one who could understand me, it was not Harvey's intellectual and liberal leanings that I prized in him most. In September it might have been different. But now I had definitely settled down to the rôle of a captive in a foreign land; I had almost learned to endure the personal inconveniences of my situation; and I was determined that I must bring away something in the nature of a system of Missouri philosophy for the edification of the people at home when the time came and I regained my liberty. Harvey was the man to help me compass this purpose. For all his unexpected divergencies from the rank and file, I could not help regarding him as a kind of epitome of the national character. He knew the speech and the customs, the heart and the soul, of the native. Between him and his friends I should have no difficulty in piecing out a life-size portrait of the creature.

The differences began to crop up between us right

away. Out of the countless discussions with which
we beguiled the Sunday evenings (Harvey did not go
"calling"), one inescapable conclusion emerged—that
whatever was sacred to me was anathema to him and
that everything that he accepted as unquestioned truth
was, to say the best for it, a string of dubious common-
places to me. He had, for instance, worked all his
adult life with his hands, but he distrusted the organizations and the hopes of the laboring-man. He was a
churchman, and he looked now to the parson and then
to the successful business man to regenerate the earth,
if, indeed, this perfect earth needed regenerating.
There was something positively religious in his worship
of success in the abstract. Given success, he seemed to
feel, and all the other virtues in the book must follow
as a matter of course. The man who had risen to the
top could not but be good and clean and sane and self-
controlled and clear-sighted as to the true values of
life. He was not only the strong man, but the benefactor of the race as well. In some mysterious manner
he was fulfilling the divine purpose while pursuing his
own interests. The reason why America was great
was because she had the wisdom to give free rein to the
ambitions of the individual. The country had been
made by its big men.

To me all this was not only far-fetched, it was
contradictory from Harvey's own point of view. For
my good friend's conduct belied his philosophy; and,
what is more, in his better moments he openly pro-

fessed devotion to a set of principles which were the
direct opposite of the thirty-nine articles of success.
These, I thought, he lived up to with a rigidity born
of natural instinct and conviction. He abhorred im-
modesty, self-advertising, aggressiveness, show, the
cold insistence on literal justness—in short, the major
qualities by which commercial success is made possible.
I was constantly learning from him the excellent habit
of giving in when I was right, of declining the things that
were my due, of minimizing instead of exaggerating
my own virtues and little superiorities. When Harvey
got some new clothes and I praised them he blushed
(the burly giant) and waved me aside with a deprecating
hand. If I said of a theme of his, "That is a neat piece
of work, colonel," he said, "Get out, you don't call
that English."

Once we bought a peck of apples in partnership for
thirty-five cents. I hesitated a moment whether to
give him seventeen or eighteen cents as my share of
the outlay, and then generously decided to make it
eighteen. Harvey tossed the pennies back and said,
"We'll call it square, old gas-pipe." When I suggested
dividing up the fruit he gave me a queer glance and then
took a few handfuls and left me nearly two-thirds of
the peck. I had thought he would count them and
pick out the biggest ones. I was using his shoe-blacking
and my East Side sense of strict dealing told me that
I ought to pay for it. But when I offered Harvey a
nickel he refused it, and when I insisted on his taking

it he simply told me that I might buy the next can. The idea had never occurred to me.

But he was not consistent even in his magnanimity. There seemed to be a shadow line somewhere in his system where self-denial ended and self-assertion began, or, as he expressed it once, where a fellow must stop giving in because the other side was doing the taking in. I do not know whether he still remembers, but I certainly have not forgotten the incident of the fountain-pen. I must say that it was not I who had asked Harvey to let me use it. But he must have observed that I had none and that I was having a struggle with an old-fashioned wooden penholder I had brought from New York, and so one night he suggested that I might see what I could do with his fountain-pen. "May I?" I asked. "Sure. Go ahead. Help yourself, any time," he said. I used it three or four times, and then I noticed that the thing had disappeared from the table. Why? Clearly I had abused the privilege. But he had said "any time," hadn't he? Now in the Ghetto no one would have granted any such unlimited rights to private property, but once one had committed himself he would have stuck it out to the end. In Missouri the rule seemed to be that you can have anything as long as you don't ask for it, and that as soon as you have accepted a liberal offer too literally you have really forfeited your privileges!

Not more than three days after this subtle lesson I engaged a laundress to call for my clothes. By the

time she appeared for my first batch I had come upon
another woman who charged more reasonably and had
given the work to her. Harvey was in the room when
the original woman showed up, and I could see that he
was listening with disapproval to what I was telling
her. As soon as she was gone he opened fire on me.
"Confound you," he said, "why did you do that?"
"Well," I answered, "I changed my mind. Haven't I
a right to do that?" "Yes," he retorted, "but you
could have let her know." I was about to answer him
that he might practise what he preached, but it occurred
to me that perhaps the American logic made a distinction between room-mates and laundresses and between
fountain-pens and soiled linen, and I said nothing.

My confusion was increasing from day to day, and
largely because Harvey and his friends worshiped
simultaneously at two distinct and opposed shrines.

Harvey had a discerning ear for music and played
the fiddle with considerable skill. I envied him the
accomplishment both because it enabled him to earn
money more easily than I did and because he got no
end of fun out of it. And yet it was a curious thing
that my friend was—I do not know what else to call it—
ashamed of his talent. When we were alone he fondled
his instrument as a loving mother fondles a child, and
played everything from college songs to nocturnes,
and studied little booklets on the art of bowing and what
not. But as soon as his Missouri friends came in to
see him he either put the beloved thing into its case and

hid it in the closet, or, if he was caught red-handed, he took on a sheepish air and spoke condescendingly of it as a frivolous diversion, and struck up "Turkey in the Straw" or "The Arkansas Traveler." Why? I made bold to ask him once, and his answer was more absurd than his conduct. He said, "It is thought a bit effeminate for a man to care for music." I could not forbear a glance at him as he said it; and the incongruity of this six-footer with his huge hands and powerful frame worrying his head lest he should not be thought masculine enough made me laugh in his face.

But Harvey knew his people better than I did. That wholesome manliness which I had so sincerely admired on arriving at Columbia had a worm at its root. It was the fashion, you see, to be masculine in Missouri, and when a thing becomes fashionable it ceases to be genuine. Those whom nature had endowed with the virtue made a fetish and a self-conscious pose of it, and those who lacked it became obsessed with the desire to imitate it. The final insult to a Missourian was to suggest that he was "sissified." There was something like a panic among the more refined of my fellow-students at the mere mention of effeminacy. Even the girls dreaded it. They, too, affected a kind of factitious burliness, a worship of the strident male, a hail-fellow-well-met air. They liked to greet one another with the jolly halloo, and the slap on the back, and betrayed an odd fondness for the big sweater and the heavy boot and the words "fellow" and "bully."

The mania was having its effect on the course of study and the whole life of the university. The departments of the arts were thrown on the defensive. The professor must adopt an apologetic tone for being interested in such unmanly things as poetry, music, or painting. Sentiment being tabooed as effeminate, it followed inevitably that whatever in the curriculum addressed itself to the emotions must be avoided like a plague.

In speaking of his friends Harvey constantly alluded to "broads" and "narrows." There was Lowry, who never failed to remind us that the particular sect to which he belonged was the only true Christian body because its bishops had been the recipients of the apostolic touch from the beginning of the world. Lowry was narrow, it appeared. On the other hand, Higgins and Moore were broad, and Harvey advised me to cultivate their acquaintance. I tackled first one and then the other, and found that they were not averse to discussion even about religion. But as soon as I betrayed myself by questioning the validity of the more fundamental doctrines of theology they informed me that certain things had better not be touched. "Broadness" seemed to consist in being tolerant toward Presbyterians if you were a Methodist, or toward Baptists if you were a Congregationalist.

Some of those boys, on the other hand, presented a problem of another kind that baffled me for a long time. When I solved it I had taken one more step toward becoming an American. It was true that *I* mowed

lawns, and washed dishes, and waited on tables, and
did a score of other odd jobs to make ends meet; but,
then, I was an immigrant without parents and without
resources. If I had the means, I thought, I would
rather not engage in all these extra-mural activities,
and devote all my time to study and recreation. But
among the other dish-washers at the club I learned there
were young men whose fathers had large farms or big
businesses in the little towns. Why, I wondered, did
they not support their sons through college decently?
Then I made the interesting discovery that they did
not want to be supported; that not to be supported
was their idea of going through college decently. I
revolved that idea through my head until I got it.
It showed me the Missourian in a new light. I
could almost forgive him his indifference to radical
discussions.

If I was by degrees being turned into an American
my friend and room-mate was learning a few things
about the Ghetto and finding them not half so repulsive
as he had thought. On several occasions Harvey listened with interest to excerpts from Yiddish literature
which I translated for him from periodicals and pam-
phlets I had brought with me. Now and then my
brother Paul sent me a few choice morsels from home—
Rumanian pastrama, or cheese, or ripe olives, and it was
gratifying to observe that Harvey smacked his lips
after sampling them. Toward the end of the winter
we had definitely formed the habit of having midnight

spreads, which never came at midnight, because Harvey was subject to a peculiar failing of getting hungry by nine o'clock, which he justified by declaring that it required more fuel to run a big engine than a small one. I also taught him to drink tea made and served in the Russian way. Harvey supplied the alcohol-burner and the pot and I furnished the tea; and every night, just when I thought he was in the thick of his mathematics or German, he would suddenly look up and give me a significant wink. Then I would look blank and he would smile encouragingly and enlighten me further by the monosyllable "feast." If I still failed to rise to his enthusiasm, he would say "Shall we?" and before I could answer he would make a dash for the corner of the room called the kitchen, and spread a newspaper at one end of the table, and announce in a falsetto voice that supper was served.

On Saturday afternoons, if there was no play in town that week, and Harvey did not have to go to orchestra rehearsals, we would go out on the back lot with a ball and a glove and I would revive an art I had not prac-tised since childhood. But the ball was much harder than the kind I had known in Vaslui, and my hands would get black and blue after an hour's catching, and Harvey would laugh every time I let a "hot one" pass without making an effort to stop it, and tell me that the essential thing in becoming an American was to get toughened up. When the baseball season opened he took me with him to one of the games, and explained its

mysteries to me, and spoke enthusiastically of its science
and said that it was the only real national sport. At
which I had to smile, because it was the very game we
used to play at home—only we called it "oina"—with a
ball made of rags and pieces of board torn out of fences
for bats. And as I looked around me and saw dignified
professors and rheumy-eyed Civil War veterans tossing
their hats in the air, I wished that my father could be
present so that I might convince him of the profound
truth I had failed as a boy to get through his head, that
an "oina" was a joy forever and not the silly childish
thing that he insisted it was.

Gradually, too, Harvey was getting acquainted with
my past history and, much to my amazement, approving of it. Once when I begged him not to let the
details of my career go any farther he looked at me in
astonishment and called me a fool. "You deserve all
the credit in the world, you bloomin' idiot," he added.
Evidently he regarded my sweat-shop experiences in
the light of heroic deeds. And thereafter he made it a
point to let every one of his friends know just the kind
of marvel his queer room-mate was, and they also—
"narrows" and "broads" alike—appeared to think the
better of me for my humble past and to show more
cordiality toward me when they passed me on the street.
"Odd, isn't it?" I kept thinking. Intellectually I
would probably have felt more at home in a European
university. But supposing even that any one could
have leaped from the sweat-shop to college over there,

would his fellow-students have forgiven him his origin, to say nothing of praising him for it?

What Harvey could *not* forgive me, and what came very near to wrecking our friendship, was what he termed my "contemptible habit" of smoking cigarettes. At first I thought that the odor of tobacco was offensive to him, and put myself to the inconvenience of going out of the house whenever I felt the desire for a smoke. But my pains seemed to go for naught; our relations remained as strained as ever. "What is the objection?" I finally asked him. "Oh, nothing," he answered, "if you can't see for yourself how picayune and insignificant the pesky things make you look." More masculinity, I reflected, and asked some one in New York to send me a pipe, adding that cigarettes were not in fashion in Missouri. Then I found that I had hit upon another snag in the American character, for Harvey apparently relished my pipe even less than he did the cigarettes. Surely, I asked myself, a pipe was not effeminate? No, indeed. But the whole business of smoking revealed a deplorable moral degeneracy. It was one of the habits that break as opposed to the habits that make, as one of those curious composite doctor-preachers who kept constantly resorting to the university and talking to men only neatly expressed it. Not exactly masculinity, then, but success.

My experiences with Harvey and with Americans generally have bred in me the conviction that no one should be granted citizen's papers unless he can "see"

a joke. A man has not even begun the process of readjustment as long as he still stares blankly at the sallies of native humor; and it goes without saying that the simplest as well as the most conclusive test as to whether a foreigner has acquired anything like a respectable command of English lies along the line of the "story." You may read and enjoy Shakespeare or Emerson; you may write a first-rate business letter in English; you may be an enrolled Republican or Democrat; but all this avails you nothing, and in your heart of hearts you are a hopeless alien. Even an interest in outdoor sports is no convincing proof that you are naturalized. It may be faked. Do you go wild over Bill Nye's *History of the United States?* Do you laugh till the tears run down your face at Mark Twain's description of a Turkish bath? Do you turn to the next to the last column on the editorial page of the evening paper and devour that before you even think of the sporting page, let alone the news? Above all, can you do your share at the dinner-table or at the marshmallow party when conversation becomes feeble and some one proposes "stories"? Then you are an American to the bone, I don't care how much you may believe in the divine right of kings and in secret diplomacy. In America—or at least in Missouri—every one is a wit, or tries to be. No one says, simply, "Pass me the salt." What he says is, "May I crave the saline or the NaCl?" just as no one asks you where you live, but where is your habitat or domicile. An American

will not talk or write a personal letter unless he can be funny. It is an excellent national trait. It makes conversation breezy. But I think it often makes it scarce.

I owe it to Harvey (who did not have to try to be a wag) that I made this jolly American characteristic, among many others, in part my own. Indeed, any inventory of my first year at college will reveal an astonishing list of things over and above what I had started out to get. The university catalogue omits quite as much as it includes. It makes absolutely no mention of the unofficial extension courses under Professor Harvey, of the practical joke as an educational method, and of the special department of personal relations for the benefit of foreign students. The peasant in Rumania says very truly that one never knows what kind of bargain he is going to make until he gets to market. I had gone to Missouri to become a doctor. But Joe Shapiro was a real prophet. Those capitalists and oppressors were making me into a gentleman.

XXI

THE ROMANCE OF READJUSTMENT

AS the summer drew near I began to look around for something to do. I would spend nearly one hundred and twenty-five dollars, I saw, between September and June, and half of it borrowed money. Harry, from whom I had got almost no help the first year, had just married and gone into business for himself, and he was giving me to understand in very broad hints that I need not rely on him the next year. Brother Paul had been out of work for the better part of the winter, and was trying desperately to keep alive while paying off some of the debts he had made in his period of unemployment. My friend, who had more than lived up to his promises, had, to be sure, agreed to lend me fifty dollars every year, but I was endeavoring to bring him out to Missouri, and if I succeeded he would need all he had to pay his own way. Therefore, if I meant to return to school next year I must find a way to earn enough to give me at least a good start in the fall. I discussed the question with Harvey and he made several suggestions. He himself was going to Joplin, where there was a lot of building and where he,

being a carpenter, always found plenty to do. I
might come along with him, and try my luck in the zinc-
mines. Or, there were the Kansas wheat-fields, where
they paid two-fifty a day and keep. A number of
students were going there summer after summer, and
returning with their hides well tanned and their pockets
well lined. Still, on second thought, he would not
advise me to tackle harvesting. I might not be able
to stand it, with my soft hands and my town breeding.

But I gave very little thought to his advice. I was
longing for a sight of New York. It would cost fifty
dollars to go there and back, but I tried to persuade
myself that I would earn enough more in the city to
make it worth while. If the worst came to the worst,
I could always get a job at the machine. I was known
there. I had friends and old pupils. Tutoring was a
possibility, particularly with my added prestige as a
college man. There was no limit to the things that one
could do in a large town. And deep down in my foolish
heart I knew quite well that all these calculations were
but a sham. In the letter I wrote to Esther I honestly
confessed that if I remained away from my own people
that summer I would feel like a man who was forced to
work seven days in the week and would be unfit to
resume work in the fall.

Then Paul somehow divined my thoughts and surprised me one fine June morning with a money order for
thirty dollars and a letter saying that he would not
forgive me if I did not come and spend the vacations

at home. Heaven alone knows where he got it, but there it was; and I sent him back a post-card with the picture of a saddled donkey and the words "Ready to Pack" underneath. The examinations had just been held, and I delayed only a few days until the instructors returned my note-books and told me my marks. Harvey was hanging over till after Commencement, because the closing days of the session were crowded with dances and entertainments and he was cleaning up a lot of money with the orchestra. He had an amused twinkle in his eye as he watched me excitedly getting ready, and every now and then he would ask: "Well, old fish, do you think we'll see you back with us next year? Or do you think you've had enough of the wild and woolly West?" And when I told him with great emphasis that nothing in the world should keep me away from Missouri until I had finished the course he slapped me on the back and cried: "Now you're talking. We'll make a man of you yet." Then he would add, "But, say, if those anarchists get a hold of you and keep you there, let a fellow know what's happening to you. Maybe we can come to the rescue."

So to New York I went, and lived through the last and the bitterest episode in the romance of readjustment. During that whole strenuous year, while I was fighting my battle for America, I had never for a moment stopped to figure the price it was costing me. I had not dreamed that my mere going to Missouri had opened up a gulf between me and the world I had come

from, and that every step I was taking toward my ultimate goal was a stride away from everything that had once been mine, that had once been myself. Now, no sooner had I alighted from the train than it came upon me with a pang that that one year out there had loosened ties that I had imagined were eternal.

There was Paul faithfully at the ferry, and as I came off he rushed up to me and threw his arms around me and kissed me affectionately. Did I kiss him back? I am afraid not. He took the grip out of my hand and carried it to the Brooklyn Bridge. Then we boarded a car. I asked him where we were going, and he said, mysteriously, "To Harry's." A surprise was awaiting me, apparently. As we entered the little alley of a store in the Italian quarter I looked about me and saw no one. But suddenly there was a burst of laughter from a dozen voices, a door or two opened violently, and my whole family was upon me—brothers, a new sister-in-law, cousins of various degrees, some old people, a few children. They rushed me into the apartment behind the store, pelting me with endearments and with questions. The table was set as for a Purim feast. There was an odor of pot-roasted chicken, and my eye caught a glimpse of chopped eggplant. As the meal progressed my heart was touched by their loving thoughtfulness. Nothing had been omitted—not even the red wine and the Turkish peas and rice. Harry and every one else kept on urging me to eat. "It's a long time since you have had a real meal," said my sister-in-law. How true

it was! But I felt constrained, and ate very little. Here were the people and the things I had so longed to be with; but I caught myself regarding them with the eyes of a Western American. Suddenly—at one glance, as it were—I grasped the answer to the problem that had puzzled me so long; for here in the persons of those dear to me I was seeing myself as those others had seen me.

I went about revisiting old scenes and found that everything had changed in my brief absence. My friends were not the same; the East Side was not the same. They never would be the same. What had come over them? My kinsfolk and my old companions looked me over and declared that it was I who had become transformed. I had become soberer. I carried myself differently. There was an unfamiliar reserve, something mingled of coldness and melancholy, in my eye. My very speech had a new intonation. It was more incisive, but less fluent, less cordial, they thought. Perhaps so. At any rate, while my people were still dear to me, and always would be dear to me, the atmosphere about them repelled me. If it *was* I who had changed, then, as I took in the little world I had emerged from, I could not help telling myself that the change was a salutary one.

While calling at the old basement bookshop on East Broadway I suddenly heard a horrible wailing and lamenting on the street. A funeral procession was hurrying by, followed by several women in an open

carriage. Their hair was flying, their faces were red with weeping, their bodies were swaying grotesquely to the rhythm of their violent cries. The oldest in the group continued mechanically to address the body in the hearse: "Husband dear, upon whom have you left us? Upon whom, husband dear?" A young girl facing her in the vehicle looked about in a terrified manner, seized every now and then the hand of her afflicted mother, and tried to quiet her. The frightful scene, with its tragic display, its abysmal ludicrousness, its barbarous noise, revolted me. I had seen the like of it before, but that was in another life. I had once been part of such a performance myself, and the grief of it still lingered somewhere in my motley soul. But now I could only think of the affecting simplicity, the quiet, unobtrusive solemnity of a burial I had witnessed the previous spring in the West.

The afternoon following my arrival I flew up-town to see Esther. She waved to me and smiled as I approached—she had been waiting on the "stoop." As she shook my hand in her somewhat masculine fashion she took me in with a glance, and the first thing she said was, "What a genteel person you have become! You have changed astonishingly." "Do you think so?" I asked her. "I am afraid I haven't. At least they do not think so in Missouri." Then she told me that she had got only ten points, but that she was expecting three more in the fall. She was almost resigned to wait another year before entering college. That would

enable her to make her total requirements, save up a little more money, and get her breath. "A woman is not a man, you know," she added. "I am beginning to feel the effects of it all. I am really exhausted. Geometry has nearly finished me. And mother has added her share. She is no longer young, and this winter she was ill. I have worried and I have had to send money. But let us not talk about my troubles. You are full of things to tell me, I know."

Yes, I had lots I wanted to say, but I did not know where to begin; and the one thing that was uppermost in my mind I was afraid to utter lest she should misunderstand and feel injured and reproach me. I did not want her to reproach me on first meeting. I wanted to give myself time as well as her. And so we fell into one of those customary long silences, and for a while I felt at home again, and reflected that perhaps I had been hasty in letting the first poignant reactions mislead me. Toward evening Esther remarked that it was fortunate I had got to town the day before. If I had no other plans, she would take me to a meeting at Clinton Hall where Michailoff was to speak on "The coming storm in America." It would be exciting, she said, and enlightening. Michailoff had just come out of prison. He was full of new impressions of America and "the system" generally, and one could rely on him to tear things open.

Of course, we went, and the assemblage was noisy and quarrelsome and intolerant, and the hall was stuffy

and smelly, and the speaker was honest and fiery and ill-informed. He thundered passionately, and as if he were detailing a personal grievance, against American individualism and the benighted Americans who allowed a medieval religion and an oppressive capitalistic system to mulct and exploit them, and referred to a recent article in the *Zukunft* where the writer had weakly admitted the need of being fair even to Christianity, and insisted that to be fair to an enemy of humanity was to be a traitor to humanity. I listened to it all with an alien ear. Soon I caught myself defending the enemy out there. What did these folk know of Americans, anyhow? Michailoff was, after all, to radicalism what Higgins and Moore were to Christianity. His idea of being liberal was to tolerate anarchism if you were a socialist and communism if you were an individualist. And as we left the hall I told Esther what I had hesitated to tell her earlier in the evening.

"Save yourself, my dear friend. Run as fast as you can. You will find a bigger and a freer world than this. Promise me that you will follow me to the West this fall. You will thank me for it. Those big, genuine people out in Missouri are the salt of the earth. Whatever they may think about the problem of universal brotherhood, they have already solved it for their next-door neighbors. There is no need of the social revolution in Missouri; they have a generous slice of the kingdom of heaven."

AN AMERICAN IN THE MAKING

Maybe I was exaggerating, but that was how I felt. From this distance and from these surroundings Missouri and the new world she meant to me was enchanting and heroic. The loneliness I had endured, the snubbing, the ridicule, the inner struggles—all the dreariness and the sadness of my life in exile—had faded out of the picture, and what remained was only an idealized vision of the clean manhood, the large human dignity, the wholesome, bracing atmosphere of it, which contrasted so strikingly with the things around me.

No, there was no sense in deceiving myself, the East Side had somehow ceased to be my world. I had thought a few days ago that I was going home. I had yelled to Harvey from the train as it was pulling out of the station at Columbia, "I am going home, old man!" But I had merely come to another strange land. In the fall I would return to that other exile. I was, indeed, a man without a country.

During that entire summer, while I opened gates on an Elevated train in Brooklyn, I tussled with my problem. It was quite apparent to me from the first what its solution must be. I knew that now there was no going back for me; that my only hope lay in continuing in the direction I had taken, however painful it may be to my loved ones and to myself. But for a long time I could not admit it to myself. A host of voices and sights and memories had awakened within me that clutched me to my people and to my past.

THE ROMANCE OF READJUSTMENT

As long as I remained in New York I kept up the tragic farce of making Sunday calls on brother Harry and pretending that all was as before, that America and education had changed nothing, that I was still one of them. I had taken a room in a remote quarter of Brooklyn, where there were few immigrants, under the pretense that it was nearer to the railway barns. But I was deceiving no one but myself. Most of my relatives, who had received me so heartily when I arrived, seemed to be avoiding Harry's house on Sundays, and on those rare occasions when I ran into one of them he seemed frigid and ill-at-ease. Once Paul said to me: "You are very funny. It looks as if you were ashamed of the family. You aren't really, are you? You know they said you would be when you went away. There is a lot of foolish talk about it. Everybody speaks of Harry and me as the doctor's brothers. Can't you warm up?"

I poured out my heart in a letter to Harvey. If a year ago I had been told that I would be laying my sorrows and my disappointments in my own kindred before any one out there, I would have laughed at the idea. But that barbarian in Missouri was the only human being, strangely enough, in whom I could now confide with any hope of being understood. I tried to convey to him some idea of the agonizing moral experience I was going through. I told him that I was aching to get back to Columbia (how apt the name was!) to take up again where I had left off the process of my

transformation, and to get through with it as soon as might be.

And in the fall I went back—this time a week *before* college opened—and was met by Harvey at the station, just as those rural-looking boys had been met by their friends the year before. When I reached the campus I was surprised to see how many people knew me. Scores of them came up and slapped me on the back and shook hands in their hearty, boisterous fashion, and hoped that I had had a jolly summer. I was asked to join boarding-clubs, to become a member in debating societies, to come and see this fellow or that in his room. It took me off my feet, this sudden geniality of my fellows toward me. I had not been aware how, throughout the previous year, the barriers between us had been gradually and steadily breaking down. It came upon me all at once. I felt my heart going out to my new friends. I had become one of them. I was not a man without a country. I was an American.

PART V

POSTSCRIPT: TWENTY YEARS LATER

XXII

JEANNE'S SENTIMENTAL PILGRIMAGE

I DON'T think I am exaggerating when I say that for five years Jeanne asked, on an average, at least twice daily to be taken home. On the contrary, I am waiving the year of courtship, when Europe was but her bargaining point; and I do not even mention the Sundays and holidays when we were together also at the noon meal. Her manner of approach was subtly impersonal. The benefit was to be principally mine.

"I should think," she would open, "that twenty years of America would be about as much as anybody would want. You are getting horribly stale. You need a change of scene. Besides, what about your own native home? I should think you would be dying to see it again."

Clearly no man can go on indefinitely withstanding this kind of unremitting and insidious barrage. Little by little my resistance was breaking down. I began to feel that I was rather fed up. And as for the old place, why it was the one thing in all the world I wanted to see. It was the thought that some day I would go back that had kept me alive. Only I had been dreaming of it so long that the craving had come to seem more agreeable than the realization. To return to Ru-

mania was like going to heaven, which, as we all know, is a good place to go to, but there is no hurry about getting there.

Therefore, one day along about the middle of June in 1920, I surprised myself by saying:

"Well, I don't know but what it mightn't be a good idea to knock off for a while. Supposing we do run over this fall. Then you can show me France and all the perfect people and things you have left behind you, and I'll take a month or two to have a look at my own country."

We set about our preparations forthwith and with thumping hearts.

It was astonishing the mass of work we had to do, the piles of things we had accumulated, the confusion of ties we had formed that must be unloosed. We had never guessed how rooted we had got in this land of our exile. My first thought had been nothing more ambitious than a flying trip. But as we went along Jeanne managed to convince me that anything less than a year would hardly be worth the pains and the expense. Consequently we had pretty much to liquidate our affairs over here. It was like emigrating all over again, only backward, and with a lot more bundles than we—or at least I—had had to worry about that other time. Jeanne, indeed, was for disposing of our household belongings, which made me a little suspicious of her designs. We could get, she argued, so much nicer things in France, so much more reasonably. Everything was so much finer and better in France, according to Jeanne.

I resisted that little stratagem. It was just that, I about decided. Therefore the house things must be stored. Besides, there was the lease to turn over, an office to be closed up, sailing accommodations to be reserved, a passport to be applied for, the rapidly melting bank balance to be withdrawn and partly converted into francs, a thousand business and family details to be attended to. And then there came an orgy of shopping. Suzanne and Louise must be fitted out presentably for introduction into their mother's social circle in Paris. Jeanne's ancient trunk and bag, which did well enough for vacations over here, were comically inadequate for such a tribal migration. My own prehistoric satchel, or whatever it was, had disappeared ages ago, along with many another precious heirloom, spiritual as well as material.

The shopping, however, was in the main on behalf of the Europeans. One could not decently return, an American and empty-handed. Jeanne had it relatively easy, both because the interval of her absence had been so much briefer and because she had kept up a correspondence with her old world. She knew approximately what she wanted, and for whom. But I had not got a letter from Vaslui in seventeen years. The few kinsfolk and friends I presumably still had there, supposing they had survived the war and the peace—where were they? What were their ages, their condition, their tastes? I had not the remotest idea. Some boyhood sweetheart—whose name I forgot—would doubtless have a few children; but I could not even make a guess about their sexes. And she herself! Twenty years ago

AN AMERICAN IN THE MAKING

I would have been sure to win her favor, maybe also her heart, with a bottle of scent. Now she would probably welcome an electric foot warmer—if Vaslui only had the current—a lot more eagerly. So I must do my gift buying at random and wholesale. About the best thing I could do was to look up the Moldavian vital statistics for 1900-1920.

About the last week in August it occurred to me that perhaps I should be getting busy about a passport.

Jeanne said, "Do we really need one? I never got one coming."

"Well," I replied, "I don't know. It only costs a couple of dollars, and it may come in useful, even if it is not required. Don't forget we are, after all, a sort of adopted waifs; Americans by the grace of an act of Congress. Besides, they have had a bit of a war over there since we came away. Traveling in Europe will be rather an official business, I dare say."

Well, it never entered my head how very formidably official it actually was. Why, going into bankruptcy, settling an estate or getting a divorce must be a lark by comparison! The four-dollar fee for the document itself was a mere incidental. So, for that matter, was the considerably heavier tax for the French visa. Our own authorities, it developed in fact, did not insist on our having a passport. But the foreign potentates whose territories we were about to pay the honor of a visit, did. The moment you put your name on a ship's manifest, it appeared, you forfeited a part of your sovereign rights as an American citizen, and surrendered yourself to the tyrannical powers of alien governments

and the awful mercies of their functionaries. We were required to fill out a questionnaire, deposit numerous photographs of ourselves, which looked so little like us that any family consisting of a married couple and two children could easily have traveled in our place, and all but had our finger prints taken.

We were asked to give a condensed account of our several life histories, our present social and economic status and our immediate prospects; to state the reasons for undertaking so extraordinary and unheard-of an enterprise as a journey to Europe, the probable duration of our sojourn, and by what frontiers we meant to enter; to describe the persons accompanying us, with their ages, sexes, relationship to us, and the like; and to conclude the sketch finally with odd details of a general character which the author of the blank regarded as too vague to reduce to specific questions. Then we must confirm the testimony by exhibiting my citizenship papers, our marriage certificate, the birth certificates of our children and a collection of sundry documents establishing our good standing in the community, our lawful wedlock, our solvency, the legitimacy of our little girls, our freedom from physical and moral leprosy, from criminal tendencies and from religious and political waywardness. Lastly, I was invited to spend several hours in the offices of the collector of internal revenue and to prove to him that I had duly and fully complied with the income-tax law.

And then, when, on the fifteenth of October, we actually found ourselves aboard a transatlantic vessel, do you think the official formalities were over and we were

allowed to take our ease in deck chairs? Not by any manner of means. I was still struggling with the baggage and trying to figure out how a stateroom of the dimensions of an apartment-house elevator could be converted into a home for a family of four for a week or ten days, when the nuisance started all over again. A diffident knock at the cabin door, and there stood before me a uniformed official with an imperial mustache. He handed me a printed paper with a bow and a magnificent flourish.

"Sorry to interrupt you, sir," he said; "police regulations."

His tone was that of a detective who has at last cornered his man.

"Very well, captain," I said in effect; "I am not going to resist. You have got me, and I'll come along like a good fellow. But can't you let me have just a few minutes till I get this prancing portmanteau up into the net there over the washstand?"

"Oh, but, monsieur," he protested, "I am not a *fonctionnaire*! I am only your humble servant, the cabin steward, and I shall be most obliged if you will take a moment now to fill this out. I will help you. And then I will send a boy to arrange your things to suit you."

On the eighth day we sighted the Scilly Islands, and on the night of the same day we thought we could see the French coast. But we did not actually touch land until midnight, and even then, as it were, just figuratively. We were not permitted to land till the next morning. The captain announced that we would sleep on board. That, however, was a loose way of talking. What

he really meant was that we would spend the night there, which was not quite the same thing. No one, I am certain, slept. The majority did not even try. For us two the sight of the European continent—consisting, for the moment, of no more than a revolving point of light—set our blood surging too violently for rest. The Americans, the wild men native to the United States, finding themselves unstirred by any inner excitement, did their best to stimulate themselves into it from without. They made merry till morning, determined that the ship's stock of champagne and other drinkables should not be troubled with another voyage.

The tips to the numerous stewards and stewardesses had been, rather carelessly, remitted after dinner that evening, so that it was best not to rely on them to continue their obsequious eagerness to serve us. Doubtless there would be porters ashore, whose tips were still an alluring uncertainty. But what with two young daughters, and three trunks in the hold and countless bags and valises in the cabin, and an indeterminate quantity of parcels and kiddy cars and loose Teddy bears and wooden donkeys and the like, a pater-familias who had not touched European soil since his own green boyhood had better be circumspect. Therefore we climbed out of our berths at sunrise, and after a lengthy and fruitless endeavor to locate the dining-saloon steward, we made a camper's breakfast on left-over fruits and odds and ends in our stateroom, flung the night clothes into the open bag awaiting them, straightened out Suzanne's hat and pulled up Louise's socks, and then we surrendered ourselves to the courtesies of the frontier police

who were now on board, and called it the end of Chapter One.

The formalities being over much sooner than expected, we were about the first to get ashore. We walked off a little unsteadily. We took in the scene with an eager and comprehensive glance. The littered harbor, the shabby sailors' cafés on the water front, the decrepit little railway waiting to take us to Paris, the bands of ragged young mendicants—not exactly an inspiring picture. And yet I felt a lump rising in my throat, and Jeanne, I thought, had moist eyes, though she denies it now. At last we were in Europe, on the hallowed ground of our native continent! And if Jeanne and I had not been ashamed of our own children and of each other I think I know what we would have done. We would have knelt down and kissed the earth under our feet.

Jeanne had not announced her coming, and there was no one at Havre to meet us. It was going to be a big surprise. Well, it was, as it turned out. But what there was of it was all Jeanne's. Already on the train I seemed to observe some slackening of the tension. Arrived in Paris, it snapped altogether. No sooner that evening were the children in bed than Jeanne dressed and sallied forth, leaving me alone with my college French to dine or starve as I might. She was off to see her friends. I offered gallantly to escort her, but she would have none of me. This was an affair of her own soul, and she required no other company. So I did not insist.

TWENTY YEARS LATER

"But see here," I called after her, "don't you go around lambasting America to your old cronies."

Toward midnight she walked in, limp and pale, a far-away look in her eye. Her obvious distress made me uneasy. But she avoided me and went straight to her room. What had happened? Had her friends divined the truth about our un-American bank balance and been cool to her? Or was someone dead? It did not seem to be that. But what it was she never told me. She did not have to. I found out for myself when I got to Vaslui.

Presently some of my wife's friends called at our hotel. When we got an apartment they all came. There was a winter of social gayety ahead of us, clearly. Jeanne seemed to be in an agony of embarrassment during these visits, which puzzled me considerably. Also it annoyed me. Was she ashamed of her provincial husband in this cultured Old World *milieu* of hers? No, it appeared to be the other way around. But I could not see why. They were quite presentable people, all of them, as far as I could judge. But then I had not woven any golden dreams about them, as Jeanne had. To me they looked like a nice assortment of European people, by and large rather above average, not so very different from Americans, class for class. There was a merchant tailor with a communard past, a doctor of Russian descent, a teacher or two, several business men and industrialists, numerous young folks. They were without exception outwardly clean, agreeable, well-brought-up people. What was Jeanne worrying about?

Little by little Jeanne began, in spite of my warn-

ings, to give her old friends little talks about America. I pricked up my ears. What was this? Irony? My wife was not knocking our adopted country. She was singing its praises! Then, by easy steps, she passed on and took a fling or two at our native continent. She led off softly, moderately; but as she went on she gained headway, and her comments were not at all unworthy of attention. I had heard Americans complain before. Criticizing Europe is one of the most popular recreations of our travelers abroad. But they were duffers at it. They never tired of the stale old song about the scarcity of bathtubs and the slowness of express trains. They rarely came within a mile of the real trouble with the Old World. Well, they should have come and heard Jeanne. I regret that I must not report her fully. It would take too much space, and it might sound like enemy propaganda.

You see, what happened was this: After a month at the hotel we went to housekeeping. We had to on account of our little girls. That was where Jeanne had made her terrible mistake—by having her children born in New York. The moment she did that the game was up. She might as well there and then have surrendered gracefully to America. Suzanne and then Louise began their careers in an American maternity hospital. As Jeanne was then a novice at motherhood, the nurse instructed her in the rudiments of infant care and discipline and recommended a well-known book on their feeding. Then afterward our family doctor did his bit to continue the insidious propaganda. The net result was that Jeanne was, without being aware of it, rearing

her babies to be Americans in the one respect that mattered. I mean food. She did attempt, consciously or unconsciously, to exert counter influences. She crooned snatches of French nursery rimes over their cribs. She hung little etchings of French scenes on the walls for them to look at. She got them French dolls. But her efforts were wasted. That complicated business which we call nationality is not an affair of speech or music or art. It is, as we all know, a matter of diet. And here, I must say, there is one thing that surprises me. How is it that nurses and doctors, especially nursery ones, have never been given their due credit as agents of Americanization? Why, the settlements and the naturalization court and the American Defense Society have nothing on them!

Suzanne and Louise, then, accustomed to beef juice and cereals, broiled bacon and finely chopped spinach, baked potato and prunes stewed for seven hours, drove us out of our comfortable hotel life in short order. They did not seem to thrive on vinaigrette and ragouts and *pommes frites*. In fact, they politely declined most of the dishes set before them. Then, after a month of reduced rations and concentrated reflection on their problem, they seemed to locate the source of the trouble. Whereupon they openly launched an agitation in behalf of their native country with the most selfish indifference to their mother's sentiments.

Said Suzanne, "I think mammee cooks better dinners than the hotel."

"Much," agreed Louise. "I don't like this *la belle France*. When are we going back to New York?"

"Let's do it tomorrow," ventured Suzanne. "I've got my doll carriage there, anyway."

Now, had we been in a position to take the young women's hint and go back at this stage, the result for Jeanne's Americanization would have been extremely unfortunate. She would have seen herself condemned to lifelong exile, a martyr in her children's cause. Luckily, and thanks largely to her own plotting, we were fixed in Europe for two years. It looked to me as if by the end of that time, assuming that the disillusioning process went on as merrily as it had started, Jeanne's naturalization ought to be pretty complete. Well, it not only went on; it kept gaining momentum. At the end of a very few months Jeanne commenced looking forward to our return to New York, not as a personal sacrifice but as a relief. The whilom exile was taking on the color of home.

But I am anticipating. For the present we could not take the youngsters home. But at least we could give them back their favorite cook. The cook did not mind. Jeanne has all the virtues of her race, and the chiefest of these is home making. Therefore she rolled up her sleeves, so to speak, and went at it with high enthusiasm. It suited her to a T. Not only would the children be better fed and happier; it would give her a welcome occupation and save us money. Industry and thrift are likewise in her catalogue of virtues. Moreover, by running her own ménage, we grown-ups, too, would get a more interesting bill of fare.

Back in New York she had been handicapped in her culinary programs by the scarcity of such fragrant

herbs as *cerfeuil* and shallots, as well as by the high cost of mushrooms, endives and truffles. White wine, without which a ragout of hare is insipid, was prohibited altogether. How in the world, she had often protested, was one to make a respectable *pot au feu* without *cerfeuil?* Here in France, by the soul of Epicurus, all these delicacies requisite to a civilized menu were plentiful and cheap. In addition, there were the glorious *pâtés* and *rillettes*, and the inimitable *boudin*—a blood sausage which in my estimation settles forever the claim of France to being a land of culture. The hotel did not go in for these things deeply enough. Hotel fare is the same the world over. It is supposed to be French. But it is not of any nationality. It aims at neutrality. It must have been designed for the palate of the council of the League of Nations.

Of course, Jeanne did get all she was anticipating—as well as a lot she was not, as we shall see directly. The thing was this: Though the choice supplies were neither scarce nor costly, the problem of getting them into the pantry was, particularly for one who had got into American ways of marketing, at once exasperating and amusing. We have all, no doubt, seen pictures and read descriptions of the treasures of the Louvre, of the fine shops on the rue de la Paix and of the picturesque cafés of Montmartre. Come to think of it, there are even some fine etchings of French market places. But has anyone yet described the tribulations of marketing in France from the housewife's point of view? If anyone has I have not come across his work.

In New York, Jeanne recalled, you went around the

corner to the Hamilton or the Washington Market, which was simply a department store for provisions. You could buy meat—the meat of every creature that bore flesh—and fish and oysters, and vegetables and fruit, all in the same shop. The grocer, too, was just next door. If it was raining, or if the baby was irritable, you could telephone. And you never had to carry your purchases home. Half an hour after you gave the order the things would come flying up your dumb-waiter shaft.

In Paris you went literally to market, in the way our great-grandmothers used to do it—with a basket, out among the carts on the open square. To secure the provisions necessary for the day, let alone Sunday, you must deal with a score or more of petty traders. It was departmentalized commerce with a vengeance. The butcher sold nothing but the meat of cloven-hoofed ruminants, in accordance with the laws laid down by Moses. The flesh of swine was an abomination to him and must be sought elsewhere. So chickens; so sea food. The woman with the pushcart who offered string beans meant what she yelled—she sold string beans and nothing else. They were not vegetable dealers, these market folk. They were commercial botanists, each with a specialty of her own. Cabbage belonged to the kale family, and the expert who dealt in that kept strictly off the leguminous species assigned to her colleague.

And how they yelled! You would have thought you were in the Italian quarter on First Avenue. And bargained, as in an Oriental bazaar. There was always a crowd of customers around every stand and cart, pull-

ing the woman in every direction. You lost twenty minutes buying peas and twenty more attracting the
attention of the onion vender. And when you finally
finished you trailed home like a pack mule, laden with
net bags and newspaper bundles—unless your democratic conscience was dead within you and you had no
compunction about marketing in the grand style with
your overworked general maid playing the pack mule
for you twenty paces behind.

But when all is said and done, I still believe that
Jeanne might have put up with these and many more
annoyances and inconveniences without permanent
damage to her European patriotism. They were, after
all, small things. Ere long, though, Jeanne, who had
left a girl and come back a wife and mother, became
aware of certain deeper phases of Old World life—
things which in the old days brushed by without touching her. The mere existence of those two little girls
somehow put significance into all sorts of things, all of
them far removed from boulevards and millinery and
art. Jeanne had never suspected herself of such a variety of philosophic interests as she now suddenly discovered. She caught herself eagerly observing not only
French kindergartens and playgrounds but also the
domestic atmosphere in which the European child grew
up, the kind of amusements and fun young folks had,
the position of the girl in the social scheme, the attitude
of boys toward girls. All this in turn was leading her
into deeper waters, such as the ambitions of the young
fellows we knew, their opportunities to follow these out,
their notions of love and marriage and the home. It was

clear to me that Jeanne was accumulating a store of mental notes on all these topics, but she rarely offered to share them. Perhaps she was afraid I might say something that sounded like "I told you so."

One day in the spring, however, she startled me by announcing her conclusions. She said:

"I know it's doing the children a world of good to be here at this age. They are getting a foundation in French such as no American school could ever have given them. And I hope that we'll be able to bring them back for a summer from time to time. But it's American girls they are going to be."

The only reply I could make to this unheralded announcement was to cheer. But my expression indicated that I felt entitled to some sort of explanation.

"When I look at poor Odette here," Jeanne went on, "and think of our little tots growing up to that kind of life, it makes me want to pack up and run away back there with them."

Now Odette, I ought to say, was the eighteen-year-old daughter of our landlady. We were now out of our Paris apartment and living in a house at St.-Cloud, that pretty suburb of Paris. The owner was our neighbor, and we were on fairly intimate terms with the family—as intimate as French traditions allow. Odette's father had been a successful painter. He was now dead; and her mother, who was a well-known sculptor, was managing to keep her little family together, partly by the proceeds of her own work, but principally by the income from property her husband had left her. Odette was an unusually attractive girl, and she possessed in

addition an abundant supply of the good qualities characteristic of French young womanhood. She was quiet and reserved, modest and serious and well-bred; in short, the perfect ideal Jeanne had, while in New York, visioned for our children.

So far so good. Maybe Jeanne still thought her an example to follow. I know she was very fond of the girl. But the life the poor creature was leading was another matter. It was this Jeanne was thinking of when she made her announcement. You see, if Odette had been the daughter of a laborer or an artisan there would have been no cause for condoling with her. Then she would have gone to work at fourteen, would have romped and danced for three or four years, would have had one or more love affairs by this time, and would have married someone she liked at nineteen or twenty. Or, had her father been one of the rich industrial bourgeoisie, her life would have been a gayer one yet. Then there would have been entertainments at her own home, and dances and the Riviera in winter, and motoring and outings and the seashore in summer, and a governess to take her to the theater and things in town. As it was, Odette was but a young lady of good family in very modest circumstances. She had a load of leaden traditions to hold her down, but no means for a respectable good time befitting her station. Young men must not come to call on her; she must not go to the theater or to a restaurant with a girl friend. Once or twice a year there might be a church entertainment for the young people; but then she must be heavily chaperoned to attend. And as madame had work to do, and was, more-

over, bored by the inane talk and pleasures of the immature, she did not always like to go; and Odette was obliged to stay at home. The sum of it was an existence beside which the life in a cloister must be exciting.

In due time, to be sure, Odette would marry. Her father had set aside a modest fund for her *dot* (dowry). If the gods were exceptionally kind to her she might even make a love marriage—by which I mean nothing more poetic than a union of her own choice. It was hard to see how that could be negotiated. The girl did not know a soul—not a masculine one, anyhow. Besides, precedent and tradition were all against such wild proceedings. In Latin Europe matrimony was not a frivolous affair left to sentiment and youthful irresponsibility. It was something to be arranged between the parents. The parties immediately concerned only became concerned afterward. Marriage was not the climax of romance; it was an alliance between families. Of course, love might come later; but not necessarily between the married couple. We had but to look at her friend Germaine to get a forecast of little Odette's future.

Along about the middle of the summer I suddenly remembered. Why, Masseuil! We had not yet been to Masseuil, to Jeanne's birthplace! And as it happened that I had some business in Tours, I suggested that she come with me.

"It will only be a couple of hours' run from there to Poitiers. We'll spend the night there, and the next day we can get a wagon and drive out to the old place."

To my astonishment Jeanne would not hear of it.

"No," she said. "Paris has been quite enough for
one trip."

I tried to persuade her. I reminded her that the capital was not, after all, her home town; that it was not
fair to regard Paris as all Europe; that she should not
let herself be discouraged by the first poignant impressions, which were inevitably disillusioning. She could
not be moved. Her mind was made up.

She said simply, "No, I prefer to keep some of my
memories intact. I don't want to return to exile with all
my illusions gone."

I thought that foolish, and said so. But I have since
been back to Vaslui, and I know that Jeanne is the wiser
of us two.

XXIII

NEARLY a whole year passed before I managed to get away. It was the most restless and discontented year of my life. Somehow, as long as I stuck in the rut back there in America I did not fret. Now I looked back at those twenty incredible years and marveled that I had survived them. The longing for Vaslui was getting so keen it bordered on pain. It was something vastly more poignant than just homesickness. It became an obsession, a downright hunger.

Time and again I paused and pinched myself to make sure I was not dreaming. I had dreamed about it so long and so often—yes, literally dreamed; back in my slum days, regretfully; later, in the Middle West, with a dull ache; more recently, with an adoring tenderness —that I could no longer think of it by daylight as a real place. How many nights, do you suppose, had I seen myself pulling into its little brick station, and heard the conductor shouting, "Vaslui, ten minutes," and found my mother exactly where I had left her, and walked up that long road to town, that Via Dolorosa of hers, and reveled in its familiar sights, and vowed that never, never would I go away again. Was there now actually such a place, or had I invented it for

some novel I was going to write? Or maybe it was like that village of Germelshausen which I had read about, and which had a trick of disappearing for a hundred years at a time. It would not have surprised me at all if, after landing somewhere in Rumania, I had stepped up to the window to ask for a ticket to Vaslui and been stared at by the girl agent in stark terror.

This dawdling abroad and not getting to the one place that was Europe to me was getting on my nerves. What did I care about Paris and all the rest as long as my Eldorado, Vaslui the Golden, was still hundreds of leagues removed? It was but a station on the way. And I felt as irritated as any traveler whose train is needlessly held up at some junction halfway to his destination.

On one occasion this tantalizing delay brought me nearly to the breaking point. Not more than a month after our landing in Europe I did succeed in wrenching myself away. I got to Prague. I stopped ten days in Vienna and a week in Budapest, almost touching the threshold of my own country. Then came a telegram, and I had to rush back posthaste to Paris. It looked as if the fates had maliciously conspired to keep me from my goal.

To me, Vaslui was something of a sacred memory. That was about all. It was the place where my father and mother had lived and died. Half the time it was the hardest thing imaginable to convince myself that I had ever been there in the flesh. I had merely heard about it from my parents, so often and so vividly that it had come to seem real. It was not in Rumania. Where

in the world was Rumania? I could as easily place Vaslui in Tennessee; but I could not make myself realize that I had ever belonged anywhere but in America.

That green youth who had emigrated twenty years before from Vaslui, and who was supposed to be no less a person than myself, was as thin as air. He was just a character in my own book, a mere invention. I could not help smiling as I went back and read of his exploits. That raw, romantic innocent who, without ever having quit his mother's apron strings, was setting out to conquer America! And then his fantastic doings in the slums and sweatshops of New York—had I ever been in the skin of that young fool? But little by little he was taking shape. Pretty soon he found his tongue, shed his steerage trappings, and wrenched himself loose from the foreign colony altogether. The dumb, gesticulating, unkempt, comic-opera alien dived down into the seething rapids of American life and came up again—a student in a Middle Western college, speaking the language of Missouri, rooting at the games, earning his way through—for all the world one of the hundred million; a sample product of the American miracle plant; a full-eared cornstalk shot up out of a Rumanian mustard seed; an American, not to be distinguished from his fellows, kneaded out of East European dough. And then, and then—he was coming right on. By the eternal, he and I were one!

But he had not conquered America, after all; not according to plan, anyway. That gave me pause. We were going back to Vaslui, he and I, but minus the million of which he had been so sure. I was not unhappy

about that lost hope, nor so much as disappointed. Why should I be? I had not even tried. I had not, when the time came, gone in for that sort of thing at all. I was taking back riches of quite another kind, things that Vaslui never dreamed were to be found in America. Yes, but how would Vaslui take that? To tell my fellow townsmen that I had come home without the one thing that people went to America for, what a ghastly failure they would put me down for! And even if they were to believe my sour-grapes tale, it would only make matters worse. It would show me up as an ambitionless ne'er-do-well. What? After twenty years in the land of gold, and not so much as a single million? Others less hopeful than I had come trailing back with theirs in half the time. They said so themselves, and gave proofs of personal grandeur and of munificence that were beyond shamming. I tell you, that was a sobering thought. You can think me vain, if you like; but I was not going home just to make a cynic's holiday. I don't mind admitting that I rather looked forward to a bit of a triumphal entry.

I called to mind that relative of mine—he has figured as Couza in my recollections, and Couza he shall remain—who first set me thinking about America. Of course, I could not hope to get all he got from my home town. He was the pioneer, after all, of returning emigrants. The public welcome at the depot, the banquets and the official reception, the admiring, cheering crowds in the streets, the hushed whispers about his skyrocket career and his vast fortune—oh, it was splendid! But somehow I was not quite sure that I wanted all that. As

a boy of fifteen I had thought it a royal show and added my voice to the resounding ovation, and maybe even dreamed of some day being in Couza's shoes. It seemed a novel kind of parade; an American was a more interesting species of performing bear. But I had found out Couza in the meantime, seen him in his East Side tenement home, and his performance revolted me. Ugh! The bumptious fraud! The stupid lies, the shabby display, the soulless misleading of poor simple people for personal vainglory! No, I would have none of that. Writing and lecturing in America had brought me as much of that counterfeit coin as I cared for. I need not go all the way to Vaslui for the small change. I was not going to set the beloved place on its ear, send my own people grasping after American shadows and make them discontented with their humble lot.

I had a very different kind of message to deliver, and the gist of it was that Couza had lied to them. I would undo the mischief he had perpetrated. I would tell them the plain truth about the land I had made my own. Couza had never emerged from the foreign colony he had tumbled into on the day of his landing. He had never touched elbows with the American reality at all. Therefore he had come dragging with him that rag bag of legends and half truths about the New World that have such a perpetual circulation in the foreign colonies. Perhaps he had not been an impostor, after all. For all I know, he may have believed those tales himself. But I had had the luck to break through the alien's barriers, strike across country and stumble on to something like the real thing. If only I could muster

the skill to make my people see what I saw; if I could paint for Vaslui America as I had come to know her; not Couza's stage paradise, but the America that lived and breathed, a land of imperfect men and human institutions, but with the blessing of heaven and the promise of salvation upon them. If I could bring that home to the people of Vaslui I should feel that all my struggles and sufferings had been worth while.

Along about August, nearly a year after my arrival in Europe, my affairs began to get straightened out, and it looked as if I might soon manage to pull away. I was almost glad now that my plans had miscarried the previous November. The delicious adventure was still ahead of me. Besides, the winter was no time to visit Rumania. In the country the vineyards would be stripped and deserted, the stubble fields gray and lifeless, the peasant hibernating in his drab homespun and his chill, underground hovels. There would be no cheerful movement on the roads; no caravans of oxcarts laden with grain and fatted poultry and wine, creaking their unhurried way to market; no files of buxom peasant lasses with flowers in their hair and bright embroidered smocks on their vigorous bodies, tripping gayly to town with baskets of eggs or sacks of beans poised adroitly on their heads. The whole scene would be overcast and gloomy. And Vaslui itself—no hubbub in the market place; no warmth or color in the busy streets; no music in the little park. Shivering, underclad, underfed children hurrying to school in the biting morning air; pinched, worried faces of men and women; windows shuttered and forbidding—the poverty and

discomfort of European small-town life in all its stark indignity.

It was not like this I wanted to see the beloved old place. In my memory it lived a spot of tender green, radiant in sunlight. Ancient elms meeting in arches above the cool lanes, the breeze casting restless shadows of lace over stone-paved courtyards and diminutive cottages. Spacious squares with long vistas in all directions, and glimpses of spires in the distance. Youngsters noisily splashing in pools on the edge of town. Here and there a weather-beaten mossy bridge spanning the Vasluiets creek, an ancient house built no one knew when, a monument set up to some forgotten hero. The inns a labyrinth of carts and *char-à-bancs*, a riot of color, seething with beasts and men. A Roman idyl. Yes, there was no month like August for seeing Rumania at its best.

Once I was really on the Paris-Bucarest express, I felt myself sobering up. I began taking stock of my own desires. What was it that was driving me, a plain, hard-headed, self-contained citizen, so irresistibly to that distant Balkan village, as if I were a romantic girl? For one thing, it dawned on me that that plan of mine of enlightening Vaslui about America was just a silly fancy. It was not at all what I was really after. I had not the slightest ambition to play the American prophet in my home town. Oh, bother, I did not crave to be another Couza, not even a reformed and beneficent one! I had no wish whatever to be made a fuss over by Vaslui. The people of the place would, after all these years, mean nothing to me anyway. If my father and

mother had been spared it might have been otherwise. As it was, there would hardly be a soul there whom I knew. One or two possibly; but they belonged more to the scenery than to the population. And wouldn't it shock Vaslui to hear who they were? Besides, they too had been dead, more than likely, goodness knows how many years!

In the name of horse sense, what was taking me in such a thumping rush to Vaslui? I am supposed to have an analytical mind, but I could not analyze my own motives in a simple undertaking like this. Anyhow, one thing was plain: I was not going to Vaslui on any lecture tour. I loathed being receptioned and lionized even in the small towns of America. To go hunting for it in my boyhood village—why, it would spoil everything that made the place dear to me! Besides, I was not exactly fitted out for a sensation. Such little prizes as I had won in that other world yonder were not spectacular enough. They did not lend themselves to public display. The chairman of the welcoming committee would have nothing to take hold of. How would he introduce me? I might whisper to him that I was once invited to lunch by an ex-President of the United States. But who would believe it? There was nothing about my exterior to back up such pretensions.

My clothes? The most modest Vasluiander going on a journey had on as good. I did not even wear a frock coat the way the royal Couza did. The letters of introduction I had were in a foreign tongue. Even my press clippings, some of which carried my photograph, would not be convincing. They might merely be reports of

some scandal I had got into, perhaps even of some crime I had committed. Did you ever try to prove to a policeman that you are an honest man? There is nothing harder in the world than to pass yourself off for what you are. Why, that whole fairy-tale career of mine, the whole amazing transformation America had put me through, would show up white against this native background! Even my schooling would mean nothing. Had I at least become a dentist or something! What good was an education anyway if it did not make a doctor of you, or the like? Even in the foreign colony back there in New York I remembered how the faces of my friends fell when, after my return from college, they learned that I had not become a doctor after all.

No, I would slip into Vaslui and out again quietly, unnoticed. It ought not to be difficult. No one knew of my coming, and no one would recognize me after all these years. There were luckily no newspaper men in Vaslui to come prying into people's affairs. At the hotel I could register as an Austrian salesman or a Russian refugee. And then I would take a week or two wandering around, treading again the precious stones of it, saturating myself with its atmosphere, living over my boyhood once more. To do it right, I knew, I should have a couple of months; but it could not be this time. Perhaps I might come again later. But I would not open my mouth to a soul.

Vaslui was not just a town where men and women lived and bargained, got married and bore children and died. It was pure scenery. It was a stage, where my childhood was, with some changes and omissions, to be

reënacted; and the actors in the performance would not, unfortunately, be the same as twenty years ago. What good would it do for me to stand up in my stall and talk to them? It would only interfere with the play and the illusion. Those players of nearly a generation ago would be out of it. The majority of them had gone to America along with me. The few who were left would have outgrown their parts quite as much as myself. They, too, would be sitting in the audience now, and no juggling of my imagination could put them back where I had left them, and where I now wanted them again just to provide me with an emotional holiday.

The old boys would be successful grain merchants or peasant innkeepers, or else bustling, middle-aged middlemen and matchmakers. The girls' case would be worse yet. They would all be married, with clusters of children hanging at their skirts. Some might be rich, and then they would be repulsively fat and self-satisfied; while the poor would be repulsively scrawny and disillusioned; and both alike would be frumpy and ill-groomed, their whilom spring and freshness gone to make room for hardened faces and grating voices. Precious little romance there. Better not go poking your foolish head in there, if you prize your memories.

The thought of my Vaslui changed, came near chilling my enthusiasm. When the train was getting into Budapest I was suddenly seized with an odd kind of terror, and all the time that it stayed there I kept debating with myself whether I ought not to beat a retreat while there was yet time. But I held on to my-

self. How would I explain my weakening to Jeanne's mocking inquiries?

And then before I knew it I found myself at home. It was odd. We had not gone more than an hour or two out of the Hungarian capital. There had been no frontier police, no passport and luggage examination. By the map we were still on Magyar soil. According to the time-table, Bucarest was a good twenty-four hours off. However it might be, as I stood there with my heart thumping and my face pressed against the window, the world I had so long dreamed about was whisking past me. There it all was—the little low, white-washed, thatch-roofed houses, with their tiny checkerboard windows painted red, and the green border—known as a belt—at the base; the well-remembered outdoor masonry ovens; the wells with their curious derrick-like levers suspended from a forked tree, at one end a weight and at the other the chain and the hook for the pail; the peasants at work in the fields, bare-footed or in raw pigskin moccasins, their embroidered smocks belted over the white homespun breeches—it was the land of my fathers, the scene of my childhood; it was home. It did not matter a straw what the political map makers said about it, what dialect the railroad inspector swore in, what flag waved over the way stations; this was the culture I had been reared in and yearned for.

The sight of these loved landmarks reassured me and made me feel ashamed of my recent cowardice. To have run away from the threshold of paradise, how mad I must have been! Now, all at once, too, my doubts vanished about what magnet it was that drew me to Vaslui.

Why, it was just this sky and this earth, these toy houses, these people and things pictured in my boyish memory! Small wonder I had failed to guess it before. It was no matter for analysis. To see was to know. I might as well have tried to chart a child's love for his mother.

And then another craving seized me, a real hunger this time. It had been gnawing me all these twenty years, until I had nearly thought it appeased by starvation. I was traveling five thousand miles to get a real meal, a meal of the kind that I had been brought up on and which was not to be had beyond the confines of my native place. And lest you should think me a worldling and a glutton, let me tell you: I know of nothing more undilutedly spiritual than to sit down at table in the village where you were born and taste again the morsels mother cooked for you when you were a boy. It is not carnal food at all, any more than the bread and wine of the Sacrament are food. It is pure piety.

Toward the end of the third day I arrived in Bucarest. It was a lucky thing that I had not visioned the capital as the land of my heart's desire, or I might have come down with a hard bump. The fact is I had no sentiment whatever about it. It stirred no memories. I had never seen it in the old days. It meant little more to me than many another European city I had passed through. It was only the last halt before my destination. Yet even so, it was a little disappointing. This shabby, sprawling, overgrown country town with a royal palace in the middle of it—was this the gilded Camelot of my boyish fancy, the splendid imperial city I had never

managed to get to? One drive through it, on the very afternoon of my arrival, behind a pair of prancing Caucasian steeds and a gorgeous velvet-gowned Russian eunuch, was all I wanted of it. My Baedeker, so voluble about every stone on the Loire, was strangely reticent about its beauties. I had vaguely imagined a volume devoted to it, like London, Paris, and Berlin—"Bucarest and its environs, with eleven maps, thirty-eight plans and three panoramas," as well as numerous little stars to single out the sights that must not be missed. Instead, that gentleman had flung it a paltry dozen pages in the guide to Turkey!

But I must admit, though it hurts me, that even they were superfluous. In any other city, if you wish to do the sights in a limited time, you must hire a guide in addition to buying one, and walk scores of blocks, and climb thousands of steps, and listen to a batch of lectures on kings and wars and architects and criminals. Bucarest is the only city I have visited that can be seen comfortably. All you need to do is to sit down in front of a café on the Calea Victoriei—Capşa's for choice—and while you enjoy your Turkish coffee or *pelin* the sights of the capital will come to you to be viewed at your ease.

Bucarest is not so much a city as a promenade. The fixtures in it are not worth looking at, and I rather think were not meant to be. If you are interested in mere buildings and monuments and that sort of thing, you can go to Rome. The flavor of Bucarest is individual, its civilization is dynamic. Bucarest is not a cluster of noble ruins like Athens or a line of proud

giants towering into the sky like New York. It is a procession, a perennial carnival. Its history is not a memory, but an aspiration. Its art is not plastic, but cosmetic. That is where it surpasses Paris and leads the world. Paris, too, has its perfume shops and scented ladies. In the Rumanian capital every other store is a bazaar of beauty requisites, and every army officer— monocled, powdered, odoriferous, lip-sticked and corseted—is so rare a sight as no amount of Baedeker stars could hope to do justice to. For contrast, there are barefooted peasants in national costume peddling fruits and nuts among the little tables, and the endless wilderness of slums off both sides of the Calea Victoriei.

I made up my mind before arriving that I would leave that same night for Vaslui. But when I did that my picture of things Rumanian was still that haloed ideal I had brought with me from America. I had not taken the realities into account. On the train from Paris my fellow travelers had warned me on no account to go about in Rumania on day coaches. The trains were so crowded that unless one started from a terminus and waited for hours in line it was impossible to get seats. It was not uncommon for passengers to stand up through a whole night's journey. The corridors, the steps, the couplings and the very tops of the cars were literally crawling with passengers. In summer the heat and the bad air were intolerable. It was by no means unusual for a woman or child to die of asphyxiation, particularly in the third-class carriages; and the amount of money you were willing to pay was no guarantee that you could get a second- or first-class seat.

AN AMERICAN IN THE MAKING

An English engineer, employed at the Rumanian oil wells, told me that he had gone a few months before from Bucarest to Jassy, and that when his train arrived two dead soldiers were removed from the roof of one of the cars. They had been decapitated while passing under a low bridge. So I was advised to travel on nothing but the international sleepers.

It seemed like a horribly splurging way of going to Vaslui, the emigrant who had walked to the first port to take ship for America, now returning in a sleeper like a giddy boyar. Supposing someone recognized me as I got out! It would get abroad and I would attract a lot of unwelcome notoriety. Then again, was there really a sleeper to Vaslui? I tried to picture the thing. It was about as easy as to imagine the Woolworth Building there. But everybody assured me that the Bucarest-Jassy express, which stopped in Vaslui every morning and evening, carried a sleeping car. It must have been doing it all along, while I was a schoolboy in Vaslui. And I had never even heard that such a thing existed. I did not see the inside of a Pullman until after I had been in America for ten years.

Sure enough, just a step from the Royal Palace Square, there they were, the offices of the International Sleeping Car Company of Brussels; and I went in and boldly asked for a ticket to Vaslui, and the clerk—who was a Rumanian, not a Belgian—was not the least bit startled by the demand. He looked as if he had been selling them every day of his life. But selling one to me was another story. He informed me without raising his head that the entire car was sold out for that night;

also for the next night, and for the one after that. Would I step in tomorrow morning? There might be cancellations. Still, there was quite a waiting list. I did step in the next morning, and every other morning for a week running. No use. It looked to me as if there must be a nigger in the woodpile somewhere. But I could not locate him. Was everybody in Bucarest going to Jassy by sleeper? No; but the ministries had a permanent reservation on half the car. The government was doing most of the traveling.

Oh! Small wonder official business moved so slowly in this beloved land of my birth. The state was eternally on the go. But what about the other half car? Couldn't he hold something for me for next week? He was very sorry; he had nothing in prospect. Then I lost my temper.

"Look here," I said, "how about reserving me a berth for All Saints' Day, or for Easter, or for the year 1931?"

He shook his head stolidly and very, very regretfully. His orders were to make no reservations more than three days ahead. And just as he said that something popped in my head—just a word—"Baksheesh!" Why, of course, Baedeker knew. This was once upon a time politically, and still remained morally, a province of Turkey, the land of the bribe.

I almost shouted it in the clerk's face. What I said was, "Oh, hang your orders! I know the rules." And I laid a hundred-lei note on the counter. "Now, just a minute," he said to me. Then over his shoulder to the young woman in the inner office, in the speech of the

land, "The American has tumbled at last." I had been cautious enough not to betray my knowledge of Rumanian. "The Department of Fine Arts," he announced, "has just canceled two places. You can go tonight if you wish."

During my long attendance on the sleeping-car man I knocked about the streets, wondering what escape there might be from this dreary town. Sipping coffee and *pelin* and watching the painted ladies and the musical-comedy officers in procession ceased to be amusing after a while. Then I remembered that I had a relative in the place. He was a Vasluiander, too, though I had never laid eyes on him. In fact, in my boyhood he was the glory of the family. As the son of mercantile parents who had contrived to become a doctor, he was held up by all the fathers of my clan as a noble example to us youngsters. I am sure it was his achievement that inspired my father with the dream that I, too, would some day rise to that dizzy height. It would be rather interesting, I thought, to meet this glittering ideal of my youth after all this time.

Finding him was not easy. Doctors in Bucarest, it developed, did not invariably permit themselves the luxury of a telephone. I should like to know how they are reached in an emergency. But after hunting for a city directory—and learning that there was no such thing—and searching for the medical association—which likewise had no phone—and communicating with the public-health office—where I was told gruffly that addresses were not divulged there—I did in the end locate my cousin through the American Red Cross.

TWENTY YEARS LATER

Thereupon I sent word to him, minutely describing my ancestry and my relation to him, and promptly got an answer with an invitation to dinner.

This last was very exciting, and ought, I felt, to repay me for all my trouble. I began picturing the feast, with my mouth watering—the fragrant *pot au feu*, the sweet-sour tomato stew, the vine-leaf croquettes, the crisp cheese *strudel*, all the dainties of my Old World past. I was also a bit flustered at the prospect of so suddenly bursting into exclusive Rumanian society. I was, after all, a plain American with a home-spun Middle Western education, wholly unversed in the higher etiquette. Would I do? At least, I must get into my "smoking," as the Europeans call a Tuxedo.

My fiacre halted before a low, one-story, rather unimposing brick dwelling in an alley-like yard, on the gate a shingle with the doctor's name and something about diseases of the skin and blood. I was welcomed by a graying, disillusioned, rather pathetic-looking provincial physician. He was in business dress. I was introduced to his two daughters, his two sons, a number of further cousins of both sexes I had never heard of. Not a trace of low gowns or evening black anywhere. The doctor, it seemed, was a widower. As the meal progressed I answered some perfunctory inquiries about my doings in the other world, and got some information about my host and my new-found family. This was Ella—little three-year golden-locked Ella when I quit home, now the mother of a young person of exactly that age. And here was Stella, who was, I thought, Betty.

No; Betty, that lovely creature who gave me so many restless moments twenty years ago, was dead, and Stella was her daughter. Of the doctor's sons, one was a physician rapidly taking over his father's practice. The younger boy had studied engineering in Berlin, and was recognized all round as an exceptionally able and well-trained young fellow; but after several years' experience he was still a mere draftsman in the government's bridge bureau. He was not getting on at all. His family, you see, were not an engineering family. They were doctors. So he was an outsider. In time he would probably arrive—in time to retire. His sons, if he should have any, and if they also became engineers, might have it easier, just as his brother who had had the prudence to follow in the parental footsteps found it comparatively smooth sailing. The usual European state of affairs, made familiar to me already in Paris. And as I listened to their account of themselves, the question kept going through my head: Where would I have landed in my profession under such a system—I, the son of a poor tradesman in a distant village? Would I ever in a thousand years have got even to college?

The girls were agreeable, gracious, cultivated young ladies, far from lacking in good looks, well read, at home in three or four languages, musical, possessed of all the virtues and accomplishments of the young women of their class and country. They were sought after socially. They had many friends. But, as I learned later, it was concern over their future that accounted for their father's gray hair and disillusioned look. Imagine it! In the western hemisphere girls like them

would have frolicked through college, played at business or some profession for a couple of years, had an active, sunny girlhood of it all, and been grabbed up in matrimony long before anyone had ever had time to start worrying about them. Eastern Europe was another world.

The doctor was not, by the looks of it, well-to-do. He had had his struggles, had married into an eminent but not wealthy family, had been forced by the standards of his professional and social *milieu* to live up to the limit of his income, and had therefore not managed to save up the indispensable fortune for his daughters' dowries. In consequence these lovely, attractive girls were in danger of not marrying, or at least not marrying desirably. There could be no more dreadful calamity in this East European world. An unmarried girl here was destined to become a dependent. Their social traditions frowned on work; they were trained for no profession. They were just decorative Victorian young ladies. It was not that the Bucarest young men were mercenary or incapable of love. But their bride's dowry was their launching into a career, their start in life. Personal preference was all very well; but, as the French put it, you cannot make your way in this world on love and clear water.

I was received cordially enough, but without that curiosity and stir and wonder that I had expected and dreaded. I was obviously not a performing bear to them; they had seen Americans before. Perhaps it would have been agreeable to be asked a little more about that other world, to have been conscious of some appre-

ciation of the miracle America had wrought in me. But then, none of these people had ever seen me before my emigration and therefore they could not gauge the vast distances I had traveled. Thank heaven for it! The doctor, in fact, did say something about another American—a brother-in-law he had in New York, who had paid him a visit just before the war. I must know him. Schmidt was his name. Had a large prosperous café over there.

What was disappointing was that dinner. In view of my anticipations, it was nothing short of a tragedy. It was a first-rate meal, you understand—the usual French cookery, the usual courses, the usual barefooted peasant girl serving it. But I could have got the like of that in any good hotel in town—for that matter, in any good hotel between Bucarest and San Francisco. Come to think of it, I could have come a lot nearer getting what I hungered for in any one of a dozen Rumanian restaurants on the East Side of New York. Still I was glad I had come. I had had a pleasant social evening, and that was better than seeing the barren, crushing ugliness of the town.

I was for a space forgetting I was in Bucarest. I was back in civilization. But before the party was quite over I was brought up with a start and forcibly reminded that I was not in Christendom, after all, but in the medieval Balkans. When the coffee was served in the drawing-room the married ladies reverted to their customary topics of conversation—duds, personalities, cosmetics and servants, each in her turn recounting with much gusto and righteousness just how often and

how vigorously she flogged her domestics. In New York servants are coddled and bribed to make them work, in Paris they are threatened with discharge, and in Bucarest they are whipped!

The next evening I really, truly started on my glorious adventure. Sharing my sleeper compartment with me was a gentleman whose pleasant duty it became to bring me a stretch nearer in the process of filling in the gap between my idealized memories of home and the ungilded reality. He was a lawyer of Jassy, on his way home. Just what impressed him with my importance I could not at first guess. Maybe, I thought, he had seen the porter lug in my bag with its many-colored labels from hotels in American cities and European capitals. But he kept up an uninterrupted evolution of bowing and scraping and mumbling polite nothings and stepping out of my way with clicking heels every time I passed him.

In the morning I arose early and stood in the corridor, watching for old landmarks. The train was now traversing familiar ground. Presently my roommate joined me. We began to talk. My Rumanian speech being a little halting, I paid him the compliment of addressing him in French. But his French proved lamer than my Rumanian. So to spare him embarrassment I switched to my native tongue. He observed pleasantly that for a foreigner I spoke Rumanian remarkably well.

"But I am not a foreigner," I informed him eagerly. "I am a naturalized American. I was born in the town we just passed, in Berlad."

As soon as he heard that his polite courtesy dropped

from him like a mask. He commenced treating me familiarly, even contemptuously. Why, hang it, I was merely one of ours! I recognized that Balkan trait quickly, and saw that I had been led by sentiment into a false step; but it was too late to retreat. It was rather hard on me. In America, where they go to the other extreme, I had sometimes found it expedient to keep my origin to myself. To have to do it in my native country all over again seemed a little too much. None the less, I took my little lesson to heart. My decision to go to Vaslui incognito was a good one on more than one count.

Soon the conductor announced that the next station would be Vaslui—just like that, calmly. Good heavens, were there people in the world to whom that precious spot was no more than a stop on the road? We arrived in a heavy mist. As my droshky went clattering up that long road I peered around in search of familiar objects, and in spite of all my efforts to keep my self-possession, I kept repeating in a whisper, "Vaslui! Vaslui at last!" Between times I acknowledged that I ought to be kicked for a sentimental idiot, and then went on mumbling some more. Arrived at the Hotel Central, I flung my bag into my room, careless of pickers and stealers, grabbed my new camera and sallied forth. I knew my way about—I was sure—blindfolded. Straight on ahead, just a step, was the hack stand; to the right, up a side street, the soda-water plant and a cluster of houses, one of which had been our first home in Vaslui after we migrated from Berlad thirty years ago. And going left, one arrived at the

little circular park where the military band played evenings, and on the edges of which, with their backs against the ornamental iron grille, sat the peasant women on market days, with their produce and their picturesque handiwork. Surrounding the park in a wide circle was the well-remembered Ring, Vaslui's Place Vendôme, with its fine shops and balconied residences. Finally, on beyond the hack stand stretched the wide Jassy road, which was the real Vaslui for me.

For the moment, however, nothing but a thick fog, with faint rays of light trying to break through. I glanced up. All ye glories, electric street lights! And that beplastered gate next door, a cinema—two cinemas —in Vaslui! That was worth closer inspection. Yes, our Charlie, our Douglas, the whole galaxy. But the hotel—why, it was no less a place than the awesome Café Central, that resort of elegance and exclusiveness. The last time I was here I dared not walk near it, always took the other side of the street for fear some fashionable lady or some officer sipping beer at the tables on the sidewalk might look at me. What had brought it down in the world—made this unspeakably shabby, evil-smelling hole of it? Maybe all of Vaslui had sunk like that. Without knowing what I was doing, I began to walk hurriedly. I must find out quickly.

Oh, merciful heavens, it was worse, a thousand times worse than I had feared! That circular park—unbelievable—it was square! The ornamental iron grille— it was wood! You could not really, honestly call it a park at all. It was a mere inclosure with a band stand in the center. I almost hoped now the mist would not

311

lift. What a fool I had been not to turn back at Budapest! If it were at least possible to think it had
changed, run down! But there was nothing to support
such a theory. The war had not come this far; there
had been no revolution. Besides, nothing of that kind
could make a circular park turn square. No, it had not
changed. There was no use telling myself stories about
it. It had always been like that. Only I had gone and
dreamed a place and dubbed it Vaslui.

To think that I had compared Blois with this—that
gem of the French Renaissance and this rubbish heap.
What, by the way, was Vaslui doing when Blois was
making itself beautiful four hundred years ago? I
looked around at the stores and the residences over
them. Ramshackle hovels built of mud. Nowhere a
house that looked as though it had stood for fifty years,
or would go on standing that long in the future. Why
was such a town ever built, and when and by whom?
American towns are not always beautiful by any means,
but they have a kind of machine-made neatness about
them and an air of hospitality. French and Italian
towns are not always comfortable or clean; but they
have color and beauty. This place lacked everything;
had neither solidity nor dignity, neither beauty nor
comfort. I must have been a monstrously clever fellow
to live down such a start.

Oh, well, I must go through with it. I struck into
the Jassy road, headed for my own section of town.
Arching elms, weather-tinted walls, distant prospects—
they simply did not exist. And that thoroughfare used
to seem so endless when mother sent me on errands.

Now it was shrunk to a mere jump. I looked for houses, names, some familiar object. It was all alien, remote, repulsive. And I thought I would find my way around as if I had never been away! Where were all those fine mansions—in one of them lived the prosecuting attorney of the county—which, as a boy of poor parents, I used to look up to with such awe and envy? Nowhere anything but dilapidation and decay and stark ugliness.

At a crossing I turned right, ran down a steep grade to have a look at the river. Now, the Vasluiets, anyway, I had not invented or magnified. We used to swim in it, fifty—a hundred strong at a time. How did we ever do it? There was not enough water in it now for a duck. It was a mere ditch with a yellow, dirty, viscous liquid through it. Well, of course, the summer was a very dry one. But those banks! A healthy boy could jump across them. Some evil pygmy seemed deliberately to have stunted and defaced the whole picture just to sicken me.

Presently I found myself in the open country. That last house there on the left, standing high up on a bank in a vast yard, was my last home in Vaslui. It was from there I had bade goodby to my childhood and my country. It was there my father and mother had died shortly after. Directly opposite—Hello, there was one name I knew! That inn and wine shop was still in the Bachman family. And a face, also—two faces. There was Mrs. Bachman, the mother of my old pal Janko. I would have known her anywhere. And Fanny, Janko's sister. Older, both of them, but not materially changed. I felt a lump rising in my throat and an eager urge to

rush up to them. But I remembered my resolve and passed on.

It was Saturday and there was no market. The highway was deserted. But in the distance a spire in yellow stucco gleamed in the sunshine. It was in the tiny hamlet of Mora Greci. That at any rate was lovely, almost as I had visioned it—that and the rolling hills and the checkerboard cornfields stretching to the horizon.

I pointed my camera at them, and decided that I must walk on out into the country. That was where the health and beauty and future of Rumania lay. But I felt irresistibly drawn to that inn and wine shop and the Bachmans. Before I knew it I found myself turned back, walking toward them. Oh, well, I would go in for a moment, just to look at them and talk a little. There could be no harm in that. I would not betray myself. They would never suspect who I was. Besides, that was rather romantic, a kind of Joseph-and-his-brethren scene. And was it not for this that I had made this long and weary journey?

I found a strange young man at the bar. The women had gone into the house. He did not know me, seemed not to take the slightest interest in me. I ordered a quarter of wine. Execrable stuff, especially in the early morning. And I had ached to come here at this season, because of the new wine! I asked him who was living now in that house across the street. He told me, and went on washing glasses. Was his name Bachman? I inquired cautiously. No, he was married to one of the girls. Which one? I pursued. I caught him

looking me over from the corner of his eye. Heigh-ho, I was slipping! Then he asked me a question: Did I know the town, his wife's family? Well, yes, I said, I did years ago; I used to go to school here, before his time.

At this point Mrs. Bachman wandered in. At close range, she looked a lot older. That was about the way mother would have looked if she had lived. What a different home-coming it would have been if I had found her here instead of Mrs. Bachman!

It may have been this reflection, but suddenly I heard myself saying, "Madama, won't you come and sit here?"

"Who? Me?" she asked suspiciously.

But she did take the chair on the other side of my little table. A mad wish came over me to take her hand. Then the bottom went completely out of my resolution.

"Do you have any idea who I am?" I asked her, all in a tremble.

She looked up at me with a troubled face. The young man precipitately disappeared into the adjoining room. Through the wall I heard excited voices, his and a woman's, the latter shouting "No, no!" Then he and Fanny burst in, and Fanny flew up to me with outstretched arms.

"Marcu!" she cried. "It's Marcu, the son of Bella! Oh, he took my heart out, that silly, saying it was Janko!"

Then I did hold Mrs. Bachman's hand. She eagerly took possession of me, shooed off the whole tribe of

them, who had come scurrying in from all directions at the name Janko, and began to pelt me with questions about her son. How did he look now? Was he rid of those beastly attacks of fever? What sort of a wife had he married? His children—they *were* the most remarkable girls in Brooklyn, weren't they?

"Twenty years!" she kept saying over and over again. "Twenty years, God bless you, he has been away, and you are the first living thing to bring me news of him! Twenty years!"

I felt my heart contracting. Poor, aging woman. She was being kept alive by but one hope—the hope that that boy of hers who had gone off on a lark so long ago would come back. But would she ever see him again? My own mother had worn her soul out yonder in that house across the road, and no one had ever come to bring her even a word from her adventuring son. How cruel life was, and how much crueller still were children!

Mrs. Bachman shifted ground. She spoke in a low, confidential kind of tone now.

"What sort of lives do you live out there? What, tell me, do you do with all the money you make?" She smiled and tried to look severe. "I do believe you get selfish and irresponsible and indifferent. Look at Janko now. When the youngest girl here was to be married we wrote him. Dowries nowadays strain a family frightfully. We had to give eighteen thousand so the young man could start this place, and it was about all we could manage between us. Fanny and the younger boys there all contributed. But Janko just

played possum, did not do his share at all. Do you think that is right?"

It suddenly dawned on me that I was in no position to answer all these tremulous questions. Why, I had not seen Janko myself these fourteen years! It seemed incredible even to me. How could I ever explain such a thing to his people here in Vaslui? Two boys brought up together, schoolfellows, inseparable; and here we were in the same city in America, separated by a five-cent ride or a five-cent telephone call, and we had not met or talked in fourteen years. There had never been an unpleasant word between us. It was nothing but the curious way America has with immigrants; our paths had diverged, that was all. We had drifted apart, Janko going into trade and I to college. Each of us had carved out his own little niche out there in that transplanted life of ours; each had married, was rearing a family, and our spheres no more touched than if we were on separate planets. It would have been very different if we had not emigrated. Therefore, Vaslui would never understand. The only course was to lie.

I said: "Maybe Janko could not afford it. We are not all magnates over there, you know. Life in Brooklyn is a little different from life in Vaslui. We earn perhaps what sounds like fortunes to you here, but it takes such a lot to live. Sometimes it's a struggle to make ends meet. As you say, Janko has five girls. So I should not be too hard on him."

"What?" Fanny broke in. "Janko not afford it? That is rich! Really, Marcu, you talk like a child.

May all our friends and well-wishers have it no worse than he! Maybe you don't know it? Then I'll tell you. Janko is rich. He has a bigger store in Brooklyn than Sharaga's on the Ring. Do you know, he has a telephone right in his own shop!"

"You don't have to try to defend him. We are proud of him, all right. We'll tell you that privately. But he is selfish, and when you see him in America, just say to him that we have not forgiven him for the way he has washed his hands of the girls and the family."

Thereupon she began rummaging in a painted chest in the corner of the room, brought out a parcel of letters with American stamps, and produced Janko's business card. She handed it to me with a gesture of clinching the argument. Bless my soul, it was worse than I had guessed! It read:

JACK BACHMAN

Dealer in

New Misfit and Second-hand Clothing
Full Dress and Tuxedo Suits
For Hire

Followed an address on Pitkin Avenue, the heart of the foreign quarter of Brownsville, and a telephone number.

I tried to appear impressed. Fanny looked at me triumphantly. But on Mrs. Bachman's face I thought I saw something that had not been there before—the first glimmering of doubt about her son's prosperity. My maybe's and perhapses had set her questioning. I told myself privately that I was a clumsy fool.

TWENTY YEARS LATER

By the time I got back to my hotel all Vaslui knew that Marcu, son of Eli, was in town. Vaslui did not need a newspaper, it had Fanny. But somehow no crowds, no band, no waving flags were in evidence. The dear old place was keeping its self-possession with infinite dignity. Three or four boyhood pals, seeing me at a little table in front, did wander over; and I noticed that though they were grown men now, they shied at my elegant stopping place exactly as we all did twenty years ago. Lupu, looking the very picture of village prosperity, kissed me and asked what I proposed to go in for. Was it to be grain, or an inn, or maybe some new line I had learned in America? He had made up his mind I was back for good. Redheaded Victor did not talk much. He seemed fascinated by my shell-rimmed goggles. Finally he ventured it: Was it weak eyes, or just a fashion? Michael had always been noted for his piety, and he thought I showed good stuff to come all that distance to pay homage to the dead. And Ilie, who had been in New York eighteen years before, inquired whether I still lived in that big tenement on Avenue B and still worked in the shirt factory; or maybe, he suggested flatteringly—maybe I was the foreman now.

There was an undertone in all these friendly inquiries that puzzled me a little. It sounded like condescension.

"Poor fellow," they seemed to say, "it has not been a bed of roses for you, has it? Well, well, you are among friends now. It's all right. We'll take you to our

bosom and help you to forget." They were terribly touched, the old dears.

I may seem ungrateful, but I did not quite appreciate Vaslui's sympathy. It got under my skin. Confound it, I was not asking anybody to sing hymns to me; but had these fellows no eyes to see the miracle America had wrought in me? Did they think my transformation was just an affair of goggles?

In some strange illogical way this encounter with the people I had so long yearned to be with set my heart beating for America more powerfully than it had ever done in all those twenty years. I felt my Americanism mounting at a dizzying rate. Not my loyalty to abstract symbols. That had been in the right place all along. But a communion of the soul. What in the world was I doing here anyway? I belonged somewhere else. I was an American. I had always been one.

Those alien men were still sitting with me, drinking coffee at my table, calling me by my first name, recalling odds and ends of their boyhood, in which in some fantastic way I was supposed to have played a part. Lupu was saying:

"What ever became of Matthew out there? He went away about your time. Foolish fellows, you two. What did you go for, anyhow? I never could get the hang of it. Some folks—well, I can understand. Chaps who got into scrapes, idlers, incompetents, sons of nobodies who had nothing to look forward to over here. But you and Matt? Golly, a funny bunch of people

you must have there. A country made up of all the good-for-nothings of the world."

So the propaganda of Couza had gone by the board. Vaslui had grown up, steadied itself and learned to see America soberly. So much to the good, at least. But the new ignorance was blacker and thicker than the old. I felt a stirring call to stand up for my adopted country, to preach Americanism to Vaslui as I knew it, to bring some light into this benighted nook of the earth. I looked at my audience. They seemed so thoroughly complacent in their own puddle, so exquisitely happy in their ignorance. Oh, fiddlesticks, why disturb them? Whom would it benefit? They would merely think I was defending myself. It would be idiotic to apologize for America to Vaslui.

That reference to Matthew Russu reminded me. He was the elder brother of Nick. Where was Nicholas Russu, that boy genius, the hero of my school days?

I turned to Victor. He used to be a fellow worshiper with me.

"That scatterbrain?" Victor made a face. "What do you want with him?"

Ilie was desperately amused at something. He started guffawing.

"Pshaw, Mark! Old sakes is all right, and all that. But you are not going to make the people in town talk about you as if you had anything in common with scum."

Scatterbrain! Scum! That only whetted my interest and my curiosity. To think of Nick still in this hole was bad enough; but that Vaslui scorned him was

incredible and outrageous. What did it all mean? Why, that boy was a wonder twenty years ago! He could not have been more than eleven when he translated all Horace's poems into such excellent Rumanian that a Bucarest publisher offered to bring them out. Later he worked out an international language, which one of our teachers sent to Zamenhof, the inventor of Esperanto, and which brought a reply from that personage, saying that the boy had made a very great contribution to the subject. In his first year in high school he made a vehicle in his grandfather's blacksmith shop which ran without visible means. It must have been operated by steam. It was, of course, a toy, and somewhat clumsy. But the mechanics teacher said Nick had a wonderful future before him, and the state inspector declared the boy to be a Leonardo da Vinci because he manifested a variety of talents.

I hunted him up that same evening. He was living in a wretched little hovel, far back in one of those alleys which I had dreamed were Italian courtyards. Only by his eyes would I ever in the world have recognized him. A neglected, haggard little man with a beard, in a motley outfit of duds, no piece of which matched any other. He greeted me mistrustfully, but brightened up when I identified myself. There was a wife, a pathetically thin little body with unmistakable traces of vanished beauty, and quite a family of children. Some were asleep, others were doing lessons by an oil lamp, two were playing that thrice-royal game of ettel-bettel in a corner. There was just one room.

We talked a bit. Nick was interested in America,

strangely enough. But I was aching to hear his history, to get some light on how that wonder boy had become this wistful misfit. It was not easy to get him to talk about himself. He was clearly trying to avoid the subject. Then I asked him to come walking with me, and noticed for the first time that he was crippled. A legacy of the war, doubtless.

"What is there to tell, dear fellow?" he said several times. "It is not anything unusual. Life has not proved so pink as it looked when we were kids. That's all."

"What are you doing?"

"Keeping afloat. What else is there to do?"

Only by hints and snatches did I piece out something like a picture of his career. He was now teaching French to a few private pupils—young ladies of Vaslui's aristocracy. He was also recording secretary to some association or committee or other. Now and then he got a little copying to do from a legal firm in Jassy. He had never got to the university. He barely managed to pull through the local high school, and that was only owing to the interest of his teachers, one of whom took him into his own home. He went to work in a shop. He had not only himself but a little sister to take care of.

But his commercial career was soon interrupted. Not being a student, he had to go into the army for three years. He had a peasant sergeant over him who did not appreciate Horace or Esperanto or invention, and he made life pretty miserable for Nick. Then he fell in love and married and got children, and the

dream of becoming an engineer receded further and further. Then he lost a child.

"Poor lamb, she could have lived. It was an ordinary case of appendicitis. But Ungar was away. There was no other surgeon in town. No money to bring Taussig from Jassy. A young fellow tried his hand at it. Not his fault entirely. There was no ether in the hospital. What do you want, dear boy? Vaslui!"

He thought of going to America. There were four children now. It was an undertaking. He got a cousin to promise him help. And then came the war. He was shot through the hip at Marasheschti. Ungar says it's tuberculosis. Nonsense! Oh, yes, he still played with his old toys. He tried to fly a year ago. Had some notion about perpendicular ascents. Vaslui laughed. He was composing a little, too. But there was only one piano in town, and he did not like bothering Bally to try his things out on it.

"What is there to tell, dear fellow?"

There was this to tell: If this was what Vaslui made of its men of genius, what would it have made of an average, plodding mortal like me?

This was the climax. Now that I was brought face to face with it, I saw that throughout all those twenty years in America this doubt had been shadowing me. Deep down in my soul, so deep that I was scarcely aware of it, these questions were constantly tormenting me: Was it worth while? Could you not have got all that America has given you—of education, of self-develop-

ment, of opportunity and of happiness—without quitting your home, your loved ones and your country?

Now I was answered. Poor Nicholas Russu was the answer.

I waited over till the next day, only to get the photographs of my parents' graves. A week before I was deploring my ill luck that I could not remain in Vaslui for a couple of months. Twenty-four hours proved quite enough—more than enough.

A month ago I landed in New York. Before leaving the pier I stopped at the bootblack parlor to have my shoes polished. They were in need of it. They had not got the treatment in Europe that they had been used to, any more than their owner.

I said to the Italian who ministered to me, "Tony, been here long?"

"Fiffy-teen yearsa, boss."

"Why don't you go home for a while? Aren't you homesick for Italy?"

"No, sir," said Tony with conviction. "No Italy for me. No good there. America fine enough for me."

"You are a wise man, Tony," said I, "and you've got a better memory than I have."

A CATALOGUE OF SELECTED DOVER BOOKS
IN ALL FIELDS OF INTEREST

A CATALOGUE OF SELECTED DOVER BOOKS
IN ALL FIELDS OF INTEREST

WHAT IS SCIENCE?, *N. Campbell*
The role of experiment and measurement, the function of mathematics, the nature of scientific laws, the difference between laws and theories, the limitations of science, and many similarly provocative topics are treated clearly and without technicalities by an eminent scientist. "Still an excellent introduction to scientific philosophy," H. Margenau in *Physics Today*. "A first-rate primer . . . deserves a wide audience," *Scientific American*. 192pp. 5⅜ x 8.
60043-2 Paperbound $1.25

THE NATURE OF LIGHT AND COLOUR IN THE OPEN AIR, *M. Minnaert*
Why are shadows sometimes blue, sometimes green, or other colors depending on the light and surroundings? What causes mirages? Why do multiple suns and moons appear in the sky? Professor Minnaert explains these unusual phenomena and hundreds of others in simple, easy-to-understand terms based on optical laws and the properties of light and color. No mathematics is required but artists, scientists, students, and everyone fascinated by these "tricks" of nature will find thousands of useful and amazing pieces of information. Hundreds of observational experiments are suggested which require no special equipment. 200 illustrations; 42 photos. xvi + 362pp. 5⅜ x 8.
20196-1 Paperbound $2.00

THE STRANGE STORY OF THE QUANTUM, AN ACCOUNT FOR THE GENERAL READER OF THE GROWTH OF IDEAS UNDERLYING OUR PRESENT ATOMIC KNOWLEDGE, *B. Hoffmann*
Presents lucidly and expertly, with barest amount of mathematics, the problems and theories which led to modern quantum physics. Dr. Hoffmann begins with the closing years of the 19th century, when certain trifling discrepancies were noticed, and with illuminating analogies and examples takes you through the brilliant concepts of Planck, Einstein, Pauli, Broglie, Bohr, Schroedinger, Heisenberg, Dirac, Sommerfeld, Feynman, etc. This edition includes a new, long postscript carrying the story through 1958. "Of the books attempting an account of the history and contents of our modern atomic physics which have come to my attention, this is the best," H. Margenau, Yale University, in *American Journal of Physics*. 32 tables and line illustrations. Index. 275pp. 5⅜ x 8.
20518-5 Paperbound $2.00

GREAT IDEAS OF MODERN MATHEMATICS: THEIR NATURE AND USE, *Jagjit Singh*
Reader with only high school math will understand main mathematical ideas of modern physics, astronomy, genetics, psychology, evolution, etc. better than many who use them as tools, but comprehend little of their basic structure. Author uses his wide knowledge of non-mathematical fields in brilliant exposition of differential equations, matrices, group theory, logic, statistics, problems of mathematical foundations, imaginary numbers, vectors, etc. Original publication. 2 appendixes. 2 indexes. 65 ills. 322pp. 5⅜ x 8.
20587-8 Paperbound $2.25

LA BOHEME BY GIACOMO PUCCINI,
translated and introduced by Ellen H. Bleiler
Complete handbook for the operagoer, with everything needed for full enjoyment except the musical score itself. Complete Italian libretto, with new, modern English line-by-line translation—the only libretto printing all repeats; biography of Puccini; the librettists; background to the opera, Murger's La Boheme, etc.; circumstances of composition and performances; plot summary; and pictorial section of 73 illustrations showing Puccini, famous singers and performances, etc. Large clear type for easy reading. 124pp. 5⅜ x 8½.
20404-9 Paperbound $1.25

ANTONIO STRADIVARI: HIS LIFE AND WORK (1644-1737),
W. Henry Hill, Arthur F. Hill, and Alfred E. Hill
Still the only book that really delves into life and art of the incomparable Italian craftsman, maker of the finest musical instruments in the world today. The authors, expert violin-makers themselves, discuss Stradivari's ancestry, his construction and finishing techniques, distinguished characteristics of many of his instruments and their locations. Included, too, is story of introduction of his instruments into France, England, first revelation of their supreme merit, and information on his labels, number of instruments made, prices, mystery of ingredients of his varnish, tone of pre-1684 Stradivari violin and changes between 1684 and 1690. An extremely interesting, informative account for all music lovers, from craftsman to concert-goer. Republication of original (1902) edition. New introduction by Sydney Beck, Head of Rare Book and Manuscript Collections, Music Division, New York Public Library. Analytical index by Rembert Wurlitzer. Appendixes. 68 illustrations. 30 full-page plates. 4 in color. xxvi + 315pp. 5⅜ x 8½. 20425-1 Paperbound $2.25

MUSICAL AUTOGRAPHS FROM MONTEVERDI TO HINDEMITH,
Emanuel Winternitz
For beauty, for intrinsic interest, for perspective on the composer's personality, for subtleties of phrasing, shading, emphasis indicated in the autograph but suppressed in the printed score, the mss. of musical composition are fascinating documents which repay close study in many different ways. This 2-volume work reprints facsimiles of mss. by virtually every major composer, and many minor figures—196 examples in all. A full text points out what can be learned from mss., analyzes each sample. Index. Bibliography. 18 figures. 196 plates. Total of 170pp. of text. 7⅞ x 10¾. 21312-9, 21313-7 Two volume set, paperbound $5.00

J. S. BACH,
Albert Schweitzer
One of the few great full-length studies of Bach's life and work, and the study upon which Schweitzer's renown as a musicologist rests. On first appearance (1911), revolutionized Bach performance. The only writer on Bach to be musicologist, performing musician, and student of history, theology and philosophy, Schweitzer contributes particularly full sections on history of German Protestant church music, theories on motivic pictorial representations in vocal music, and practical suggestions for performance. Translated by Ernest Newman. Indexes. 5 illustrations. 650 musical examples. Total of xix + 928pp. 5⅜ x 8½. 21631-4, 21632-2 Two volume set, paperbound $4.50

HEAR ME TALKIN' TO YA, *edited by Nat Shapiro and Nat Hentoff*
In their own words, Louis Armstrong, King Oliver, Fletcher Henderson, Bunk Johnson, Bix Beiderbecke, Billy Holiday, Fats Waller, Jelly Roll Morton, Duke Ellington, and many others comment on the origins of jazz in New Orleans and its growth in Chicago's South Side, Kansas City's jam sessions, Depression Harlem, and the modernism of the West Coast schools. Taken from taped conversations, letters, magazine articles, other first-hand sources. Editors' introduction. xvi + 429pp. 5⅜ x 8½.   21726-4 Paperbound $2.00

THE JOURNAL OF HENRY D. THOREAU
A 25-year record by the great American observer and critic, as complete a record of a great man's inner life as is anywhere available. Thoreau's Journals served him as raw material for his formal pieces, as a place where he could develop his ideas, as an outlet for his interests in wild life and plants, in writing as an art, in classics of literature, Walt Whitman and other contemporaries, in politics, slavery, individual's relation to the State, etc. The Journals present a portrait of a remarkable man, and are an observant social history. Unabridged republication of 1906 edition, Bradford Torrey and Francis H. Allen, editors. Illustrations. Total of 1888pp. 8⅜ x 12¼.
                    20312-3, 20313-1 Two volume set. clothbound $30.00

A SHAKESPEARIAN GRAMMAR, *E. A. Abbott*
Basic reference to Shakespeare and his contemporaries, explaining through thousands of quotations from Shakespeare, Jonson, Beaumont and Fletcher, North's *Plutarch* and other sources the grammatical usage differing from the modern. First published in 1870 and written by a scholar who spent much of his life isolating principles of Elizabethan language, the book is unlikely ever to be superseded. Indexes. xxiv + 511pp. 5⅜ x 8½. 21582-2 Paperbound $3.00

FOLK-LORE OF SHAKESPEARE, *T. F. Thistelton Dyer*
Classic study, drawing from Shakespeare a large body of references to supernatural beliefs, terminology of falconry and hunting, games and sports, good luck charms, marriage customs, folk medicines, superstitions about plants, animals, birds, argot of the underworld, sexual slang of London, proverbs, drinking customs, weather lore, and much else. From full compilation comes a mirror of the 17th-century popular mind. Index. ix + 526pp. 5⅜ x 8½.
                    21614-4 Paperbound $2.75

THE NEW VARIORUM SHAKESPEARE, *edited by H. H. Furness*
By far the richest editions of the plays ever produced in any country or language. Each volume contains complete text (usually First Folio) of the play, all variants in Quarto and other Folio texts, editorial changes by every major editor to Furness's own time (1900), footnotes to obscure references or language, extensive quotes from literature of Shakespearian criticism, essays on plot sources (often reprinting sources in full), and much more.

HAMLET, *edited by H. H. Furness*
Total of xxvi + 905pp. 5⅜ x 8½.
                    21004-9, 21005-7 Two volume set, paperbound $5.25

TWELFTH NIGHT, *edited by H. H. Furness*
Index. xxii + 434pp. 5⅜ x 8½.   21189-4 Paperbound $2.75

THE METHODS OF ETHICS, *Henry Sidgwick*
Propounding no organized system of its own, study subjects every major methodological approach to ethics to rigorous, objective analysis. Study discusses and relates ethical thought of Plato, Aristotle, Bentham, Clarke, Butler, Hobbes, Hume, Mill, Spencer, Kant, and dozens of others. Sidgwick retains conclusions from each system which follow from ethical premises, rejecting the faulty. Considered by many in the field to be among the most important treatises on ethical philosophy. Appendix. Index. xlvii + 528pp. 5⅜ x 8½.
21608-X Paperbound $2.50

TEUTONIC MYTHOLOGY, *Jakob Grimm*
A milestone in Western culture; the work which established on a modern basis the study of history of religions and comparative religions. 4-volume work assembles and interprets everything available on religious and folkloristic beliefs of Germanic people (including Scandinavians, Anglo-Saxons, etc.). Assembling material from such sources as Tacitus, surviving Old Norse and Icelandic texts, archeological remains, folktales, surviving superstitions, comparative traditions, linguistic analysis, etc. Grimm explores pagan deities, heroes, folklore of nature, religious practices, and every other area of pagan German belief. To this day, the unrivaled, definitive, exhaustive study. Translated by J. S. Stallybrass from 4th (1883) German edition. Indexes. Total of lxxvii + 1887pp. 5⅜ x 8½.
21602-0, 21603-9, 21604-7, 21605-5 Four volume set, paperbound $11.00

THE I CHING, *translated by James Legge*
Called "The Book of Changes" in English, this is one of the Five Classics edited by Confucius, basic and central to Chinese thought. Explains perhaps the most complex system of divination known, founded on the theory that all things happening at any one time have characteristic features which can be isolated and related. Significant in Oriental studies, in history of religions and philosophy, and also to Jungian psychoanalysis and other areas of modern European thought. Index. Appendixes. 6 plates. xxi + 448pp. 5⅜ x 8½.
21062-6 Paperbound $2.75

HISTORY OF ANCIENT PHILOSOPHY, *W. Windelband*
One of the clearest, most accurate comprehensive surveys of Greek and Roman philosophy. Discusses ancient philosophy in general, intellectual life in Greece in the 7th and 6th centuries B.C., Thales, Anaximander, Anaximenes, Heraclitus, the Eleatics, Empedocles, Anaxagoras, Leucippus, the Pythagoreans, the Sophists, Socrates, Democritus (20 pages), Plato (50 pages), Aristotle (70 pages), the Peripatetics, Stoics, Epicureans, Sceptics, Neo-platonists, Christian Apologists, etc. 2nd German edition translated by H. E. Cushman. xv + 393pp. 5⅜ x 8.
20357-3 Paperbound $2.25

THE PALACE OF PLEASURE, *William Painter*
Elizabethan versions of Italian and French novels from *The Decameron,* Cinthio, Straparola, Queen Margaret of Navarre, and other continental sources — the very work that provided Shakespeare and dozens of his contemporaries with many of their plots and sub-plots and, therefore, justly considered one of the most influential books in all English literature. It is also a book that any reader will still enjoy. Total of cviii + 1,224pp.
21691-8, 21692-6, 21693-4 Three volume set, paperbound $6.75

PRINCIPLES OF STRATIGRAPHY,
A. W. Grabau

Classic of 20th century geology, unmatched in scope and comprehensiveness. Nearly 600 pages cover the structure and origins of every kind of sedimentary, hydrogenic, oceanic, pyroclastic, atmoclastic, hydroclastic, marine hydroclastic, and bioclastic rock; metamorphism; erosion; etc. Includes also the constitution of the atmosphere; morphology of oceans, rivers, glaciers; volcanic activities; faults and earthquakes; and fundamental principles of paleontology (nearly 200 pages). New introduction by Prof. M. Kay, Columbia U. 1277 bibliographical entries. 264 diagrams. Tables, maps, etc. Two volume set. Total of xxxii + 1185pp. 5⅜ x 8.   60686-4, 60687-2 Two volume set, paperbound $6.25

SNOW CRYSTALS, W. A. Bentley and W. J. Humphreys

Over 200 pages of Bentley's famous microphotographs of snow flakes—the product of painstaking, methodical work at his Jericho, Vermont studio. The pictures, which also include plates of frost, glaze and dew on vegetation, spider webs, windowpanes; sleet; graupel or soft hail, were chosen both for their scientific interest and their aesthetic qualities. The wonder of nature's diversity is exhibited in the intricate, beautiful patterns of the snow flakes. Introductory text by W. J. Humphreys. Selected bibliography. 2,453 illustrations. 224pp. 8 x 10¼.   20287-9 Paperbound $3.25

THE BIRTH AND DEVELOPMENT OF THE GEOLOGICAL SCIENCES,
F. D. Adams

Most thorough history of the earth sciences ever written. Geological thought from earliest times to the end of the 19th century, covering over 300 early thinkers & systems: fossils & their explanation, vulcanists vs. neptunists, figured stones & paleontology, generation of stones, dozens of similar topics. 91 illustrations, including medieval, renaissance woodcuts, etc. Index. 632 footnotes, mostly bibliographical. 511pp. 5⅜ x 8.   20005-1 Paperbound $2.75

ORGANIC CHEMISTRY, F. C. Whitmore

The entire subject of organic chemistry for the practicing chemist and the advanced student. Storehouse of facts, theories, processes found elsewhere only in specialized journals. Covers aliphatic compounds (500 pages on the properties and synthetic preparation of hydrocarbons, halides, proteins, ketones, etc.), alicyclic compounds, aromatic compounds, heterocyclic compounds, organophosphorus and organometallic compounds. Methods of synthetic preparation analyzed critically throughout. Includes much of biochemical interest. "The scope of this volume is astonishing," *Industrial and Engineering Chemistry.* 12,000-reference index. 2387-item bibliography. Total of x + 1005pp. 5⅜ x 8.   60700-3, 60701-1 Two volume set, paperbound $4.50

THE PHASE RULE AND ITS APPLICATION,
Alexander Findlay

Covering chemical phenomena of 1, 2, 3, 4, and multiple component systems, this "standard work on the subject" (*Nature,* London), has been completely revised and brought up to date by A. N. Campbell and N. O. Smith. Brand new material has been added on such matters as binary, tertiary liquid equilibria, solid solutions in ternary systems, quinary systems of salts and water. Completely revised to triangular coordinates in ternary systems, clarified graphic representation, solid models, etc. 9th revised edition. Author, subject indexes. 236 figures. 505 footnotes, mostly bibliographic. xii + 494pp. 5⅜ x 8.
60091-2 Paperbound $2.75

THE WONDERFUL WIZARD OF OZ, *L. F. Baum*
All the original W. W. Denslow illustrations in full color—as much a part of
"The Wizard" as Tenniel's drawings are of "Alice in Wonderland." "The
Wizard" is still America's best-loved fairy tale, in which, as the author expresses
it, "The wonderment and joy are retained and the heartaches and nightmares
left out." Now today's young readers can enjoy every word and wonderful picture of the original book. New introduction by Martin Gardner. A Baum
bibliography. 23 full-page color plates. viii + 268pp. 5⅜ x 8.
20691-2 Paperbound $1.95

THE MARVELOUS LAND OF OZ, *L. F. Baum*
This is the equally enchanting sequel to the "Wizard," continuing the adventures of the Scarecrow and the Tin Woodman. The hero this time is a little
boy named Tip, and all the delightful Oz magic is still present. This is the
Oz book with the Animated Saw-Horse, the Woggle-Bug, and Jack Pumpkin-
head. All the original John R. Neill illustrations, 10 in full color. 287pp.
5⅜ x 8.
20692-0 Paperbound $1.75

ALICE'S ADVENTURES UNDER GROUND, *Lewis Carroll*
The original *Alice in Wonderland*, hand-lettered and illustrated by Carroll
himself, and originally presented as a Christmas gift to a child-friend. Adults
as well as children will enjoy this charming volume, reproduced faithfully
in this Dover edition. While the story is essentially the same, there are slight
changes, and Carroll's spritely drawings present an intriguing alternative to
the famous Tenniel illustrations. One of the most popular books in Dover's
catalogue. Introduction by Martin Gardner. 38 illustrations. 128pp. 5⅜ x 8½.
21482-6 Paperbound $1.00

THE NURSERY "ALICE," *Lewis Carroll*
While most of us consider *Alice in Wonderland* a story for children of all
ages, Carroll himself felt it was beyond younger children. He therefore provided this simplified version, illustrated with the famous Tenniel drawings
enlarged and colored in delicate tints, for children aged "from Nought to
Five." Dover's edition of this now rare classic is a faithful copy of the 1889
printing, including 20 illustrations by Tenniel, and front and back covers
reproduced in full color. Introduction by Martin Gardner. xxiii + 67pp.
6⅛ x 9¼.
21610-1 Paperbound $1.75

THE STORY OF KING ARTHUR AND HIS KNIGHTS, *Howard Pyle*
A fast-paced, exciting retelling of the best known Arthurian legends for young
readers by one of America's best story tellers and illustrators. The sword
Excalibur, wooing of Guinevere, Merlin and his downfall, adventures of Sir
Pellias and Gawaine, and others. The pen and ink illustrations are vividly
imagined and wonderfully drawn. 41 illustrations. xviii + 313pp. 6⅛ x 9¼.
21445-1 Paperbound $2.00

Prices subject to change without notice.

Available at your book dealer or write for free catalogue to Dept. Adsci,
Dover Publications, Inc., 180 Varick St., N.Y., N.Y. 10014. Dover publishes more
than 150 books each year on science, elementary and advanced mathematics,
biology, music, art, literary history, social sciences and other areas.